C000128356

Peggy Cole's
Countryside Year

Peggy Cole MBE

Dedicated to my past and present neighbours
and friends throughout Suffolk

Peggy Cole's Countryside Year

© Copyright Peggy Cole 2002
Illustrations © Sonya E. Burrows
Edited by Miriam Clift

First Published by LUCAS BOOKS 2002

ISBN 1903797-08-X

© Copyright 2001. All rights reserved. No part of this publication may be reproduced, stored in a retrieval system or transmitted, in any form or by any means, electronic, mechanical, magnetic, photocopying, recording or otherwise without the prior permission of the copyright holders.

Printed by: Winsor Clarke Brackenbury Ltd: 01473 254817

Contents

Foreword

Peggy Cole's Country Matters column has been essential reading in the Monday edition of the East Anglian Daily Times for many years. The wise words from this most famous of Suffolk country "gals" have entertained and enlightened hundreds of thousands of people.

Peggy's Columns evoke memories of Suffolk past, of simple, uncomplicated lifestyles, and of innocent childhoods spent in the unspoiled Suffolk countryside of decades long ago.

I am delighted that Peggy's words have been gathered together and published in this book. I am sure it will provide many people with a great deal of pleasure - whether they are "good old Suffolk boys and gals" or simply people who have grown to love this beautiful part of the world.

TERRY HUNT
Editor, East Anglian Daily Times
January 2002

January

JANUARY

Although Christmas decorations have become commercialised, the tradition goes back to the old Roman ceremony of Calennig. The Romans used this pagan symbol of fruitfulness at the change of the year, and I wonder if the Christingle service has its origins in the Calennig. The large orange or apple which forms the basis of the decoration represents the world; the three hazel rods on which it stands, decoratively carved, the Holy Trinity; a candle represents the Light of the World and sometimes ears of corn were stuck in the orange. The evergreens and holly surrounding it were reminders of the fruits of the earth and flour was often sprinkled over the top to represent snow. Another hazel rod is stuck into the side of the orange to form a handle for at one time, it was the custom in Wales for the children to make these Calennigs on New Year's Eve and then carry them round from house to house the next morning, holding them out and singing;

'A Happy New Year to you, and a Gift to me'.

No doubt January (Black Janiver) has earned its bad name, but country folk find plenty of good words for the first child of the year. It is true that there often comes snow and ice, frosts, mists, darkness and floods, but they are needed in the circle of the year and there comes also beauty, colour, warmth, song, birth and work to bring hope and cheer. As one of my brother Ronnie's sayings goes, 'You must have a winter to get a summer'.

In January the sun and the heavens in which he runs are already preparing for spring. The earth may still be lapped in hard frost and chilling rains, but no foulness of the weather can destroy January's great gain - the longer light. The sun mounts higher above the mists of the horizon; his shadows grow daily shorter and steeper, recovering from their lank exhaustion behind every grass-tuft in the December fields. With longer daylight comes more active evaporation. There is a freer movement of air, owing to the changes of temperature produced by the sun on his course. Even when the earth is cold and backward, spring still gains ground in the sky. The light has a firmer quality of whiteness and reveals a hundred quiet tones and contrasts of colour which were hidden or lacking under darker skies.

The woods are transformed to a magical loveliness by a sudden snowstorm. In the quickly fading light, farmers, shepherds and cottagers watch the snow with country eyes. The farmer knows that his winter wheat will grow green and strong under the blessing of snow. The shepherd hastens to bring in his sheep to the lambing pens he has made by piling straw stuffed into hurdles to break the icy winds.

Under the snow, violets, snowdrops and primroses are safely sleeping, while in the trees shivering rooks are holding numerous council meetings. The finches, tits, jays, magpies and other hard-billed birds seem to find sufficient food in seeds and hibernating insects to survive a month of snow and frost although they may draw nearer to the warmth of human homes to seek scraps. After quite an absence, the blue tits return to the bird tables amusing everyone with their antics as they try to eat the food that is suspended. They arrive from nowhere, alight on a piece of fat and quickly make a hole in it. Hanging upside down, they occasionally stop to look both ways as if to see what is about before returning to the business in hand. What a lot of pleasure they give.

One often sees tracks made by the fox, hare, rabbit or squirrel in the snow and the faster the pace the fewer the tracks as hind feet, followed by fore feet, leap precisely and economically over the white surface. Many a tale of tragedy or escape is told as the tracks of predator and prey come together and only those of the predator moving away. The stalking spoor from bush to bush, the sudden leap, the smudged area of capture - all are plainly marked in the snow.

Then overnight the bitter east wind is suddenly gone, bringing by contrast a morning when the air is almost warm. The snow melts away in a flood of water and under the rain in the leafless boughs the tender notes of the robin become fuller and more prolonged. When you are working in the garden you will soon have one coming to see what you are up to, and they can get very cheeky. Children love to hear the story of the robin covering the babes in the wood with soft leaves to keep them warm. It won't be long before you see them carrying a great beak full of soft moss or leaves. The female ceases to sing, or to defend her territory, and moves towards her partner while at the same time looking out of the corner of her eye at the old kettle hidden in the hedge, which she will use for her early nest. We always say that St Valentine's Day is the day robins choose their mates, but somehow I think it's long before then.

January

I have a bird table, and this month I can see the blackbirds with their feathers fluffed out making them look quite fat, however, I have been surprised recently to find out the weight of some of our birds. The heaviest is the swan at about 15lb or more, with the golden eagle next at 9-10lb. Seabirds like the cormorant and gannet are around 7lb and wild geese may tip the scales at anything from 5-9lb. Apart from these heavier birds, many of the small perching birds such as finches, tits and warblers, weigh less than one ounce. Some weigh very little - tree creepers and chiff-chaffs weigh but two drachms, and the common wren is even less. (A drachm is equivalent to one-sixteenth of an ounce.) Even a swift will register only one ounce and a blue-tit less than half an ounce, and think of the song power of the nightingale, which will weigh only three-eighths of an ounce! Knowing this, we can understand how important it is to feed the birds in severe weather. The cold weather claims the lives of many tiny creatures, the wren being one that suffers the most. A warning at this time of year, if you are cleaning out nesting boxes, don't put wood preservative inside the boxes or round the entrance. If you are thinking of making a box, do apply the preservative outside at least three to four weeks before the nest box is to be put up.

Plough Monday is the first Monday after 6th January, so-called because it was formerly the day on which work on the farm resumed after the Twelve Days of Christmas and spring ploughing began.

'Plough Monday next after that Twelfth tide is past,
Bid out with the plough, the worst husband is last.'

Before farmers and farm labourers started to work with their ploughs, they would give them a good clean and decorate them. These would then be hauled to the local church to be blessed, and to pray for a good harvest before the start of the new year's work. The Sunday service was abandoned at the Reformation, but in recent years services of blessing for farm work and tools have been revived in many of the little churches. I think it would be nice for more of these services to be held for say; gardeners and allotment holders. Plough Monday would be the start of the field work, provided the weather was fit. The young men left work early to get dressed up, with horse brasses, bells and ribbons. They called themselves 'jacks' and the name given to ploughs was 'bullocks'. A decorated plough would be hauled around the village and a man would dress as a woman, demanding money from every householder or passer-by as a contribution towards keeping the Plough Light alight in the church throughout the year.

This is what Thomas Tusser wrote in 1580, conjuring up a picture of industrious ploughmen hard at work on countless farms at the beginning of the season. But how much actual work was ever done on this day is very uncertain because the principal feature of the day was not ploughing but the ritual dragging about of a decorated plough. Men wore fanciful costumes of various kinds, usually adorned with ribbons and any sort of ornament including, in some districts, horse brasses. Included in the company would have been a man dressed in women's clothes, called the 'Bessy' who carried a collecting box. The plough was drawn through the streets and up to the doors of the houses where gifts of money or food and drink were provided. In the Middle Ages a part of the money collected was used to support the 'Plough Light', maintained by the Ploughmen's Guild in the parish church. This light burned before the altar and was never allowed to go out. These lively Plough Monday celebrations gradually died out at the beginning of the twentieth century, although their memory still lingers in many villages, where a service is still held with a plough standing to be blessed in the church, and prayers are offered for a plentiful harvest in the coming year.

The flu bug is the biggest drawback to this month, it has made so many families ill in some way or another. Next will be chicken pox and I can remember how as children we had to stay in bed with curtains drawn to shade our eyes. Mother would dab the afflicted areas with calamine lotion and warn us not to scratch. She told us that as soon as the rash had all come out we should soon feel better, but, looking into the mirror, this took a lot of believing. German measles was another illness that my brother and I had as young teenagers, and the only good thing about these infectious complaints was the time we had off school - some three weeks. We even had a fire in our bedroom, the only time I remember this happening. Then the old nursery fireguard was put round the fireplace and hot water bottles put in the beds to make sure we kept warm. Once we were over the worst, we played games such as ludo or snakes and ladders and read comics. We had our meals in bed - Mother would bring us basins of hot Bovril with bread soaked in it and a lemon drink made from lemonade crystals. We thought this a great treat.

Over the winter, my mother would give us Cod Liver Oil, and Fish Malt - how I hated this - and every night our chests were rubbed with Camphorated Oil

My daughter-in-law has tried to teach me lace making. 'All you do,' she explained,' is pick up a bobbin and place it over another bobbin.' Although it looked so easy, somehow I think it will take me a long time to work out the wonderful patterns they create. The history of bobbins and beads is fascinating; beads are fixed on a wire and put on bobbins and are then called spangles. So many lace makers have a passion for highly decorated bobbins and the English are intensely proud of theirs. It was not until I was reading Spangles and Superstitions a booklet by Christine and David Springett who are well known in the lace business, that I found out that there are so many bobbins. They are made from all types of wood, and decorated bone, glass and ivory bobbins are also sought after. Belgian lace makers mainly use plain bobbins whilst the English craftsmen love colourful ones. Glass beads came from all over Germany while vast quantities were also made in Amsterdam and Venice, and often beads were bartered with African tribes. The history of all beads used for spangles makes fascinating reading.

Spangles are put on bobbins to stop them from rolling when in use. Bobbins that are made either from wood or bone and inlaid with spots of pewter are known as leopards. In the Bedford area it was said that using such a bobbin would protect the lace maker from arthritis and rheumatism, which must have been the bane of many who practised this craft.

Many lace makers were superstitious and were only too ready to pass on their beliefs to others. Buttons, for instance, of particular types can have great significance. Should a lace maker become engaged, she would use a button from her fiancé's waistcoat to spangle a bobbin, inscribed with their names. On the other hand, a trouser button had a very different meaning; when a spinster who had been 'on the shelf' finally managed to catch herself a husband, her friends would take an 'old maid bobbin' - one very thin and plain - and spangle it with a single trouser button. There are several superstitions associated with death and if one occurred in a lace maker's family, then it was said that her working lace pillow would be put into mourning by changing all the colourful beads on the spangles to black ones.

There are many different stories as to what happened to a lace-maker's equipment on her death. Some say that each of her friends would be invited to choose one of the bobbins, while another says that the entire equipment would be burned. However, I know that there are lace makers today who are the proud owners of bobbins that originally belonged to their grandmothers, so perhaps not all the stories are correct.

Although January marks the opening of the year and a brand new beginning with spring not that far away, our ancestors didn't see it that way. To the Anglo Saxons it was 'wolf month', because there were dangerous and hungry animals on the prowl.

It doesn't take much to discover that the better days are not far away. On a fine day the crows may already be busy in the tree tops. The males are out to attract mates, and not only does he perform a kind of clumsy dance, but he may even produce a few chosen 'words'. Some people may think it's only a rattling, grating noise high above. However, according to tradition, St Cuthbert treated crows with a great deal of affection, and they were a constant companion to him on his travels.

Does it cost less to live in the country than in the town? Many townsfolk think that life is both easier and cheaper in the country - vegetables and fruit grow in the garden, the hens lay eggs and that is the picture they have. On the whole, I feel that housekeeping is more expensive in the country than in the city. Of course, any shopping expedition nowadays tends to end up with a moan about rising prices. No doubt fruit and vegetables do cost less if you grow them yourself but they certainly cost more if and when you have to buy them. Don't forget you have the cost of seeds and tubers and as for the eggs - the hens have to be fed as well as looked after and they don't lay all year round. Taking it all the year through, I think it is fair to claim that the backyard hen's eggs cost more than the eggs from the shops.

In our village, fish comes our way only once a week, and we are lucky that we still have this service - of course it is bound to be more expensive than in town. Household replacements and all the many things besides food that a housewife needs to buy usually involve a trip to town and you then have to think about petrol or bus fares. The thrifty town housewife can cut her costs if she chooses, by visiting street markets, by shopping around competitive stores and by snapping up perishable foods at closing time.

Don't think that I'm grumbling, there are many compensations to living in a village, and I would not live anywhere else, even if it does cost more!

Of the many changes in the habits and ideas of English people during the last hundred years, none has been more striking than the attitude towards the observance of Sunday. The Lord's Day used to be looked on as a time of rest after a long week of toil, consisting of a 70- or 80-hour week.

All the material needs of the day were prepared on the Saturday, clothes to be worn were already laundered and repaired, boots and shoes had to be cleaned and polished, even food necessary for Sunday was prepared and cooked the previous day and cold dishes were accepted. Children were not allowed to play games, little girls were not even permitted to play with their dolls. Weekly religious periodicals were the reading for the day, as well as the bible. Of course there were no Sunday papers and ALL shops were closed.

Years ago, when you lived in a tied cottage, you were expected to go to church or chapel or the 'governor' (master) would want to know where you were on the Sabbath. To attend church services was one way of keeping a roof over your head.

It's not often today that we hear people talking of their 'glory hole'. When we were small children, everything was put in the cupboard under the stairs - shoes and boots, toys, Kilner jars and anything else that was not in everyday use. Modern houses have fitted cupboards so there is no longer a need for the good old glory hole. In our house, my mother used to make rag and wool rugs and she would keep all the bits of material in a box or large sack then, during winter evenings, out this would come from the glory hole. One year, as she took the box out, mice began running everywhere. They had moved into her rag box and made it their winter home. As country folk will tell you, they try

9

and get into the warm for the winter and would soon find a hole in the stud and plaster houses. That year, even in our brick house, they found a small space to squeeze in to make themselves comfortable.

Travelling around the countryside covering many thousands of miles throughout the year, I am amazed at the lovely village signs there are. We have to thank the royal family for the growing popularity of these decorative emblems. As long ago as 1924, the Duke of York, later to become King George V, made an appeal at the Royal Academy banquet for the revival of the old practice of displaying village signs, and since then the royal estate at Sandringham has given active support to the movement.

The 1953 coronation was commemorated by the erection of a number of signs, the Festival of Britain in 1951 was the occasion for others to be made and then came the Queen's Silver Jubilee when more signs appeared.

In the villages around where I live, many of the signs have been designed by Mary Moore and made by her late husband, Hector. The pictures usually have a story behind them; take Easton village - their sign depicts the famous crinkle-crankle wall, while a huntsman and hounds represents the Easton Harriers. Grundisburgh has the main panel depicting heraldic features of the Garland, banner of the second Baron Cranworth.

Brandeston has a lovely sign depicting the arms of the Revett family, builders of Brandeston Hall and benefactors of All Saints Church, built mainly in the 14th century. The Rév. John Lowes, vicar of Brandeston for 50 years, was hanged for witchcraft in 1646 at the age of 80 years. The thatched cottage was reputedly used as an occasional refuge by Margaret Catchpole, whose uncle lived in Brandeston.

At first glance, Hasketon sign looks like a rural scene with two heavy horses, plough and ploughman on a furrowed field. Birds hover above what appears to be a setting sun. In fact, this is the striped and crinkled underside of a field mushroom. Apparently, the world's largest recorded mushroom is attributed to Hasketon.

Monewden sign commemorates the Queen's Silver Jubilee - the church is shown on rising ground indicating its reputation as the highest point in Suffolk. A wheatsheaf represents the farming life of the village and a wheel, the trade of the wheelwright, continued in the village up to the present time. I was lucky enough to see the sign in Mary Moore's workshop when it was brought in for repainting.

Charsfield village sign features a church, with its interesting Tudor porch, similar to the Wolsey Gate in Ipswich, a field gate and a wheatsheaf illustrate the farming aspect, the basket of apples is a reminder of the extensive local fruit growing and the shield is that of Sir John Leman, 17th century lord of the manor.

Kettleburgh has one of my favourite signs showing Ketyl, the Viking settler who cleared the land and founded a community giving the village its name. The crown reminds us again of the Silver Jubilee of our Queen.

Pettistree is another favourite, with the main panel showing a farming scene, a pair of Suffolk horses ploughing, with St Peter's Church in the background. The sign also bears the Prince of Wales' plume of feathers to commemorate the wedding of Prince Charles and Lady Diana Spencer. A plaque on two sides of the post depicts St Peter with his symbol, a key.

Ufford commemorates the famous Crisp's horse of Ufford, foaled in 1768, the foundation stallion of today's breed of Suffolk horses. The stylised crown and waves on the sign refer to King Wuffa, the 6th century King of the East Angles whose palace was nearby.

Laxfield depicts more village history, including the shield of the Wingfield family who financed the building of the church tower. Flames and the date 1557 refer to the burning at the stake of John Noyes for his adherence to reformed religion. A medieval plough team of oxen, a pair of Suffolk horses ploughing, and a steam locomotive show the long tradition of agriculture and recall the days when Laxfield was a busy station on the Mid-Suffolk Light Railway.

The Snape sign depicts an Anglo-Saxon ship, recalling the ship burial found in the last century, a monk represents the old priory, the original bridge (now demolished) and delicate wrought-iron work suggests the reeds at the riverside and a curlew. The latter, whilst indicating birdlife in the area, also provides a link with the composer Benjamin Britten who lived locally, and whose work was much influenced by the local landscape.

So many of the signs depict the Suffolk horse; Trimley St Mary's sign shows

11

a Suffolk horse and waggon together with the Silver Jubilee symbol, and the little village of Hoo's sign depicts simply a horse. No doubt this was because the horse was used in every part of the work of growing crops, turning the soil, sowing and reaping, and without it the work would have been very hard indeed.

The lovely art work on the Melton sign which used to stand outside the Phyllis Memorial Maternity Home, is now removed since the 'Phyllis' is no longer used. The sign was made for the fiftieth jubilee of the home which was founded by Sir William Churchman in memory of his daughter.

There are many more village signs not mentioned here and I suggest you take a ride out around the villages to see some of the lovely craftwork for yourselves - you won't be disappointed.

'If the Kalends of January be smiling and gay,
You'll have winter weather till the Kalends of May'

This saying was quoted to me by an old Buckinghamshire countryman - it is an old saying of labourers and hedgecutters. It is good to hear the Roman word for the first three days of this month. Many people think that the first three days of the year rule the weather during the first three months, and are the presage of the weather in September. Folk in the old days would take great notice of the first moon of the new year, and Kilvert, in his diary, speaks of the moon as 'a very keen moon'. He added that 'the Greeks used to throw a kiss to the sun as a welcome each day'

Another old saying was 'The last twelve days of January rule the weather for the whole year'. One of the comforting things about this modern age is that old beliefs and customs die hard. St Agnes' Eve (21st January) is still treated with due regard in some parts of the country. This is the time when a girl may see her future husband or at least find out who he is by baking a 'dumb cake', so called because nobody is allowed to talk during the making of it. Her initials were then pricked in the cake and overnight those of her future husband would appear.

Farmers and corn merchants should take note of the weather on 25 January -

January

St Paul's Day;

'If St Paul's be fair and clear,
It doth betide a happy year.
But if it chance to snow and rain,
Then will be dear all kinds of grain'

One of the old country skills that has not been forgotten is thatching. Rodger Chilvers, the thatcher from Pettistree has made a wonderful job of thatching the old barn at Wantisden. Rodger told me that all the reeds he used were local as were the 'brawtch'(hazel sticks used to fix the reeds on to the roof). In fact the only thing to be brought in was the wire netting. I have memories of helping my father to thatch the corn stacks when the harvest was done. I would help him 'pull the straw' - water was thrown over a heap of straw then it was pulled out and put into a yoke, which the thatcher carried up on to the roof. After the whole roof was done, the top was decorated with curves or zig-zags - the same decoration used on the barn at Wantisden. The barn is a fine piece of craftmanship, and should last more than 70 years.

Wood-pigeons are a common bird in East Anglia, and have inspired many legends and beliefs. One saying is, 'When the pigeons go a-benting, then the farmers go lamenting'. It is also said that these birds never go short of food, except when they are obliged to feed on the seeds of grass, which ripen before the crops of grain. The seed stalk of grass is called the 'bent', hence the term 'benting'.
Doves, and to a certain extent pigeons, have always been treated with respect. The dove is a universal emblem of peace and in earlier times, they were thought to be messengers of the three classic fates. It was also believed that anyone who slept on a mattress filled with pigeon feathers would die - a belief easily disproved.
Another old country rhyme associated with birds

'Cuckoo, oats and woodcock hay,
Make the farmers run away'

13

This referred to an agricultural belief that, if spring was so backward, and oats could not be sown until the cuckoo was heard, or the autumn so wet that the late crop of hay had to be left until the woodcock arrived, farmers were certain to suffer considerable losses.

I can remember my father telling me, 'Should a robin die in a person's hand, that hand would always shake'. Some people still believe that a robin entering a house signifies the death of someone in that house.

The wren is another bird that causes superstition, although not so highly respected as the robin, 'The robin and the wren be God Almighty's cock and hen'. Then there is the saying that, 'A martin and a swallow are God Almighty's shirt and collar'.

Walking with my little dog through my neighbour's orchard, the ground was crisp with frost and I could hear the bells ringing out from Bredfield church. A pair of magpies, bright as a black and white decoration, were flying from tree to tree. These birds have always given me a sense of astonishment and I can never get used to their beauty although I have seen them all my life and heard their curses hurled down as they flew overhead. The combination of colour is spectacular and even after a dirty meal, you never see a dirty-looking bird. There are still many superstitions about the magpie but here is an old way of reversing the bad luck which is said to follow them and that is to bow with courtesy and say 'Good morning Mr Magpie or Mrs Magpie'.

All this goes back to a close and intimate connection with nature; a friendship and a realisation of the life of others besides man.

It is so nice to get out again and be able to walk up the lane and watch the new shoots appearing and green grass coming up, as if looking forward to spring. The cunning old cock pheasant always amazes me - it has been said that the wiliest bird that flies is the wild goose, but I believe that the pheasant is more cunning. To see a cock pheasant in the breeding season crowing in triumph and defiance reminds me of a proud barn-door cockerel. I always think they know when the shooting season is finished. From by back bedroom window I have seen a cock pheasant for the past two years, fly up into an apple tree - always the same tree - for his night's sleep. Somehow he has managed to survive the local shoots. The best place to see this fine bird is in a wood in late October when the trees have lost most of their leaves. Standing in a clearing, surrounded by the red of the dying season, the yellow of maples and the rich tawny tones of beech and oak, his own plumage matching these autumn fires. Then, with every turn of his proud head, he shows a flash of purple and green, breathtaking in its beauty.

The myths, legends and lore associated with dogs are many and have a tendency to contradict each other. For instance, a black and white dog is generally held to be lucky in England while in India it is the opposite. In Scotland, a strange dog in a house means a new friendship but in Lancashire, if one is followed by a dog that simply won't go away, it is an omen of death. However, I am sceptical as I have often been followed by strange dogs without any consequences good or evil. At one time, mad dogs must have been a good deal more common and their appearance caused widespread alarm. In this respect, a dog that howled on Christmas Eve was killed because it was feared that it would go mad before the year was out. We are all acquainted with the phrase 'A hair of the dog that bit you' but at one time, it was no more than the literal truth. If someone was bitten by a mad dog, it was believed that if they ate a hair of this dog it would cure the madness brought on by the bite.

There are other sayings, not often heard nowadays - one such is when referring to people in country districts who are content to do nothing for themselves but rather to expect other people to keep them. It is often said of them that they 'will neither work nor want', or 'He never did a hard day's work in his life and never had a wet shirt' or 'He's yan of them born tired never-sweats'. A cold weather saying is 'There's a good steward abroad when there's a wind frost' meaning that the cold will make the men work hard even without supervision. Another old saying is that 'Two hids (heads) are better than one, even if they're only ship's (sheep's) heads'. Years ago, I remember an old man saying to me, after watching two pretty girls go by; 'Some o' these young gals put more muck on their faces than a farmer dew on an acre o' land in a year'.

With all the winds, one can't help watching the birds in the sky, and as my brother and I watched some rooks flying round and round, he said 'They are going round in a basin - that means rough weather is coming'. In Norfolk the jackdaw is another weather prophet, there is a saying, 'When three jackdaws are seen on St Peter's Vanes together, then we're sure to have bad weather'.

15

I wonder how many houses still have a horseshoe nailed to the lintel or door; iron was regarded as a powerful defence against fairies and witches while the crescent shape of the horseshoe, the symbol of the moon goddess and of fertility, brought good fortune to the household. Usually the horseshoe was fixed with its points uppermost so that the luck would not run out, but in early times it was attached with the open end downwards, as a charm against witchcraft.

There is a belief that one should throw an old shoe over the threshold when a member of the household leaves home in order to wish them success, but, if they should forget something and return immediately, disaster will follow unless they sit down before setting out on their journey again.

In spite of the television, the hearth is still the focal point of family life and I remember the days when we all sat in the kitchen near the fire or range, especially in winter. The Romans record that this was the dwelling place of the domestic gods and there is a saying that the fireplace or inglenook was the home of brownies or fairies who brought good luck to the household. Some people still leave a piece of coal burning when they go up to bed to keep the fairies warm.

In some parts of Britain, when families moved house it was traditional to take a few cinders from the old fireplace with them to the new one, so that family ties would remain unbroken. When chimneys smoked or the fire refused to catch, housewives did not blame the wind or draughts, but witches, and many people were convinced that the iron poker, laid across the grate, would cure the troublesome fire. Some of the older generation still use a poker to draw a cross on the hearth stone of a new fireplace before lighting the fire, and some say they can foretell the future by the movements of the embers gathering at the back of the fire.

A flake of soot hanging on the grate is said to foretell the arrival of a stranger, while coals burning in a heap, with a hollow in the centre, or divided into two parts, signifies a parting. When there is a spluttering from a piece of coal, this meant a quarrel in the household, but, as my old aunt used to tell me, if you gave the fire a good old stir with the poker, this would prevent the quarrel. A live coal falling from the grate was a sign of a wedding in many parts of the country, while a spit on the hearthstone brought bad luck. Throwing items in the fire had many mysteries; do not throw egg shells into the fire, or the hens will stop laying, while anyone who burns bread is said to be feeding the devil.

At one time there were many little gatehouses next to stations occupied by railway workers and their families. The gates that kept road traffic from the railway lines when trains are due were operated manually, and were usually the wife's responsibility. Before opening the gates to road traffic, it was essential to have a thorough knowledge of the train timetable to know if a train was due. You could set your watch by the trains and many a time I have seen my father pull out his pocket watch from his waistcoat pocket to check the time with the trains. The gatekeeper had to be an early riser, as the first train arrived at about 6am. The penalty for oversleeping was being roused by a crash as the train went through the gates. This carried a stigma that would last a lifetime.

I was born at Easton and I can remember walking to Framlingham with my mother pushing my brother and sister in the pram. If the railway gates were closed we would get very excited, waiting to see the fast train thundering by just in front of us. I should think the gatehouse must have shuddered violently with the vibration of their passing.

The gates used to fascinate me; the lamp was a large, square structure with bull's eye lenses, coloured alternately red and green. When placed on the gates at night, its red eye glowed a warning in whichever direction was closed to traffic. The mortality rate was rather high and several cats, with much-shortened tails had literally escaped death by inches.

I admire the sewing seen at shows and exhibitions, they are works of art and patchwork and quilting have become very fashionable in recent years. Patchwork was practised in Egypt over 3,000 years ago but it was not until cheap cottons became available from India that it was established in this country. From the 18th century onwards, it flourished, and the Americas became the centre of this fine art when the Pilgrim Mothers came from England, taking much of this material with them to get them started.

Any kind of new or old material can be used, or a mixture of both, provided that it is all of the same weight and will not fray. Silk and cotton should never be used together. Templates are often used and these can be made in all shapes and sizes, the most popular being the hexagon. The finished articles can be used as a bed cover or for hanging on the wall. A popular patchwork item used to be a 'love cushion', made up of pieces of material from father's shirt, mother's blouse and baby's first dress.

Quilting is another sewing art in which you have two layers of cotton with a layer of cotton wool in between - these are joined together by means of running threads that curl and twirl in many artistic patterns, forming the material into a warm and soft cover. Although quilting is also a very old art, it had a special vogue in the 18th century when a lot of men wore quilted waistcoats with lovely embroidered flaps over the pockets.

Today there are so many beauty products on the market, but in days gone by women relied on the products of the kitchen and the fields to keep them beautiful. Recipes were written down and passed on from mother to daughter in neat little books, and in one such book the author says, 'Beauty can be deare. Always wash in rain water, never water from the well, and use a little cream skimmed from the milk, with honey taken from the hive.' It was the cost-free flowers and herbs of the field that best served the cause of the early country-woman's beauty. We know from history that Helen bathed her face in the dew, Cleopatra washed in asses milk, Elizabeth I scrubbed her blackened teeth with sage leaves and Nell Gwynn boiled burned cabbage stalks to make a black dye for her 'jet curls'.

Burdocks and plantain were dug up to make astringents and the oil squeezed from the house leek was used for chapped lips and hands. Special teas made from parsley, rhubarb and nettles had their uses in clearing up yellow complexions after the winter and to dissolve the rheumatics drink one pint daily. For relaxation there was the bran bath and the lavender pillow was used for inducing sleep. Women liked to look beautiful, and if they could not sleep, a pot-pourri of rose leaves, thyme, rosemary, lavender, lemon verbena and mignonette would be placed in a dish by the bedside.

The face pack was known even in great-grandma's day. If there was any yeast left over after baking, it would be mixed with rain water and spread on the face until it dried - this was also supposed to close up large pores and was a good treatment for pimples and whitlows. Egg-yolk and honey banished wrinkles; all you had to do was to wash in hot rain water then spread unbeaten egg white on the face, leaving it to dry then removing it with cold rain water and smoothing on a mixture of milk and almond oil. After this, the lines should have disappeared.

Teeth were cleaned with salt, soot, chalk or dried sage and rubbed with fresh strawberry leaves. Toothache was dealt with by clove oil; I remember my mother rubbing this on our gums if we had a toothache and raw garlic and brandy was also used. No doubt, even if the brandy did not cure the problem, it produced a feeling of relief.

Eyes were bathed in infusions of fennel, cold tea and salt solutions. To remedy bags and wrinkles under the eyes, small bags of raw potato were placed on them at bedtime. However, great-grandmother's words of wisdom were that the greatest beautifier of all for eyes is to think noble thoughts, for this is the expression that gives the look of the soul - wisdom indeed.

REMEDIES

'On January 31 never go to bed with cold feet or a cold heart'

The hedgerow was the medicine chest of the Middle Ages; with all the variety of edible plants and fruits, the people of those days wasted nothing. Roses, thyme, sage and wormwood were all used in medicine. Coltsfoot is common in our hedgerows and was collected by the Romany people to make a syrup which was used as a cure for bronchial trouble. The celandine was also collected by the gypsies and the juice of the stem was used as a cure for warts.

January is also the month for head colds, so I will give you two suggested remedies which were given to me, to relieve the suffering, although there are no real cures. These have stood the test of time. One is Blackcurrant tea, made by pouring boiling water over a muslin bag filled with blackcurrant jam. The other is a treacle posset. Put a pint of milk in a saucepan and bring almost to the boil. Add two tablespoons of treacle and the juice of a lemon. Boil slowly until the curd comes off, then strain and drink very hot, preferably in bed - it suits a January night.

Another old fashioned helpful cure is to take two eggs and break them into a basin. Add two tablespoons of rum and two teaspoons of sugar and beat these together. Heat one mug of milk to just below boiling point then pour the mixture into the hot milk. Drink this and you should soon feel your limbs come back to life.

I have been given a good cough mixture recipe by Nigel Wynn of the Woodbridge Complementary Healing Centre - he says it is very good and can vouch for its effectiveness.

Dice one large onion, take a jam jar and cover the base to about a quarter of an inch deep with a good quality brown sugar. Next add a similar layer of the diced onion, followed by another layer of sugar. Repeat this process until the onion is used up, and complete with a final layer of sugar. Leave this to soak for 3-4 days, by which time the sugar will have liquified. Strain off the sugar liquid through a muslin, or similar strainer, into a second container and warm gently on a low heat. Stir in an equal quantity of honey and continue warming and stirring for five minutes. Remove from the heat and stir for 1-2 minutes until the mixture cools. The syrup is now ready to be bottled.

Often when we felt a cold coming on, we took a hot basin of onion gruel (onions cooked with salt, pepper, a lump of margarine and a little milk). We ate this hot then it was up to bed. Country people still say the onion is one of the best cures. Some of the common pieces of advice concerning colds are to 'sweat out a cold' and to 'feed a cold'. One way to stop a cold developing was to suck a raw onion, or to inhale the smell of freshly cut onions. When you were ill in bed, a half onion would be standing on a plate on the windowsill and would be changed each day to take away any infections. My mother always rubbed our chests with camphorated oil or goose grease. We kept our feet warm by cutting brown paper to the shape of the foot, rubbing the paper with tallow candle wax and placing it inside our socks. We also rubbed the candle grease on paper and put this on our chests to keep the cold out.

Mustard plasters were used to reduce inflammation or relieve back pains and as late as the flu epidemic of 1918, linseed poultices were ordered for the treatment of pneumonia.

Many herbs were used in the old remedies, and most cottage gardens had an important corner for growing herbs and roots for medical purposes. Many people will remember senna tea and castor oil - cures for constipation, not forgetting Beecham's Pills said to be 'worth a guinea a box'. We were often given brimstone and treacle and had to lick a dessertspoon of half treacle and half flowers of sulphur, which tasted as unpleasant as it looked. So many ointments and embrocations were used; I can remember my father having a bottle of white horse oils in the shed. He got my mother to rub these on his back when it was bad and he said it always relieved the pain.

We have a lot to thank our ancestors for, in the way of cures. The gypsies always say that a cure is close to the disease. Thus the dock leaf grows near the nettle and willow bark, said to cure rheumatism, is found beside the water that causes it. They used foxgloves to cure heart disease long before scientists discovered that digitalis - the drug obtained from foxgloves - was good for the heart. Nettles were used to cure skin diseases, they are very rich in iron which improves the complexion, and ground dandelion was used to cure diseases of the liver.

RECIPES

Everyday country food might seem simple but is tasty, warming and substantial, and will see you through any working day. Years ago, there were specific times of the year for slaughtering animals, when fresh meat was available and for the rest of the year there was only bacon or salt pork or beef. Cheese was made mainly in the spring and summer and although there were hard cheeses which lasted through the winter, the lighter cream and curd cheeses had to be eaten fresh and were only available when the sun shone and the cows were out to grass. Vegetables obviously had their seasons and so there were times when there were plenty of fresh ones around while at other times there were only dried beans and peas. We only ate parsnips and Brussels sprouts after the first frost had touched them as this made them eat so much sweeter - as I have proved many times in the eating.

Nowadays we are spoilt for choice, then the two main parts of the country diet were salt meat - mainly pork and bacon - and cheese, the others were beer and bread. Wheat flour was used to make puddings, dumplings and plain cakes, mixed with lard and perhaps sweetened with currants.

The country food did require long, slow cooking which might seem extravagant in terms of fuel, but since most cottages had an open fire or kitchen range burning all the time, the same amount of fuel was used whether the cooking pot was on or not.

Parsnips

The parsnip is a wonderful vegetable, often known as the Lent Vegetable because it was much used in Lent. It is a root that will stay quite happily in the ground all winter without being destroyed by the frost - in fact frost improves the flavour, making it much sweeter. One of the best uses is to make parsnip wine (years ago this was known as 'Parson's Wine).

4lb parsnips
8 pints water
2½lb sugar
Juice of 2 lemons
8oz raisins, chopped
1 tsp wine yeast and nutrient

Scrub and boil the parsnips without peeling them. Do not boil too long or this will make the wine cloudy. Strain on to sugar, lemon juice and raisins. Cool the liquid until lukewarm and add the yeast. Cover and leave for ten days. Strain into jars and seal with an airlock. This wine is best left for a year before drinking - just right for next Christmas.

Pea and Ham Soup

Some kinds of food are particularly appropriate for really cold weather. There are often ham bones and oddments of meat left over from the festive season. I never throw mine out to the dustbin or to the birds as it's the time of year to get the soup pan on the go! The day before you think of having this good wholesome food, you will need to soak some dried peas, dried butter beans, haricot beans and lentils in a bowl of water. My mother used to put a lump of bicarbonate of soda as big as a hazelnut in with the pulses, it was supposed to be a charm against flatulence. You will need a ham or bacon bone for pea soup, to give it flavour - even a knuckle of ham will do.

After soaking the pulses, put them into a large pan with the ham bones. Cover with water and slowly cook for two to three hours. I also add any vegetable that is available, diced and cooked for at least three quarters of an hour of the cooking time. Served with Suffolk dumplings, it is as good as Christmas Day lunch!

Marmalade

This is Seville Orange season, and in all our years we have not found any bought marmalade quite as good as the home-made variety. You will need fruit cutting boards, a basin for the pips, a pan for the shredded fruit, a cloth for constant wiping of fingers and very sharp knives. An added bonus is a good programme on the radio - its no good trying to watch TV as your eyes must concentrate on the job in hand.

I always use:

2lb Seville oranges
1 lemon
4 pints water
4lb sugar

Peel and cut up the oranges, saving the peel and the pips. The pips are put in a net bag in a bowl and covered with water to steep overnight. These are then boiled up with the peel the next day, strained and the water added to the marmalade pan.

All the other ingredients are boiled together until they reach setting consistency. When making ginger marmalade, I add 8-10oz chopped preserved ginger during the last five to eight minutes of boiling, or you can use crystallized ginger.

For another flavouring to your marmalade, try replacing one pint of the water with one pint of pineapple juice . For a dark Dundee-type marmalade, use one tablespoon of dark treacle with the sugar, this gives a slightly bitter taste and a rich, dark colour. A miniature bottle of Cointreau or Armagnac can also be added.

During the cold weather there can be snags to making marmalade, as you can't keep the windows open for too long. If you do, clouds of steam billow above you and the icy blast cuts the air around the cooker. If condensation gets out of hand, you are liable to have it dripping down your neck. Of course, if you wait until the brew is safely done, you may combine operations by spring cleaning the ceiling at the same time. Think of the satisfaction you will have, the ceiling and walls cleaned and rows of vintage marmalade in store!

February

S.E.Burrows
2000

FEBRUARY

February is described as the 'Gateway to the year', the month of transition from winter to spring; a month of promise with longer days and brighter hours. In the country the silver skies are deepened with blue and gold. The country walks have catkins, no longer drab and grey, but golden brown or a pale green tipped with carmine, and wild willow palm burgeons in silver buds. Some country folk smile and talk of an early spring as a 'Coltsfoot Spring', but so often the weatherwise remind us of fickle April to come with the bleak dark boughs on blackthorn hedges covered in white blossom, like drifts of snow, and speak of a 'Blackthorn Winter' with a shudder. The blackbird is beginning to sing more, and you can see a tiny tinge of gold appearing at the base of his beak - this will slowly spread until his whole beak becomes crocus yellow. House sparrows too are smartening themselves up, as the grey patches that have obscured their black bibs for the last few months are fading away.

Traditionally, Candlemas (2 February) holds the key to the month's weather, for if the day is fine, then much of the winter's harshness is said to be still to come. Another old saying is that 'When the wind's in the east on Candlemas Day, There it will stick till the 2nd of May'. According to a German proverb, 'The badger peeps out of his hole on Candlemas Day and if he finds snow, walks abroad, but if he sees the sun shining, he draws back into the hole'.

Candlemas goes further back than Christianity. Candles have been symbolic of life and resurrection since ancient times, and therefore are closely associated with the returning of spring and the growth of crops. In the days of the early church, Candlemas - being the end of the early church's Christmastide - was the time when people's thoughts turned to spring. Beeswax candles were used in churches as it was traditionally held that the bees came from heaven. The procession and blessing of candles at the time went back to the pagan torch processions, when people would march around the fields, bringing light to invigorate the soil before the spring sowing. Candles are still blessed in churches in many places for use in the coming year, and tapers are lit in honour of our Lord and the Virgin Mary.

Snowdrops, a symbol of purity, are also called Candlemas Bells or Mary Tapers. At Woodbridge an old tradition has been held since 1738, where

Peggy Coles Countryside Year

instructions were left on the gravestone of a George Carlow that bread was to be given to the poor on Candlemas Day.

There seems to be no shortage of 'spadgers' - the Suffolk word for sparrows. House sparrows are very happy and pleased with themselves as long as they are in the company of their own kind. A lone sparrow is as distressful a sight as a single starling on a chimney pot or TV aerial. These little chaps have the strong character of an individualist, yet are essentially social birds. They must not only be 'in' with other sparrows, but also be near to man. The sparrow is one of the very few birds which has voluntarily elected to live close to us. Using his sharp wits, he has managed to keep a full crop ever since that wise decision was taken as far back as biblical times when sparrows learned that the safest place to build a nest was under the eaves of the temple. From then on they have adopted man's abode as shelter. Every house we build is a potential site for sparrow tenants and it is possible to have them in residence any month of the year.

While other birds are forced to waste a great deal of time and energy in defending their territory, in long migratory flights and even in singing to advertise their presence, house sparrows concentrate on looking for food where it is most likely to be found and easily picked up. When half a dozen sparrows have found a good patch, you often find another fifty have turned up to join the feast before you can turn round. They sit on my rooftop and watch for me to come out to feed my chickens, then they follow me up the path and, when the gate is opened, they are in the run feeding with my birds. They are no fools; even when working in the garden they are with you, watching in case food is about to appear.

As spring comes, the sparrow wastes little time, for once the courting is done, he keeps the same mate for life. There are cock fights in plenty but it's really little more than springtime madness. One never sees sparrows flying very far or high and they have none of the aerial lightness and grace of the finches and tits. A flight no higher than the gutter on a roof is quite enough to see 'what's cooking' in the next field or over a couple of garden walls.

In the oral history by George Ewart Evans The Crooked Scythe Mrs Tom Jay recalls that there was a Sparrow Club, members of which used to go round the

28

farm stacks at night with netting. The sparrows caught in this way would then be skinned and put into a stew, with a piece of pork. Sometimes they were put into a basin with a suet crust on top and this was called a 'Sparrow Dumpling'. I can remember that my father used to go sparrow hunting at nights, but I can't ever remember my mother cooking them. However, no doubt they helped to provide many a meal in years gone by.

A farmer once said to me 'I'm blest if I know what to make of sparrows. I hate 'em when I see 'em and if I don't see 'em, I worry because I think there is something wrong with my place'. There is a saying that if sparrows dust bathe with hectic and hasty abandon in the fine tilth of your seed beds, it will soon rain. Some people curse sparrows, but the world would be a poor place without their cheerful chirping in the eaves of our houses. In the bible, we are told that 'two sparrows may be sold for one farthing yet one shall not fall to the ground unnoticed by the Creator'.

The first week of February is said to be courting time for the birds, and St Valentine's Day the day when they chose their mates. Rooks have been repairing their nests ready for the breeding season. They hold noisy meetings known as rook parliaments, and seem to take more time to get started in the mornings. They will be in the rookeries for long periods before they fly off in search of food. In the past, you would have seen them repairing their nests almost everywhere, but town rookeries are much less common than they used to be.

In cold weather several blackbirds will appear on one patch, and I am amazed that they spend so much time and energy getting rid of would-be competitors. Their fights are quite alarming, with one blackbird setting into another with much vigour. The search for food is abandoned for a short while, during which time the supply often disappears as other species take their share. When a blackbird is in its own territory it flies at its enemies, and when they reach the boundary of their territory they take up the 'threat' display fanning their tails and raising their beak into the air. There is such a contrast too - one minute the blackbird seems to be trilling sweetly, if softly to itself as it sits in a prominent position on the hedge - the next minute it is having a fight with another of its kind.

Peggy Coles Countryside Year

I was recently clearing out some old cards, which I had kept for years, and I came across one card my late mother had given me. It was my grandmother's funeral card, and very different to the cards we send today. It was like a small postcard, with flowers drawn on it all in black and white with a little verse and her name on the back and a note of where the funeral and interment was to be. There was something special about these sad little cards, with their black-edged envelopes.

We no longer have the old characters who dug the graves, there is still the odd man who has to do the job by hand, but most often a small digger comes in and takes all the hard work out of the digging. I remember the old gent who came into our villages on a small moped with a spade and fork tied on to the carrier. I don't know how he drove around like that, but as far as he was concerned he had the right of the road, and all other driver had to swerve to avoid him! He was a kind man, and I used to take him a flask of tea and a cake - I knew it was hard work digging a grave as my husband used to dig them and I would help with filling them in. Sometimes it would be a double grave, six feet deep. He would dig it the day before the funeral and often there would be heavy rain in the night and the grave would fill up with water so we had the extra job of getting it out. It was a craftsman's job getting the grave the right shape and size. Sometimes they had to be lined with hanging ivy and flowers pinned around the sides.

Most people wore black clothes to funerals, the men wore black armbands and the ladies black hats. Funerals used to be big and grand - most of the villagers would attend, and there would be a big spread to eat afterwards. Today, many of the churchyards are full and most people have to be cremated.

For many years the commercial manufacturers have been turning out Valentine cards by the million, and a token of undying love will be sent to sweethearts all over the world. Years ago, country love tokens - country swains or wooden valentines as they were called, were sent to the ones we loved. These were painstakingly hand-made and were real labours of love. Made of pressed, frilled or embossed paper with decorative hearts, cupids and flowers painted by hand with delicately phrased lines of verse which made every wooer a poet laureate, if only for a few hours.

Those who were really skilled ventured to add paper roses, a piece of ribbon or silk, pressed flowers or coloured feathers arranged decoratively. Although these creations were sometimes sent anonymously, the receiver would always know the giver. They were greatly treasured and often handed down from one generation to the next. There are collections, including some very fine examples in the Victoria and Albert Museum in London and at the Castle Museum in York.

As well as valentine cards, it was also customary to give a gift of a more practical nature as a love token, though if they were highly valued, these tokens were kept unused - possibly as part of the young lady's 'bottom drawer'. Welsh love spoons, butter prints and lace bobbins were all made and scratched designs, initials and pierced hearts added. It must be remembered that the person making such objects may only have had the simplest blade to work with, by the flickering light of a candle late at night after a hard day's work. The love spoons would be intricately carved with circular holes, wheels, stars and quite fragile designs; sometimes the handles were flat and bore beautiful carvings such as keys, doves, knots or the name of the recipient. Most of the designs were symbolic; two spoons projecting from one handle meant 'we two are one', if the handle bore wheels 'I'll work for you' and hearts said plainly 'I love you'. Spoons with one large bowl and several smaller ones meant that it was hoped that a large and happy family would follow.

People often say 'Get February over with, then we can look forward to the spring'. Already we see the swelling buds on the tips of twigs and many other signs of new birth. Some birds are singing away as dawn breaks, and my mind goes back to the music we used to have. Years ago it was simple and mostly played in pubs. Many had no music teaching - if you had a good ear and memory, it was soon picked up on a concertina. Sometimes one had a mouth organ, and always men's whistling was as clear as a bird's. I can remember when whistling was solely for men's pleasure, and women were not encouraged to whistle:

'Whistling women and crowing hens deserve to have their heads cut off'

I can remember in the early 1950's, most men in villages used to cycle to work, and you could recognise them by their whistling. My father would often say,

'So and so was late for work this morning' - he would know his whistling. Years ago, Revival meetings sent a wave of tunes around the country. The revivalists chose good rousing settings for their cheerful hymns, and the music of them flew from one to another - 'See how does it go?' they used to ask, and the tune was whistled and sung, passing from one to another with minor alterations. The hymn 'When the roll is called up yonder I'll be there' was a favourite with man and boy. The man milked his cows to its tune, and the ploughman sung to his horses and cattle, whistling in all weathers.

The piano was an important part of many households, and many a song was sung around it. The musical box used to be a Sunday treat, a mahogany box about two feet high, which stood on the parlour sideboard. It had a key and when wound up would play many fascinating tunes. John Howson, who wrote Many a Good Horseman went around the villages and recorded interviews with musicians and singers. It was lovely to hear the old boys singing and playing the accordian, and some played the bones - two white meat bones, dried and cleaned, which they would tap on their knees. I have heard many a good tune played with bones and on a mouth organ.

Flowers have a wonderful language of their own. The rainbow coloured Iris was the bearer of good tidings, white heather for luck and myrtle orange blossom for wedded love. Fennel meant strength, columbines (granny bonnets) meant folly, daisies for innocence and rue, which flourished in most gardens, meant regret, but changed on Sundays, when it was taken to church for grace. The so-called 'bunches of misery' were lavender for distrust, mint for suspicion and marigold for pain.

There was a great interest in flowers when Dutch artists poured their delight in flowers into their paintings. Then birthdays were 'flower days'. Spring blossoms come from children on Mothering Sunday, and lilies decorated churches at Eastertide (the Madonna Lily being the symbol for purity). Later children were christened with flowery names - Daisy, Lily, Rose, Poppy and Violet. We all know the red rose means love, and the exquisite moss rose, with its sheath of green, was a confession of love. A full-blown rose, with two rosebuds meant secrecy, and the wild rose, picked from the hedgerow and presented in the fields said 'I wound to heal'. 'A red and a white rose together meant unity, but a yellow rose meant jealousy. I love Lily-of-the-Valley, which always meant happiness, and was so often a young man's offering to his sweetheart, making them one of the most treasured of flowers. Sprays of white Jasmine meant amiability, blue and brown velvet pansies meant 'Think of me', blue periwinkle from grassy banks and woods brought pleasing remembrance and lasting happiness. Sage was for long life, and esteem, and a spray of ivy was always there for friendship.

There are rules in the presentation of flowers, reversed with their heads downwards, they gave the opposite meaning. A bunch of wheat, picked from the harvest fields, meant riches, and a single straw meant agreement, but a broken straw meant a quarrel. A dandelion clock was used to question love - the famous 'She loves me, she loves me not'.

We had a lot to thank Nature for in our childhood days, the fields were our toyshops, where we used to make toys from anything we found in the pastures. The flowering spikes of the Plantain were picked for the game of 'Soldiers' with a bunch of green flowering heads. We then picked out the likely warriors and challenged another soldier flower to combat, and when his head flew off, a fresh one was taken from the bunch, took his place and we fought on. We picked rye grass, which we called 'Tinker, tailor grass' and we counted the little ears to find out whom we should marry - 'Tinker, tailor, soldier, sailor, rich man, poor man, beggar man, thief'. Then we used to say 'This year, next year, some time, never'. We even used acorn cups to drink spring water running from the banks. Pea-shooters, pop-guns and whistles were all made out of hollowed elder stems. Hazel saplings, which grew in abundance, were used for fishing rods, and hawthorn leaves, showing their small lovely rosettes in early spring, were called our 'bread and cheese'.

Washing day was always on a Monday, and I think this was because the men were at home some of the weekend and could help to carry the water for the coppers. Men and elder sons filled copper baths and bowls for washing and rinsing water, because not all cottages had a pump or well and pond water was mainly used. If the pond was a long way from the back door it meant a long trek to cart the water. Sometimes too, it would have to be strained with a piece of net or muslin to get the weeds and pond life out. Then, in winter time, the ice had to be broken on the pond to get the bucket into the water. Saturday night was always bath night and some of the very dirty clothes were put into the tin bath and covered with used bath water to soak over the weekend.

Situated in the backhouse, 'backus', the copper boiler was built in one corner heated by a fire underneath and with a flue behind. It stood about three feet high and held about ten gallons of water - some old farm cottages still have a boiler in the backus. Sticks were gathered to light the copper, and firewood and coal were piled on to keep it burning and to keep the water boiling. Not just coal and firewood, but any available rubbish such as paper, rags, old shoes or wellies would be 'stuffed up the copper hole'. I once put one of my father's best shoes in the fire as it had fallen into a pile of rubbish - I never heard the last of that for many years! The water from the weekly wash was never wasted as it was used on the garden - the soapy water helped to keep the white fly and caterpillars off the vegetables. The copper was also used for boiling the Christmas puddings and for brewing beer, and very strong it was too!

Also standing in the 'backus' was the mangle which was used to wring out excess water and also to press linen. Woe betide you if you were not careful, to catch your fingers between the rollers! Sometimes it took three or four days to dry washing in the winter. If it was wet outside on washdays, lines were strung from the ceiling beams and the washing pegged on. We would just get it all dried and ironed, and then be ready to start the whole process again the following Monday.

There is an old rhyme for washing day:

'Those who wash on Monday have all the week to dry,
Those who wash on Tuesday are not so much awry,
Those who wash on Wednesday, one hesitates to blame,
But those who wash on Thursday, wash for shame
'Those who wash on Friday, wash in need
And those who wash on Saturday are sluts indeed.'

My grandchildren get great pleasure from going through my needlework box - the button box has many tales to tell of where the buttons came from. Discovering old buttons is a most fascinating hobby. Buttons have been widely

February

used as both fasteners and decorations since the sixth century. During the last two hundred years they have been used on military and civilian uniforms to denote rank and status. In the USA decorative buttons have been collected since the 1930s while in Britain the interest is growing.

Some of the first buttons were made from small pieces of cloth sewn into a tight knob, and some of the best British buttons were made in the 18th century, including Wedgwood jasper medallions, carved pearls and engraved silver buttons. Between the two World Wars few decorative buttons were produced as women's fashions did not require them. Covered fabric and glass buttons were used on children's clothes and rubber buttons on Liberty Bodices.

Recently I was shown a large collection of buttons which ranged from metals including alloy, aluminium, brass, bronzed alloy, copper, gilt, lead, painted metal, pewter, English silver, steel, tin, zinc and filigree (fine wire work). Enamelled buttons are a work of art in themselves with their pretty colourings. Then there are glass buttons, such as peacock eye, paperweight and opaque - these were made from black pressed glass with metal dies and were very fashionable during Queen Victoria's long widowhood. I also saw ceramic, horn, bone, wood, shell, bakelite, papier maché leather and fur. The back of the button can be nearly as important as the face particularly if there is a shank (a loop for sewing the button on). The collector told me her collection started when her husband gave her an enamelled button he had found in the River Deben, and she became hooked on this fascinating hobby.

In February the moles are getting busy and we see large molehills appearing beside the road and in the banks. A rare sight in the countryside today is of a row of skinned moles left on a fence or gate to show the farmer that the mole catcher had been at work. The sad fact is that while moles become no fewer in number, professional mole catchers are steadily dwindling in number, and there are many areas entirely with none at all. The days are gone when a young man, fond of an open-air life and anxious for an independent lifestyle, could be trained and taught the secrets of the countryside.

The mole catching season lasts from September (after harvest) until June, but in the season it takes really bad weather - snow, fog and very hard frosts - to stop a catcher from working. Catchers seem to have an uncanny knowledge of where to look for mole runs and where to put their traps. Going into a field he has not 'caught' before, the trapper will first walk round the boundaries, looking in the hedgerows and ditches for signs which will show him where to find the main runs. They generally run into the field from the hedge and from these the moles push out smaller runs as they search for worms. A mole will eat more than its own weight - anything up to sixty earthworms - in a day. Molehills are often seen in gardens and on the roadside but I asked my friend where he begins to look for moles and, while I am sure that he was keeping many secrets to himself, he admitted that he looks first in damp ground near brook courses, canal banks and railway embankments. It is said that the grass turns yellow over mole runs. They seem to be conservative creatures and not easily cleared from a particular spot - my friend told me that he kneels in the same place to set his traps as his father knelt forty years ago. When we were young, as soon as moles were caught and removed from the traps, they were skinned and the carcass left on the fence or gate as evidence to the farmer of the mole catcher's success. The professional catcher would fasten the skins onto wooden boards to dry before sending them away to be made into a moleskin waistcoat - these were highly prized by many people. In a good year, a catcher could catch three thousand or more moles.

The damage a colony of these pests can do to a field of roots, sugarbeet and so on is enormous - a whole crop can be uprooted and ruined. Where poison was used, it was usually strychnine powder on the worm, but this killed the worm and moles don't like to eat dead worms when they can get live ones. In our gardens we try some of the old methods, such as putting holly leaves in the runs, or disinfectant, and some people even use mothballs, but as my mole catcher friend says, traps are still the best method of ridding ourselves of these pests. When you buy a mole trap, put it in the ground for a few days until the newness wears off, and then once you set the trap in a run - never in a mole hill - make sure that you keep any light out.

Moles are active both day and night with periods of work which are almost continuous and last about four and a half hours alternating with rest periods of about three and a half hours, which time they spend in the nest. Because of this, some people will tell you to watch one hour after dawn, midday and again at teatime.

February

When I speak to local school children they are always amazed at the things we used to have to do in my schooldays. I went to Kettleburgh school, now made into a house, where there were two classrooms with dark, sloping porches where the washbasins were situated. Outside toilets (buckets) were very smelly at times and the bigger boys would wait until the girls were sitting down when they would lift up the back board behind the pail and get a stinging nettle to tickle our bums. We received school milk in one-third pint bottles. Some of the children would stand these bottles underneath the radiators to warm the milk and it would get a brown skin on the top - this put me off milk for the rest of my life. Mrs Atkins used to cook our school dinners in her house, up the lane past the school, and we took turns to help her fetch it and take the pots and pans back again. My brother slipped over one day with a jug of custard so that meant no custard with our chocolate crunch that day. We took it in turns to wash up and to help in the school garden.

We had to walk along roads and fields to be in time for school and we were often sidetracked; looking for birds' nests and picking wild flowers. The teacher had a lot of jam jars around the classroom full of wild flowers and shrubs. I can still smell the tar in the summertime. The playground was of tar covered only in sand so we would often get tar on our clothes. Mother would try to get it off with margarine as soon as we got home and we changed into our old clothes. There was a list of jobs to do after school, such as fetching the milk in a can, collecting sticks for the fire and hogweed or cow humble for our tame rabbits - it was no good picking a bunch, we had to take a hessian sack to fill. Maybe we didn't have TV's or computers, but life in the country was quite full for youngsters. We knew the names of all the birds, animals and flowers of the countryside. We knew where the best primroses, oxslips or five-fingers grew and often we would pick up a baby rabbit or hare.

The roads in those days were empty except for a few lumbering horse-drawn vehicles, and maybe the odd van or car, so we were able to play for hours on the roads with our hoops, spinning tops and hop-scotch. We were always pleased to find a lump of chalk in the fields for drawing on the roads - there was no money to spare for buying chalks. My piece of chalk was my pride and joy and would be hidden in a safe place so that my brother could not find it. The hoop would help us on our way to school as we would run or trundle it along with a stick. Us girls had wooden hoops, but the boys had iron rings called a rim, which were made by the local blacksmith. Sometimes we would use an old cycle wheel with the spokes taken out.

The most treasured possession in those days was a pocket knife or shut-knife as it was called. These would be carried everywhere and be used to cut sticks from the hedgerows to make bows and arrows. We all knew where the best sticks were growing and the girls had to wait until the boys had cut theirs and then hope that they would cut some and help us to make our bows and arrows. Sometimes we would make a pop-gun by cutting young, pith-filled shoots from the elder tree, pushing out the centre to form a barrel. Some of them had a spring fitted (a metal strip from Mum's stays!), and we used them to shoot dried peas or small stones. Another joy was our carts, made out of orange boxes fitted onto a pair of old pram wheels. We played about in these during the week and then used them to carry home sticks for the fire on a Saturday.

We used to make 'dens' at the bottom of the garden or near a wood. They were made from twigs, old boxes and dried grass and were a hotch-potch affair of old fire guards, corrugated iron sheeting and old planks of wood - anything we could lay our hands on. A hole was left in one side for an entrance, which we could crawl through, and we fixed up shelves on which the girls would soon place jam jars filled with wild flowers. An old sack was put on the floor and a tin box held our treasures. These included rubber bands, pencils, marbles, string and lumps of chalk from the fields and used in many of our games. There would be room for about four or five children and getting dirty was all part of the fun. We used to take our lemonade or bottles of water and jam sandwiches to eat. Our dens had an atmosphere of adventure and plans were made for the day ahead, with the children from next door joining us.

When we were children there was much more freedom, there was no law against children riding on farm implements and vehicles and we loved to ride on the horses and wagons. We would walk for miles down dark lanes and in the woods, looking for mushrooms and blackberries.

In those days there were no televisions, but we all listened to the 'wireless' (radio), and I remember my late uncle, Morry Bugg of Saxmundham, telling me that it would take all day to install a wireless in the home. There was the tall aerial and insulators to fix and a bucket full of earth sunk in the ground to carry the earthwire. Inside the wireless there would be a grid bias, a high tension battery and an accumulator - which had to be charged up each week. Then to complete the outfit, there would be a large loudspeaker. Not everyone had a wireless in the early days, but most cottages would have a harmonium. This would often have been handed down from the previous generation. Families would gather round, especially on a Sunday night and sing good old 'Wesley' hymns. In fact, this was probably the first kind of music they knew.

REMEDIES

Nature has given us many gifts and the country woman has known of them for centuries; most had a sound knowledge of the healing properties of herbs, which had been acquired naturally as a child. When she was ill, she watched her mother gather different herbs, finding where they were growing, noting their particular taste and smell and learning how to prepare them. But then the so-called wonder drugs made by white-coated men and women in large factories changed all that. For this reason, people thought that they must be better and more effective. Nowadays we are not so sure and many are asking if the old herb and natural remedies are not better after all. We seem to have come full circle and herbs are once again being widely used - not just by cranks but by qualified and experienced doctors as well.

'Sage, hibiscus and marigold,
Excellent herbs had our fathers of old'

Rheumatism

I can well remember how my father used to carry all sorts of items in his pockets but it was not until years later that I realised what they were for. There would be a potato to ward off rheumatism, one of the most common of remedies; the smaller and harder the potato became, the less likely you were to suffer from the complaint. Apples were another aid as was drinking a glass of dry cider every day. No doubt this was very pleasant, although I do wonder if it really cured 'the screws' as we call rheumatism. Another cure is to take a teaspoon of cider vinegar every morning before breakfast. Eating celery cooked in milk is supposed to be good while I have been told that a teaspoon of celery seeds infused in a cup of boiling water and taken three times daily brings relief. Garters were once worn as a preventive measure. These would be made in summer from dried eel skins stuffed with lavender. The garters would be buried in peat, between layers of mint and would be ready to wear in the autumn.

Headache

A most effective relief for a headache was to lie down with a cloth wrung in vinegar on the brow, tied in place with a large handkerchief. As children we always knew when we came downstairs in the morning if Mother's head was tied up then we had to be quiet

Burns & Scalds
If we burned ourselves, Mum used to get a piece of clean rag and soak it in cold water and then put it on the burned place.

Chilblains
First thing in the morning, put your feet in the chamber pot.

Sore Throat
We used to tie a stocking around our neck before going to bed. I have been told the dirtier the stocking the better, but we only used clean ones!

Sickness
If one felt sick, it was said that you had been eating pork at the wrong time of year, as pork should only be eaten during the months with an 'r' in them.

Toothache
When we had toothache, Mum used to put a clove in the tooth. We had to try and keep it there, hoping the pain would go away.

Nosebleed
Put a door key at the back of the neck - the big old-fashioned iron keys not a little old Yale key!

Earache
If we had earache, Mum would roast a small onion, wrap it in a bit of white rag and then put it in our sore ear.

Hints During Cold Weather

To prevent the lock on a car door from freezing in cold weather, cover it with sticky tape

Keep the plugs in baths and washbasins when not in use so that the drips do not make the waste pipes freeze

When hanging out the washing in winter and on a freezing day, add a small handful of salt to the final rinsing water - it will help to stop clothes from freezing

Make sure that vegetables are well covered - once potatoes are frozen they will soon turn black and are no good for cooking

A few drops of glycerine in the toilet cistern provides an excellent anti-freeze

When boiling the kettle for tea or coffee, put spare water in a flask to use later in the day

If you have a stone bird-bath, tip the water out each evening as it will only freeze, and may crack the bowl

Remember, every mile is two in winter!

RECIPES

Suffolk Rusks

This plain little cake is made all over East Anglia, and at one time it was always a tradition to bake them on a Friday when doing the weekly baking - my husband took two in his lunch box every day.

9oz Self-raising flour
3oz lard, butter or margarine
Pinch of salt
2 eggs, beaten
Enough milk to mix

Sift the flour and salt, rub in the fat and add the beaten eggs and a little milk to mix to a pliable dough. Roll out to a half-inch in thickness and cut out into small rounds. Put on to a greased baking tin and bake in a fairly hot oven, Gas Mark 5, 200°C until golden brown.

Once they are cooked, split in half with a fork and put back into the oven for 10 minutes or so, until crisp and brown.

Light dumplings

There are many different ways of making a good light dumpling - some call them 'swimmers' or 'floaters'. A very light dumpling as follows:

Mix together 4oz self-raising flour a pinch of salt and enough water to make a soft dough, form into small balls and drop into soup or stew, making sure it is on the boil. The dumplings should boil for 10 to 12 minutes.

A more crusty dumpling uses 4oz self-raising flour, 2oz shredded suet, a pinch of salt and water to mix. Form into small balls and boil in soups or stews for 20-25 minutes.

Some people add an egg to the mixture, and chopped parsley makes a nice flavour.

Ginger Beer Plant

Mother used to make this and we used to love it. We took it into the harvest fields, or when we came home from school we would go and get a stone bottle from the pantry floor and fill our glasses. It looks rather like mud when you first make it, but it will start to clear after a day or two.

Blend one teaspoon of fresh yeast with one teaspoon of sugar. Add $1^1/4$ pints of tepid water.

Feed daily with one teaspoon of sugar and a heaped teaspoon of ginger for ten days. At the end of this period decant the liquid, whether it is required for ginger beer or not, and halve the sediment. If you wish, you can give a friend the other half, or you may like to keep another plant grown from the second portion of the sediment.

To make the beer, make syrup by dissolving 1 $1/4$lb sugar in 1 pint of water and bring to the boil. Add the juice of three lemons and six pints of cold water to the boiling syrup. Decant one pint of the ginger fluid and add this to the syrup, bottle and leave lightly corked for two hours. Then cork tightly and leave to mature for at least ten days. Do not fill the bottle too full or they may burst.

Onions

It used to be said that an old-fashioned farmer's wife's home would not be complete unless a good string of onions hung in the shed. An onion boiled in milk and flavoured with nutmeg, taken as hot as possible, was used as a 'scarecold' and onion gruel made with milk as a cold cure. Knowledgeable folk also used their onions to top a welsh rarebit for supper. They also used to roast them, cut them open and butter and season them, top them with cheese before browning them to crispness under the grill, making a delicious cheesy crust.

Nowadays many country women use onions for entrees, savouries, curries and garnishing. Sometimes they are boiled and cooked slowly in a casserole, and they are also stuffed with mince, liver and bacon then served with mounds of mashed potato and a little pork dripping.

Onion Pie

This is a recipe my mother used to make.

2lb onions
1/2lb bacon
2 eggs
2oz pork dripping
Seasoning
Short pastry:
6oz plain flour
3oz butter
Water to mix

Skin and chop the onions and fry slowly in some of the dripping, chop the bacon into small pieces and add to the onion. When cooked, but not browned, cool and add beaten eggs with butter and seasoning and mix thoroughly.

Line a shallow tin with pastry and pour mixture in, cover with another thin layer of pastry and bake in a moderate oven for about 3/4 hour. You can also change the topping by adding cream to the beaten eggs and using breadcrumbs, dabbed lavishly with butter, instead of pastry, for the covering.

Stuffed Onions

4 large onions
3/4lb good minced beef
6oz breadcrumbs
1 tbsp mixed herbs (parsley, thyme, marjoram)
1 egg beaten
Dripping or oil for roasting

Peel and boil the onions whole in salted water for 1/2 to 3/4 hour. Scoop out the centres, chop them and mix with the minced beef, breadcrumbs, herbs and beaten egg. Pile the mixture back into the part-cooked onion shells, stand them in a dish with the dripping or oil and bake for 1/2 to 3/4 hour in a moderate oven (180C or Gas 40) until they are brown on top.

45

By February we begin to tire of winter vegetables. Some of the less familiar ones are well worth trying, such as Sea Kale, Celeriac, Kohl Rabi and Red Cabbage. Try cooking some of the more familiar vegetables in different ways. Brussels sprouts are very good fried in deep fat, but the fat must be very hot so that they are crisp and brown outside and juicy inside - drain well before serving. Brussels sprouts pickled go very well with cold meats. Celery stewed until tender, then coated in batter and fried, make tasty fritters.

March

2000
S.E.Burrows

MARCH

Catkin time is here - watching March winds sending yellow pollen flying is a delight to see and the horse chestnut buds are breaking, shedding their sticky brown scales. This is the beginning of the agricultural year, and you will often hear the country man saying 'A peck of March dust is a thing, Worth the ransom of a King'. But it should be a bushel instead of a peck of dust. We need a dry month in which to get on with the spring sowing. It all rests on the weather, and invariably March is a fickle month. Days cold and bold alternate with soft mild spells as winter strikes its last blows. The increasing actinic power of the sun even on cold days, hurries forward flowers in sheltered south-facing nooks, and the double notes of the chiff-chaff delight the ear as the yellow-brown form of the first summer migrant sings and swings from the bare branches of budding trees.

I always find March a restless month - whether it comes in like a lion or a lamb makes no odds. Although I know full well that nature is moving forward, there is a feeling of a gap in March before the great breakthrough into April and spring, when nature gets on with it in a big way. The fickle wind fills the lungs as one stands on high ground and it leaves one feeling a little breathless and the eyes and ear lobes smart if there's a touch of 'east' about it, as there so often is. This is typical of March - everything is, as it were, just out of reach and it's a job to be patient and wait for things to happen. As sure as God made little apples and big 'uns, the time will come and nature will unfold its intent. It's a month of laughing and crying, with skies as mild as milk one day, and the wind chasing the rain over the earth the next. March is a promise - it's not spring, yet it is a farewell gesture to winter. All in all it's a month of excitement. The earth has a fresh smell, as one has not scented it for many a long month and one's nostrils 'imagine' the perfume of the violet in some secret place.

Once you see the tractors out pulling the land down with cultivator or disc-harrows, and watch the soil change from beige to warm brown as the sun and winds dry the freshly moved soil, suddenly you can feel, hear, see and smell the spring. England's spring, the loveliest spring in the world, and before you realise it, it is shirt-sleeve weather.

The nesting season is on the way, song thrushes begin to build in the bare hedges - they usually lose some eggs from their nests to the jays or magpies, and the missel thrushes will be making their nests in the forked tree branches around the garden. Only the hen will be sitting on the eggs for the male will be singing loudly in the tree tops.

Daffodil buds show green among the upright blades of their foliage in the flower border, small iris reticulata and crocus are all coming into bloom. In woodland, the ground is covered with the early blossoms of wood sorrel, wood anemone and wonderful primroses. These plants have rested all winter and now they are bursting out all over the countryside, and there is a saying that when you can stamp on five daisies, Spring is here. Whenever I see primroses, I think of my childhood. I often used to get into trouble for being late home from school, as I would go hunting for different kinds of primroses. 'Five fingers' as we called them, were like a cowslip, but had big blooms on the stems. These were a rare find, and we would not tell other children where these flowers grew, it was our secret. Violets, blue and white, would fill our cottages with their scent.

This was also the time of the year when we used to go into the woods with father, helping him to cut pea sticks and bean poles before the sap had risen. When we were on our way mother would call after us, 'Bring me a new linen prop'.

March is the traditional month for the exhibitions of so-called madness among hares. On the skyline, if you are lucky, you will see two or three hares tearing across the field one after the other at breakneck speed; they jump, twist, turn and kick. Suddenly they stop, frame up for a boxing match, give a few sharp blows and then off they go again. Sometimes in their excitement they throw away their usual caution and run foolishly into grave danger. I suspect that a handsome lady has something to do with this; she turns the boys' heads and they fall to quarrelling about her. So seriously do they take their love affairs that they forget their traditional foes.

Hedgehogs now emerge from their winter quarters, and start to feed up on insects. Toads and frogs will be spawning, and I can remember when March was the month for chick hatching. Some farmers used to like to get early hatchings, so they would have point of lay pullets ready for September. The incubator would be cleaned out ready for the eggs, or farm workers would be looking for a broody hen towards the end of the month to put 13 eggs under her. Neighbours would often lend a broody hen, and sometimes gamekeepers would come round and buy any broody hens that you had - broody bantams made excellent mothers.

If you look closely at a dog rose, you will see that the sepals in the centre of the flower are not all the same. The legend is that long ago there were five brothers, each of whom had a beard. When two of them decided to shave theirs off, one of the others was in doubt about what he should do, for while the two with beards urged him to keep his, the other two begged him to shave it off. Whichever piece of advice he followed would not meet with general approval. At last he had an idea to please them all - he shaved off one side only. If you examine the dog rose you will usually find that little points grow on both sides of two of the sepals, two are without points and the fifth has them on one side only.

A friend asked me recently if I had ever known a rat to attack a rabbit. I thought he was pulling my leg, but he told me that he was walking by a woodland stream one evening when he suddenly heard a distressed squealing close at hand. He said he was amazed to see a baby rabbit rolling on the grass with a large brown rat clinging to its back. As he was crossing the stream, he then saw a slim shape slide through the grass to the struggling pair and seize the rat from behind. The rat screamed at this unexpected attack, let go of the rabbit and turned to fight off his attacker - a stoat. When the rat relaxed its grip, the rabbit ran a few yards and collapsed, apparently dead, but then seemed to recover and slipped off down the field. He told me he watched the fighting pair, the cries stopped and he saw the stoat standing by the dead rat. Turning in the opposite direction taken by the rabbit, it went off. I know that a stoat will tackle and kill a rat and even a small chicken, but I had never previously heard of a rat hunting a rabbit.

When I was a young girl, I used to help with feeding and cleaning out the chicken huts on the farm where my father worked. One day I saw two rats enter one of the small huts, they did not notice me. When they appeared again, one was on its back clasping to its breast an egg from the hen hut and the other was dragging the first by the tail held firmly in its teeth. They made straight for a hole in the earthen floor under the wall and the egg was put aside. Then one backed into the hole and the other pushed the egg into it. Rats are very intelligent and versatile creatures who seem to be able survive in any environment!

Although I love to see the birds in my garden, there is one visitor with whom I get rather cross at this time of year - the pigeon. I walk up the garden path and watch them fly off the spring greens, then, as soon as my back is turned, they are back again to destroy as much as possible of the brassica crop. Fond as I am of seeing the pigeon flying around, it does not recompense for the loss of my green vegetables. Even as my brother and I are wondering how we can protect our spring cabbages, I hear the sudden 'clap-clap' of wings above and look up to see my enemies gliding peacefully overhead towards the nearest tree. We stick bottles painted red on bamboos and dot them among the plants, even stretching pieces of string over them with jangling bits of tin. Sometimes I have made a scarecrow but the pigeons watch our efforts from a distance and keep away for a few days, but hunger very soon moves them into attack. I have a shrewd suspicion that the pigeons understand my fondness of garden birds.

We all get a little annoyed when we find early primulas and crocus decapitated by sparrows who also have a habit of taking dust baths on the newly sown beds. Even the jackdaws come early every spring looking for suitable chimneys to nest in. However, I look forward to any sort of bird which comes into the garden, over the years there have been many absentees, and on balance, I believe they have as much right to eat and live their lives as we do.

With warmer, sunny days coming, I have noticed the fly coming out of its winter hiding. An old lady once told me about a fly trap her parents used to have for when there were swarms of flies in her house, always at meal times.

A fly bottle was put on the table - a conical glass vessel about six inches high and the same across the base. It stood on feet that were raised half an inch from the plate, a trough about an inch wide and deep ran inside the bottle all round the central opening at the bottom. Some sugar was sprinkled on the plate to attract the flies, which eventually flew up into the dome. The trough was filled with beer or vinegar, into which many flies fell within an incredibly short time. There was a terrific buzzing noise as they flew about inside before falling into the liquid. The bottle was emptied by removing the stopper at the top.

March is a superstitious month and I am sure that there are many who, like myself, on the first day of March say the magic words 'Hares or white rabbits'. You can go further and look out for an even-leafed ash tree:
'An even-leaved ash, and a four-leaved clover
You'll see your true lover before the day's over'
The name clover is a corruption of the word 'clava', meaning a club, and we preserve this emblem of good luck on playing cards - the suit of clubs. I remember that my father always kept a hare's pad in his pocket throughout this tricky and romantic month.
Crossroads are places of ill-omen. One should always avoid crossroads when out walking although whilst riding or in a two or four-wheeled vehicle, the metal parts will protect you from evil. At all costs, you must never stop in the middle of a crossroads and try to get your bearings.
Dogs have many superstitions attached to them. One is that if a dog whines persistently for no good reason, it is a sign of misfortune coming to the family, while howling in the night foretells a death or some calamity. Another saying is that if a dog howls persistently in front of a house where someone is ill, the person will die. This belief is strengthened if the dog belongs to someone in the house. Should the dog be driven away, but return to howl again and if any dog suddenly howls three times and then falls silent, it is a sign that a death has just occurred nearby. If a strange dog comes to your house, it is a sign of a new friendship, but if one crosses your path on your wedding day it is a bad sign, and to avert misfortune, the couple must give each other a kiss. When out walking, if you meet three white dogs

together, they will bring you good luck, and even better, if you are on your way to a business appointment, your project will be successful. When a visitor arrives, a dog often senses their intentions towards you; barking means these are not so good, while if it welcomes with enthusiasm, their coming will bring good luck.

The light of a candle can tell you your fate; if the flame burns blue, there is often a death in the family, if the flame sways and moves around - even if there is no draught - windy weather is coming, and if the wick refuses to light, there will be rain. A spark foretells the coming of a stranger or a letter. To light a candle from the fire in the hearth is considered to be unlucky, and for the same reason never light three candles with the same match.

Coal is considered lucky, and a piece of coal that has been given to you, wrapped in a piece of cloth should be carried in your pocket or handbag for good luck. If you find a piece of coal when out walking, if you pick it up, spit on it and throw it over your left shoulder and walk on without looking back while making a wish, your wish will be fulfilled. Coal is one of the lucky gifts the 'first-footer' brings as he enters your house on New Year's morning.

I am sure you have heard the cock crowing in the morning - if he crows at nightfall he is trying to tell us that bad weather is on the way, while if he crows at midnight, he is foretelling a death in the neighbourhood.

On seeing the new moon, you should turn the coins in your pocket for good luck, and if you hear the cuckoo whilst out walking, turn over your loose change and make a wish. Also when putting on new clothes for the first time, put a small coin into the pocket and you will always have plenty of money whilst wearing the garment. Another lucky omen - if when sweeping your house you notice a coin lying in the dust, pick it up and put it in your purse or pocket, even a small coin should bring you luck.

A gypsy would never use a caravan until the spider had spun her web across the doorway. This was because a spider would not spin her web if the wood was damp - as soon as the web was spun, the caravan was dry and ready to be occupied.

The last days of March are said to be days borrowed from April and these, proverbially, have meant bad weather, often called the blackthorn winter as the blackthorn is in bud at this time. This borrowing legend also occurs in France and Spain and people would not borrow or lend on these days.

The day after St David's Day is St Chad's Day and gardeners used to say, 'Sow peas and beans on David's and Chad's be the weather good or bad'. Another old saying is that the last three days in March are called blind days and no seeds should be planted. The weather is often windy and stormy at this time and tradition has it that these days have been borrowed from April.

Many people collect picture postcards, but the golden age of this hobby in Britain was from the closing years of the 19th century to the end of World War One, when postage increased from a ha'penny to one penny. During the Edwardian period, collecting postcards was a national craze and every drawing room in the land had its postcard album. This was usually kept beside the aspidistra and the family bible on the table by the window. In the years of the Great War alone, it was estimated that 25 million postcards were produced. The majority of these wartime cards were of a special kind, producing a deep feeling of nostalgia. Young men during the war years often sent silk postcards, and all sorts of postcards were produced by the leading manufacturers of the day. The artists were in great demand to keep up with supply. One of the most popular themes was of food and farming in general. Hardly surprising considering the acute shortage that faced the nation at that time. The most prolific of the comic artists was Donald McGill who worked incessantly at creating colour-wash drawings which sold in their millions. He produced up to nine cards a week and many of the farming cards were sent to the troops in France. They were real morale boosters and were wholeheartedly approved by the War Ministry. Brightly coloured country scenes were the most popular with the troops as, at that time, much of Britain's family and social life still revolved around the countryside. Common country scenes, like tilling the land and harvesting were a boost to soldiers in the wretched conditions of the trenches. Not much has changed today; country views and farming scenes are still very popular.

Although we have lost many of the old crafts of our villages, basket making is still going strong. It is one of the oldest and most universal in the world today and large quantities of baskets are in common use in spite of all the plastic containers. Baskets are used by agricultural workers, fishermen and distributors of all kinds of food. Nobody can say exactly when the first baskets were woven and traditional baskets have changed very little. The shapes, patterns of weave and materials used have remained the same throughout many centuries, as have the names of different types of basket. A 'skep' was used for potatoes, by beekeepers for collecting a swarm of bees. Lobster and crab pots were 'Cherry-chips', while the most popular shopping basket was known as the 'sitting hen'. This name came from Scotland where the basket was used for carrying broody hens from one croft to another, as it was once the custom to borrow a broody hen from a neighbour. At one time, the fishermen of Great Yarmouth and Lowestoft used a lot of baskets, but plastic trays have taken over now, and the herring ladies who used to come down from Scotland all used large baskets. Laundries had basket-work hampers, and I can remember when working at St Audry's Hospital, we had large hampers for the linen, but as the years went by, these were exchanged for cardboard boxes.

Years ago I remember there was an old basket maker, Joe Pipe, who lived with his sister Rose in Grundisburgh. He made some wonderful baskets and both my mother and I bought strong linen baskets from him - I still have one of his baskets. He was a real character and would go round the pubs collecting orders. He used to say 'Make you one - what size do you want? Have it next week'.

The Basket Makers' Company was established in 1569 and still exists, although its records were lost in the Great Fire of London in 1666, when the Guildhall was destroyed. The motto of the basket makers is 'Let us love one another'. It is nice to know that the blind and disabled are still trained in the art of basket making and many of the teachers are members of the Guild who have left their own trade to help the disabled and to share their experience. During the last war, the War Office commandeered all willows and two million panniers or willow hampers were made and used for dropping stores by parachute. I have been told that Dutch farmers in the Arnhem area were still using some of the panniers dropped during the Battle of Arnhem for storing bulbs up until a few years ago.

Years ago, countrymen would study the moon, as this was supposed to determine the sowing of the crops. There are certain superstitions attached to the moon at particular times - the harvest moon riding high meant dear bread, a full moon at Christmas foretold a poor harvest while a new moon coming on a Saturday or Sunday meant foul weather and bad luck almost everywhere. In Cornwall, a Saturday moon was called 'The Sailor's Curse' while in Norfolk, a new moon on a Saturday, if it comes once in seven years, comes too soon. I know some people in this area who will say 'Saturday's change and Sunday's full, never brought good and never will'.

'On Mothering Sunday above all other
Every child should dine with its Mother'

I am very lucky as the mother of two good sons to have their love, phone calls and visits, it's these little things that make a mother feel loved and not lonely. I feel sad when I hear of anyone who has argued with their parents and do not keep in touch. Why not forget the past and go and visit on Mothering Sunday. We are not on this earth for long so why make ourselves and our parents unhappy. Just remember that life is short, so be happy and make someone else happy as well - you only have one mother, so take care of her!

Mothering Sunday is the fourth Sunday in Lent, and used to be a holiday for apprentices and daughters to visit their mothers carrying a present of violets, a trinket or a Simnel cake. The name 'Simnel' is probably derived from the Latin simila meaning fine flour, but there are different theories by various writers, and I like the story of Simon and Nelly. Long ago there lived an honest old couple rejoicing in the names Simon and Nelly. It was their custom at Easter to gather their children about them and thus meet together once a year in the family home. The fasting season of Lent was just ending, but they still had some unleavened dough left over which had been used to make bread during the forty days' fasting. Nelly was a careful woman and it grieved her to waste anything, so she suggested that they should use the remains of the Lenten dough for the basis of a cake to feed the assembled family. Simon readily agreed, and further reminded his wife that there were still some remains of their Christmas pudding hoarded in the cupboard, and that this might form the interior of the cake and be an agreeable surprise to the young people after making their way through the less tasty crust.

So far, things went on harmoniously, but when the cake was made, a subject of violent discord arose. Simon insisted that it should be boiled, while Nell, no less obstinately, contended that it should be baked. The dispute ran from words to blows for Nell, not choosing to let her province in the household be thus interfered with, jumped up and threw her stool at Simon who, for his part, seized a besom (broom) and applied it with right good will to his wife's head. She now seized the broom and battle became so warm that it might have had a serious termination had not Nell proposed a compromise that the cake should be boiled first and afterwards baked.

Accordingly, the big pot was set on the fire and the stool broken up and thrown on the fire to boil the water, while the besom made fuel for the oven. Some eggs, which had been broken in the scuffle, were used to coat the outside of the pudding when it was baked. This new and remarkable production became known as 'the cake of Simon and Nelly' but soon, only the first half of each name was preserved and, joined together, it has ever since been known as the Sim-nel or Simnel cake.

This charming tale came from a booklet given out to visitors years ago by Mrs Spriggs of Princess Café, London Road South, Lowestoft. The tearoom seated fourteen people and items for sale included Hovis Bread, baked daily and Vienne Bread, noted as a cure for indigestion - especially suitable for Afternoon Tea, price one penny to three pennies, and Princess Raised Pork Pies, sixpence and one shilling, larger sizes; ten pence per round.

Recently I was getting my baking equipment out to make some scones and could not find my scone cutter. I ended up using a stainless steel wine glass to cut out my scones. Later I found my cutters in the back of the cupboard in a basin. All this set me thinking about the old tin utensils we used to buy at the ironmonger's shop years ago - how I loved looking in these shops. Nowadays most utensils are made of stainless steel, plastic or have a nonstick coating. Most of the utensils in the Victorian kitchen were made of tin, and I can remember my mother's kitchen with all the tin and metal equipment. First there was the paraffin can under the sink or in the shed, this would be used most days to fill up the oil stove and was made of strong tin. Then there were little oil cans we used to oil our cycles - it is difficult to buy these little oil cans now. Almost every item of kitchen equipment was supplied by the ironmonger.

Knives were of steel but not 'stainless' and quickly became spotted and marked. We cleaned them with knife cleaning powder, and there were even knife cleaning machines, into which you would put the knife, turn a handle and get your knives clean. There were knife boards for carving the Sunday joint - if you were lucky enough to have one. Fathers would go outside with the carving knife and sharpen it on the back-door step. After rubbing the knife up and down on the step, the blade would be as sharp as a razor.

We had wire toasting forks for toasting bread in front of the open fire, and we would then eat the toast oozing with dripping. Since there are not so many open fires today, toasting forks are not much used, although I'm sure the toast tasted better made in this way. Skewers are another item we don't see much nowadays. Most butchers would use a skewer in your meat to hold it together, and many still do, but if you buy meat from a supermarket, then it is wrapped in plastic.

A tin kettle was always singing away on the edge of the fire, or on a trivet, and if the heat was too high, you could soon burn the contents of a frying pan, which were usually made of thin tin. Candlesticks were made of stronger tin, and there were also many sizes of repair kits. As I remember, you could buy a square of cardboard, with up to four rings of tin and cork, a nut and a bolt. With this kit you could mend a hole in a kettle or cooking pot. Most people don't worry about repairing cooking utensils today.

Lastly, I cannot forget the old tin baths, which came in all different sizes. Now I keep these in the garden planted up with flowers. Visitors have remarked that these baths are now antiques and should be taken care of. They were hard times, but the utensils were of good quality and very useful.

St Patrick's Day
'One leaf for fame, one leaf for wealth,
One leaf for a faithful lover,
And one leaf to bring glorious health.
All are in a four-leafed clover.'

There are many legends about St Patrick, the patron saint of Ireland. He was born in 85AD on the banks of the River Severn and at the age of sixteen was captured by pirates and taken to Ireland as a slave, where he worked as a shepherd in County Antrim for six years. Escaping he landed in Gaul and travelled to Rome, where he was imprisoned for a time. Later he returned to Ireland to preach and convert the people to Christianity, in particular, the pagan king Loigaine. He used the three-in-one leaves of the shamrock to explain the Holy Trinity, and was also supposed to have banished snakes from Ireland.

St Patrick's Day is the day for potato setting in Cheshire, and for planting cabbages in North America.

It is curious to learn that something that originally began in the days of ancient men and continued through the ages is now a popular hobby. Many of the people who collect horse brasses do not know the original meanings of the symbols they contain - usually it is the gleaming brass work which attracts the buyer.

The use of horse brasses had its beginnings in the days when primitive man believed that every object, whether living or dead, contained a 'spirit' and these spirits were either good or bad. Daily life for such people was a constant struggle to live; to seek and kill enough food and find safe shelter, facing overwhelming odds and sudden, violent death. So it was that such people believed that charms could protect them against the evil spirits of death, and used the symbols of good spirits - two of these being the sun and the moon. They also believed that certain metals contained good spirits, so these charms were created from bronze, iron and brass, and hung around horses' necks for protection.

There were three main types of brasses, the disc or sun brass, the crescent or moon and the heart brass. Certain designs were more common in particular districts. Some references reveal that the carthorse, walking or trotting, was to be found in Sussex, the windmill in Lincolnshire and the owl near Leeds. Some had religious subjects, such as the 'Flight to Egypt', but with the disappearance of the cart and plough horse, the need for creating horse brasses died out while collectors came to the rescue and recognised the skill and care that went into the craft. Nowadays the craft mostly survives in country craft centres, antique shops and folklore museums.

25 March is Lady Day - the first day of the legal year until the English calendar changed in 1752. Rents were due, tenancies were reviewed, commenced or terminated and it was New Year's Day. Things have changed now, but one old saying states that if Good Friday or Easter Sunday falls on Lady Day, there will be a national disaster within a year.

Easter weekend is special for many; the greatest religious festival of the Christian year. For some it's the start of the holiday season, others will be busy in their gardens, some will be out on their boats, while churches will be decorated with the first spring flowers. Families go to services together, and children have great fun hunting for Easter eggs. Because Easter comes in spring many pre-Christian customs are concerned with fertility and renewal. Wearing new clothes on Easter day will ensure good luck for the year. Years ago, it was only the rich who followed this tradition, but as the years went by, most family members managed to have something new to wear for Easter. Many will claim to dance as the sun comes up on Easter morning, and a lot of churches hold their first service as the sun comes up.
The egg is the symbol of life - hence the Easter egg. The ancient Teutons believed that at Easter time rabbits laid eggs, and this was the origin of the Easter bunny. To refuse the gift of an Easter egg, was to refuse the friendship of the person offering it. If your Easter morning egg had two yolks, this meant great prosperity. Eggs, blessed at Easter, warded off illness, and rolling Easter eggs downhill was a favourite Easter game - the idea being to cross the finishing line with an unbroken shell. The winner would be rewarded with a year of good luck.

There are a great many customs in various parts of England concerning Easter eggs. In the past, pask, paste or pace eggs were given beautiful mottled designs by boiling them hard inside the coat of an onion, with the juices of various herbs and flowers, such as broom used as dyes. Some pace eggs were simply dyed and decorated with tallow. Another technique was first to dye the egg black or some bright colour, the dye then being scraped off with a pen-knife to make a design - all sorts of designs were created, like lovers' knots, birds and coloured ribbons.

Unexpected patterns and tones appear when eggs are wrapped in leaves, skins, petals and grasses and then boiled. Patience is required for this since the work is fiddly but it is surprising what you can end up with. Onion skins will produce a terracotta effect and blades of grass make a criss-cross pattern. Petals from the crocus give a veined greeny, yellow-red appearance, and a leaf pattern can be designed by using the shoots of wild cow mumble. There are many other wild leaves to experiment with and you will be surprised at the results. Once you have decided on your leaves, grasses and so on, tie them around the egg with strands of cotton, this will give a marbled appearance, then wrap them carefully in cling film. Place each egg in boiling water separately , then, when the shell has taken the dye, lift out gently. Remove the cling film and leave the eggs, still wrapped in the grass or leaves until quite dry.

Another method of making your own original Easter eggs is to immerse the egg in hot water for a few minutes and then use a tallow candle to inscribe a name, a face or a pattern suitable for the person to whom it is to be sent. The warmth of the egg makes it an easy process. The inscribed egg is then placed in a pan of hot water and saturated with cochineal or some other dye. Because the part over which the candle has passed is impervious to the dye, when the egg is removed from the pan this part remains white on the coloured background.

Three or four days either side of Easter, young men and boys used to go out Pace egging, collecting eggs for themselves and acting the pace egg play, which is the Easter version of the ancient mumming play. They still do this in some regions, only now the children go round Pace egging and the old play, once the essential heart of the custom, is forgotten.

Whether we like it or not, the donkey is of unique interest - whereas it is possible to steer a horse almost anywhere by a gentle pressure of the knees or a touch on the reins, the ass appears incapable of observing any such discipline. The animal may be strong, courageous and even swift, but it is always to some degree unmanageable, although just as intelligent as the horse.

I am told that donkeys are descended from the grey wild ass of Africa, and the habits of the desert-loving wild beast have been passed down to the domestic animal. A donkey's temper is closely related to the barometer - like Badlam's ass, the donkey speaks loudly in protest and warning before a storm. He is comparatively high-spirited when the air is warm and dry, but subdued into sullen sluggishness in wet weather. He hates mud and will often refuse to cross a brook, yet he delights to roll in the sand and dust. Country men always say that you should buy a donkey in wet weather so that you can see his faults and sell him when the sun is bright and warm.

The ass has played a humble part in the rough and dusty highways of history, and it is certainly at its best in the eastern setting of the hot, dry lands. The transport ass has always suffered from being overburdened, and one can see from bible stories how hard he used to work, and still does. Donkeys are still working, and even in the lowliest stables of the Holy Land, donkey bridles are well kept and adorned with brightly coloured blue beads to ward off the 'evil eye'. The little saddles are also well kept , with saddle bags attached on either side at the rear often bound along the edges with silver and blue tapestry. Of course it was a donkey that Jesus chose to carry him on his triumphal entry into Jerusalem, and the donkey still bears a cross on his back in memory of his hour of glory - not such a lowly beast after all.

The time has come for frogs and toads to mate and spawn and, as if at a given word, they have emerged from their hibernating quarters and set forth on the annual pilgrimage to the waters where they themselves were spawned. It's a slow, laborious walk as, one by one, they reach the water's edge and wade in to push off into deeper water. Some come singly while others have already mated and the males are mounted like jockeys on the backs of the females.

Once in the water, the males begin their singing, a watery, purring sound that continues night and day whilst breeding is in progress. Only a sharp frost at night will hush the choristers, for the cold makes them sluggish and takes away the desire to mate. Sometimes during these early spring nights the frosts are so severe as to form a sheet of ice over the pool. Then the toads will sink to the bottom of the pond, burying themselves in the mud until the spring sunshine melts the ice and warms the water.

The poor old female has to put up with several males all trying to cling on to any part of her anatomy and, burdened by their weight, the helpless female sinks to the bottom of the pool. Eventually the surplus males, realising the pointlessness of holding on, release their grip and only the rightful one remains with the female. Unlike the frog which lays its eggs in large, irregular shaped masses, the eggs of the toad are laid in long chains which measure anything up to ten feet in length and contain as many as five thousand eggs. These chains, or strings of spawn become wound around water weed and submerged tree branches as the female moves about whilst laying, and so they become anchored and will not drift about the pool or sink to the bottom.

The breeding habits of frogs are much the same as those of the toad, except that frogs spawn earlier - usually at the end of February or beginning of March. The male frog mounts the female in much the same way as the toad, but he can be cruel in embracing his partner so tightly that he can sometimes crush her chest and kill her.

Weather in March can be fickle, and logs of wood are still needed to keep our fires going. When you are next out for a country walk, think of the following words and how much trees mean to us:

'Ye who would pass by and raise your hand against me, hearken ere you harm me,
I am the heat of your hearth on the cold winter nights
The friendly shade screening you from the summer sun
And the fruits are refreshing draughts, quenching your thirst as you journey on.
I am the beam that holds your house, the board of your table,

The bed on which you lie and the timber that builds your boat.
I am the handle of your hoe, the door of your homestead,
The wood of your cradle and the shell of your coffin.
I am the gift of God and a friend of man
Ye who pass by, listen to my prayer
Harm me not'

Handy Hints
1 Electric toasters can be difficult to clean. A flat paintbrush will be most handy to remove all traces of crumbs very easily
2 When making a fruit salad, try soaking the oranges by covering them with boiling water and letting them stand for five minutes. You will find that the white, pithy part will come off quite easily, leaving the skin and flesh quite clean and easy for slicing
3 Knives and forks which have been used for fish should be rubbed with the rind of a fresh lemon after washing. You will find that no flavour or smell of the fish remains
4 To remove iron mould stains, cut some rhubarb into small pieces, put into a saucepan, cover well with water and boil for 10-15 minutes. Strain off the solution and soak the stained part in the hot liquid. It may be necessary to repeat the process once or twice.
5 Patent leather shoes may also be cleaned with glycerine. Rub well into the leather and polish with a soft cloth
6 Some uses for glycerine:
A mixture of two parts glycerine and one part lemon juice makes an excellent cleansing lotion for the skin. Apply it sparingly and rub well into the hands.
Glycerine may be used for loosening glass stoppers in bottles when they cannot be removed by any other means. Apply it with a paint brush around the top of the stopper and it will gradually soak between the two surfaces and help to lift the stopper.

RECIPES

Simnel Cake

6oz butter
6oz caster sugar
3 large eggs and 1 egg white
8oz plain flour
Pinch of salt
$^1/_2$ level teaspoon ground cinnamon
$^1/_2$ level teaspoon ground nutmeg
4oz glace cherries, cut into quarters
12oz mixed, dried fruit
Finely grated rind of 1 lemon
1lb almond paste
Milk if necessary
Icing sugar for rolling

Grease 7in round cake tin, line with greaseproof paper and grease the paper. Cream the butter and sugar until fluffy. Lightly whisk the whole eggs and gradually beat into the creamed ingredients. Sift the flour, salt and spices over the surface and fold into the mixture. Add all the fruit and the lemon rind, folding together to give a smooth, dropping consistency. If too firm, add a little milk. Divide the almond paste in half. Lightly dust a surface with icing sugar and roll out one half to make a 16cm (6$^1/_2$in) circle. Spoon half the cake mixture into the prepared tin, place the round of almond paste on top and cover with the remaining cake mixture. Press down gently with the back of a spoon to level the surface
Bake in the oven at 150°C /Gas Mark 2, for 2$^1/_2$ hours. Cool in the tin for 1 hour. Divide the remaining almond paste into two. Roll out one half to a 17cm (7$^1/_2$in) circle and make the rest into eleven small balls. Lightly beat the egg-white and brush over the top of the cake. Place the circle on top, crimp the edges and, with a little of the egg-white, fix the balls around the

top edge of the cake. Brush the almond paste with the remaining egg-white and place under a hot grill for 1 to 2 minutes, until the paste is well brown. Tie a ribbon around the cake before serving.

Hot Cross Buns

1lb strong flour
1 tsp salt
2oz butter
1 egg
$^{1}/_{2}$ pint milk
1oz fresh yeast or $^{1}/_{2}$oz dried yeast
1oz sugar
1$^{1}/_{2}$oz chopped peel
2oz sultanas

Add the yeast and sugar to the warm milk and leave for 5 minutes to become frothy. Add the melted butter and egg. Warm the flour and sieve with the salt. Put yeast mixture into a mixing bowl and add warmed dry ingredients plus fruits and spices. Mix to form a soft dough and then beat well until the mixture leaves the sides of the bowl. Cover with a cloth and leave in a warm place to prove.

When doubled in size, knead and shape into buns. Cover with a greased polythene bag to prevent a skin forming, and leave to prove again for 15-20 minutes. Place a small cross of pastry on each bun and brush the top with a little milk and sugar glaze. Bake at 200°C for 15 to 20 minutes

Furmenty

This dish was served steaming hot in basins and in Thomas Hardy's The Mayor of Casterbridge, Mrs Henchard said, 'It is very nourishing after a long, hard day's work'

1 teacupful clean new wheat
¹/₄lb mixed fruit (currants, sultanas etc)
2oz flour for thickening
2 pints milk
2oz sugar
Nutmeg to flavour
Cream for serving

Cover the wheat with 1 pint of the milk in a bowl and put into a slow oven or slow cooker and leave overnight. Transfer to a saucepan and add the rest of the milk, sugar and a little grated nutmeg. Thicken with flour, mixed with milk, add the fruit and bring to the boil. Serve hot with cream
Furmenty is an alternative spelling but probably the same dish is an old yeoman farmer's dish and was made mainly at Christmas. The old custom was to serve a small bowl on Christmas Eve and offer it to friends or any stranger who came to the door. Furmenty takes a lot of cooking - up to twelve hours.
Fluffin - as some people called it - was made with barley instead of wheat and the recipe was to simmer enough barley and milk until it is as smooth as velvet, then add grated nutmeg and sugar to taste and a few drops of rum or brandy. I was told that whichever corn was used it needed to be washed thoroughly and soaked overnight before cooking.
Kibbled (broken) wheat should be simmered then a knob of butter, sugar, cream and rum added and I am told it is as near a liquid spice loaf as one can imagine - delightful and fragrant. It has also been described as 'gruel with its best clothes on'. There are many versions of this old dish and I came across this recipe in one of my old cookery books; put the wheat into a big earthenware covered bowl, cover it with water and put the bowl in the warm oven for three days - it will turn soft and jelly-like and is delicious. Add cream and sugar and eat like porridge. The process of slow cooking was called 'creeing' when applied to any corn being cooked and is an old word from the french 'crever'.

To improve an apple tart, try sprinkling 2-3 tablespoons of orange juice over the apples. This gives a delicious flavour and is an improvement at this time of the year, when they are sometimes dry and tasteless.

To weigh golden syrup when making gingerbread or puddings, it is advisable to weigh or measure the syrup accurately. Try dusting the scale-pan with a good sifting of flour. You will find that the syrup runs without sticking to the pan. Another tip is not to let the syrup get too hot when making gingerbread as it toughens the cake.

You might smile at the following recipe - called 'Paradise Pudding'

If you have a good pudding, pray mind what you're taught
Take sixpennyworth of eggs, when they're four for a groat
Take of some fruit, which Eve once did cozen
Well pared, and well chopped, at least half a dozen
Six ounces of currants, and pray wash them clean
Else they grate on your teeth if you know what I mean
Six ounces of bread, let the maid eat the crust
The crumb must be grated as fine as fine dust
Six ounces of sugar won't make it too sweet
Some salt and some nutmeg to make it complete
Complete did I say? Oh no, you must add
Six ounces of suet, or all will be bad
To these you may put, if pleasant and handy
Some nice lemon peel and a spoon full of brandy.
Three hours let it boil without hurry or flutter
And serve it up hot with some good melted butter
Adam tasted this pudding, thought it wonderfully nice
So Eve gave her husband a very large slice!

April

S.E.Burrows 2000

APRIL

April showers come suddenly and unexpectedly but just as soon go away. An old saying goes 'You won't be likely to get a wet shirt if you tap the weather glass of Nature'. Chaffinches call 'tec-tec' before rain and woodpeckers 'drum', rooks tumble in the air like fan-tail pigeons and caw to beat the sound of tractors at spring sowings. Moles cast up busily, feeling the increased humidity in the soil when worms become easier prey. Flocks of sheep feed ravenously, and cows lie down to keep a dry place for the night. Telegraph wires often hum out a message of coming rain, distant sounds come as clear as a bell and your long sight suddenly seems exceedingly good. One of the most common and reliable ways to forecast the coming of rain is that the dandelion closes its petals before a shower.

April can be a flippant month of high winds and cutting showers, but these winds help the arrival of an ever-increasing host of birds winging their way to spend the summer in this country. Martins and swallows 'God Almighty's bows and arrows' begin to arrive, to be followed by the swifts. There is a quaint belief that if a large gathering of swallows congregates around a house, someone in the house will die, and the spirit of the deceased is thought to fly away with the birds. Towards the end of the month the nightingales arrive, having also flown some two to three thousand miles from their warm grounds in the South. I have often stood outside my house at a very late hour to listen to the song of these birds - a moving experience of Nature at its best.

This was the time of year when the cattle were turned out into the meadows for the night after having been shut in the cattle yards throughout the winter months. How pleased they were as they roamed around, with flying tails. It was also lovely to see the old carthorses nibbling at one another's necks under budding chestnut trees, with their halters hung on the gate post. As a child I used to watch in amazement as the animals first ran around after being confined in the stable all winter.

April sees great activity in the cottage gardens. Workers are anxious to make full use of the extra hour or so of daylight, spades and forks gleam in the last

73

rays of sunlight. The evening meal can wait, the air is sweet with the smell of newly turned soil and rich well-rotted manure. A well-ordered, freshly sown kitchen garden proclaims an act of faith. The man that bends his back in April for the practical purpose of setting seeds in the drill is also bowing his head in a prayer of supplication and looking towards the fruits of July and the harvest he hopes to gather. He stands erect and looks back over his work at the well-raked plot, drilled and trodden into neat straight lines, each marked with a stick bearing an empty seed packet and he can see the burgeoning rows of broad beans and green peas that will soon appear and the long ropes of onions hanging on his cottage wall, ripening in the September sunshine. He has implicit faith that if he plays his part, Providence most surely will not fail him. Seasons may vary, dry spells are good to ripen fruit, wet ones good to swell the root, but a harvest of one sort or another we know we will have.

The birds are nesting in hedges and banks and in trees and shrubs around the houses. High up in the untrimmed hedge is the magpie's nest which, from ground level, seems just a clumsy bundle of black thorny twigs but climb up to it if you can and you would see that there is, after all, a rough and ready artistry about it. A lid of twigs covers the top and a ragged opening in the jabbing, prickly structure resembles a crown of thorns and would defy any intruding fingers. So different from the little wren, whose nest hangs in one of my clematis, a dear little nest artfully woven of hair, moss and tiny scraps of leaves. No man's fingers could possibly have made so neat an object and there she sits close, hour after hour, rocking gently in the wind. The blackbirds sit tight when discovered, watching the intruder with a shining black eye and slips off the nest to safety only at the last moment.

There is a legend about the wood pigeon and the magpie. The magpie undertook to teach the pigeon how to build a more substantial nest. The pigeon, instead of being a docile and interested pupil, kept repeating her old cry of 'Take two Taffy, take two'. The magpie maintained that this was a most un-workmanlike manner of proceeding as one stick was as much as could be managed at a time to advantage. The pigeon kept insisting otherwise until, in a violent rage, the magpie gave up the task, saying 'I say one at a time is enough and if you think otherwise, you may set about the work yourself for I will have nothing more to do with it'. Since that day, the wood pigeon has built her slight platform of sticks and compared with the large structure built by the magpie, looks to be a most inferior substitute.

This is the month during which many families will make well-intentioned but almost always unsuccessful attempts to bring up some young wild creature which has been abandoned by its parents. The half-fledged blackbird, the baby rabbit or the young starling which comes suddenly down the chimney like Father Christmas - they throw themselves on our mercy and we take them on. They seldom survive long; the caresses of our children, an empirical diet and sometimes, alas, the cat, combine to shorten their lives. They have, after much argument, hardly been christened when there has to be a funeral behind the tool shed. They have the touching charm of the helpless and they arouse in us - though not in the cat - the protective instinct. Unfortunately, they take an entirely different view of their inability to look after themselves. Their parents spoil our fruit, eat our vegetables and block our gutters with their untidy nests, and these helpless, uninvited guests will do the same if they survive our hospitality. However, we do what we have done in other springs. We bring out the breadcrumbs or the lettuce and charge the fountain-pen filler with milk, we shut the cat in the outhouse and, very occasionally, we save a life.

As children we would walk miles, climbing through hedges and over barbed wire fences - never mind if we tore our clothes - the important thing was to find those first spring flowers or the first frogspawn. Armed with jam jars, we would search among the weeds of country ponds, the spawn looked like jewels shining in the water. How cross our parents were when we filled the tin baths and all the buckets we could find, so that when Mother needed these containers to get water or to do the washing, they could not be used. Every year we were told off, but we still used to bring the frogspawn home.

Towards the end of April we would set off with an old dessertspoon tied on a piece of nuttery wood and hunt for the nests of moorhens, or waterhens as we called them. These birds would make a nest in the reeds or in the branch of a tree which had fallen into the pond. We were not too happy if the nest was towards the middle of the pond as this required good manoeuvring and a steady arm - so often we would get an egg on the spoon then drop it into the water. Sometimes we would get home with the eggs and would be disappointed to find blood in the yolks because the mother bird had been sitting on them for too long. It was best to leave one egg in the nest so that the birds would keep laying more. Moorhens can be very cruel birds; they will kill a duck's small family as they come out of the nest into the water. For this reason country folk had no time for the moorhen.

Sometimes in the early spring, just before harrowing time, peewits nested both on the ploughed land and on the unturned ground, and we often took their eggs since these would have been destroyed by the harrow later on. Readers may think that this was a regrettable thing to do, but fifty years ago there were many more birds around and to find eggs to eat added a little variety to the monotonous diet of the farmworkers' families. Nowadays this is an unheard-of delicacy

This is the time of year when watercress looks its best growing in streams, the bright, gleaming green of the flat leaves covering the streams. Today we have to be careful as some places in the wild can be polluted, and it is safest to buy it from the greengrocer. When we were children, Mother used to send us to get a basketful for tea. It grew in nice clear water, there was so much of it and it was so fresh. Boiled eggs chopped up with watercress made very nice sandwiches and it would also improve any salad.

While we were getting the watercress, we also looked to find the first flowers of the month. Among the earliest would be the prickly gorse with its golden pea flowers. It is always best in April, scenting heaths and sandy places. Later we would find the Snake's Head Fritillary, which has now become scarce. Lords and Ladies Cuckoo Pink (Arum Maculatum) was another plant we loved to see. It was called 'Lords and Ladies' because the roots were used to make the starch for fine lace and ruffs. The richly scented sweet violet was one of our favourite to gather. This was always the flower of love and was considered to have great virtues, especially for the eyes. We would often get wet feet trying to pick some Marsh Marigold Kingcups (Caltha Palusiris) out of the streams or the wet meadows.

Years ago, this was the time of the year when Mother used to put the eggs under a broody hen and it was always a baker's dozen. The baker's dozen is twelve for the baker and one for the devil and this came about because loaves would shrink after a while and as there were heavy penalties for selling short weight, the baker would always add an extra loaf to make up for the lost weight. The extra loaf was called the 'vantage loaf', and when breadmen delivered loaves to the houses, they were given one for every twelve they sold and that was their payment. I still put a baker's dozen eggs under a broody hen and keep up the old superstition that an odd number is supposed to be lucky. It was said that if you only put twelve eggs under a hen, they would all be cock birds. The best time for doing this is at sunset, but we would never put eggs under a broody hen on a Sunday.

There are various superstitions about eggs; when you have eaten an egg, you must not burn the shell - it should always be smashed. It was said that if an eggshell was burned, the hen that laid it would not lay any more. Country folk of many years ago thought that witches used eggs for evil spells and for trying to make ships sink at sea, so they were smashed. Even old sailors to this day will tell you that they never mention the word 'egg' when at sea, they used to call them 'roundabouts'. Double-yolked eggs meant a death in the family and one with no yolk at all was generally unlucky, some people called these 'wind eggs'.

In April the dandelion is coming into its full glory. It may be a common weed, but it has a beauty of its own. The sides of the roads and lanes are studded with them now and they shine out from the young grass like little suns. Each golden head consists of scores of tiny florets which together make a neat yellow circle. As young children we used to pick them and then get teased by the older children who said we would be wetting the bed as we had picked dandelions. Herbalists use the root for medicinal purposes and the white 'milk' which exudes from the stem when the dandelion is picked was a sure cure if rubbed on warts. The young leaves are as good as lettuce for salads, and my mother used to cut up the leaves and mix them in the chicken meal - it was supposed to do the poultry good.

When I was a girl April was always spring cleaning time. Mother used to buy tins of distemper and packets of ceiling white. There was a lack of labour-saving devices, detergents and polishes, mother's two hands were her equipment, together with her enamel pail and plenty of soda. No wonder her hands used to look so red as there was no money to buy rubber gloves.

The Victorian cooking range was a demanding monster which required hours of toil to keep it shining brightly and working efficiently. Not only in spring did it need cleaning but every week. It was necessary to remove fender and fire irons, rake out all the ashes and cinders, throwing in some damp tea leaves to keep down the dust. Then the flues were cleaned and the steel parts polished with Bath brick and paraffin, the iron parts black-leaded and polished and the hearthstone washed and polished. After the stove was done, the coconut matting was taken up with the rugs and put over the garden hedge.

Whitewashing the ceilings was an awful job as cottage ceilings were always flaking and the first job was to scrape off the old paint before putting on a fresh lot. However, this had to be done as the ceilings were blackened with smoke from the fire and the oil lamps. Mother would tell us not to walk about indoors as she didn't want us to cart the flakes everywhere on our shoes. The ceilings were painted with 'ceiling white', a powder which was bought in one or two pound bags and mixed to a paste with water. Often you ended up with more on yourself or the floor than on the ceiling, but when it was finished, it left an attractive scent in the room. Walls were next; they were brushed down and there was distemper all over the place but there was a nice clean smell after it was all done. Most of the woodwork was painted with dark stain, curtains were washed with Rinso or Lux Flakes.

The warm glowing shades of reds and browns which had been used in curtains and covers throughout the winter months were removed, cleaned and put away. In their place to herald the coming of spring, out would come the bright colours of fresh chintzes for curtains and chair-backs and white cotton covers on chests of drawers and old military boxes for storing clothes. These had been boiled in the copper, rinsed with a Reckitt's blue bag then starched. We even had a new tasselled fringe for the mantelpiece. Sunlight soap was used for giving a good scrub up. All the little bits of soap were cut into small pieces, covered with boiling water and kept in an old stone jar. It set like a jelly and when we came to use it for washing and in the copper, we just lifted it with our fingers. The furniture was given a good polish with Mansion polish and the windows were cleaned with newspaper and a little vinegar in the water to give that extra shine.

The kitchen and pantry were distempered and this involved moving out all the heavy furniture and equipment. In the pantry there was the meat-safe, pickling jars and bottles, the bread crock and all the crockery, cutlery and food for the whole family. Being a cool room, usually situated on the north side of the house and very cold in winter, it was ideal for storing the buckets of drinking water collected from the pump in the garden. There were stone bottles of home-brewed beer and eggs in pails preserved in isinglass for future use. All of these had to be moved out so that the walls could be freshened up.

Washing was a major part of spring cleaning and the copper would have been filled the night before from the soft water butt or the pond. A lot of soda was used in those days to soften the water so that less soap was needed. All the household items were boiled and then put through the mangle. When dry they were ironed, this was done on the kitchen table, which was covered with old pieces of blanket topped by a length of clean sheeting. The iron was a 'flat iron', heated on the kitchen range and wiped with a clean cloth before use. Some people used a patent slip-on ironing shield or 'slipper', which was put on over the heated iron and stopped any marks being made on the clothes. A later type of iron was the 'box iron' in which a triangular piece of stone was made red-hot in the fire and then placed inside a box-like container, which opened at the back. Although this sounds old-fashioned, it was very effective, bearing in mind that electricity was unheard of in most country cottages until well after the Second World War.

Understandably, there was not much cooking done in spring-cleaning week. We often had potatoes baked in their skins, perhaps some cold pickles and some cold cooked rabbit but there was always plenty of bread if we were hungry. Mum would give us rounds of bread and dripping or sometimes bread and margarine with a little sugar sprinkled on top - this was a real treat. If the rhubarb was fit, we would have some cooked with custard, otherwise no pudding. We were always pleased when the spring cleaning was finished.

Mother Nature is wonderful at this time of year, whether in the garden or the countryside - there are so many different shades of green setting off the spring flowers.

I am often asked 'How do you make spring flowers last longer?' Just think of trying to arrange a bowl with Crown Imperials with their high-shouldered bells, tulips, irises and possibly a few late hyacinths. The flower arranger will tell you that green oasis is a boon to use with a lot of flowers but it is not so good for the soft stems of spring flowers. A piece of wire netting in the water is a good means of support. There are quite a few tales of making flowers last in water, such as adding lemonade, aspirins, pennies and sugar. Adding pennies or aspirin to the water has no visible effect on cut flowers, although they do help to prevent the growth of micro-organisms. Alcoholic drinks do provide good nutrients for the flowers as they contain sugar, but the flowers are just as happy with either sugar or fizzy lemonade. A drop of bleach in water to clean the containers thoroughly will also help. Remember that tulips are heavy drinkers, so check the water frequently to make sure that the stem-ends are covered.

Here are a few tips to make your cut flowers last longer.

Anemones - put flowers into 1/4 cup of vinegar to 2 cups of water for 1-2 hours

Carnations and Pinks - put in cold water only, but cut stems between notches. Add about one-third fizzy lemonade to two-thirds water and they will last for weeks

Chrysanthemums - crush stems and hold in boiling water for 2-3 minutes, then put into cold water

Daffodils - place in one inch of cold water for 1/2 hour, then arrange in more water

Irises - cut above white stems under water, dip into boiling water for one minute and place in deep water

Evergreens - submerge in a bath of water overnight

Primroses - dip stems in boiling water for 30 seconds, then place in cold water

Tulips - pierce each stem just below the flower with a pin

I was once asked where 'Bed and Breakfast' could be found and this started me wondering how people got by years ago. Nowadays, it is one of the country's biggest and most honourable home industries, and it's my guess that this became popular in the 1920's when the bicycle became popular, and little notices would be hung on the garden gate. A friend who used to cycle a lot told me that he used to pay five shillings a night at premises that were often recommended by the Cyclist Touring Club. One time, he thought his luck was in when he was only charged four shillings - but when he woke up in the night, another traveller was snoring on the other side of the double bed! Beds in those days ranged from the high-sprung trampoline type to the sort of downy feather type which was very welcome on a chilly night. A washbasin with running water was still something of a novelty and there might well have been a large earthenware bowl and the sort of ewer in which, if we are to believe Charles Dickens' account of a really cold night in Paris, the water was 'liable to freeze with a sharp report'. There would have been flowery wallpaper with a text such as 'Jessica's First Prayer' hanging over the bed head, with another religious text or two thrown in to keep it company. Often faded photographs of the landlady's kith and kin would feature prominently.

Gradually the bed and breakfast industry smartened itself up and the sign 'Vacancies' hung, not only outside cottages with roses round the door, but on premises calling themselves guest houses. Breakfast was always the big attraction - as it still is today, with plates of egg, bacon, sausages and tomatoes preceded by porridge and ending with unlimited toast and marmalade.

There are many superstitions regarding trees. Ash was known for its magical properties which supposedly cured a child of rickets and an ancient custom was to pass the child naked through a cleft of a tree trunk which was then bound and sealed with clay. As the tree healed, so did the child.

Elder was considered to be unlucky if brought into the house - my mother would not let us children bring it indoors - perhaps this was because it was said that the Cross was made of elder. The scent of the flowers was believed to poison anyone who slept under the elder. However, I think this is a wonderful shrub as not only the flowers but also the berries can be used for wine making. Hawthorn was frequently used for the maypoles which symbolised joy at the return of summer. Country folk used to hang sprays of hawthorn outside the cowsheds to be assured of a plentiful milk supply. It was considered seriously unlucky to bring hawthorn (may) flowers into the house.

Hazel has become most widely known for providing the wood for divining, or dowsing, rods used to locate underground water sources and other objects. I don't know how this technique works, but I have seen it for myself. My late uncle was a water diviner. He always told me it had to be a stick cut like a letter Y, from a hazel (Corylus Avellana). Hazel divining rods have been used throughout the British Isles not only to search for water, but also to pinpoint hidden treasure and the whereabouts of serious crime. That is until the seventeenth century when such practices became too closely associated with witchcraft and were stopped. Hazelnuts have been regarded as fruits of wisdom.

For children, the hazel was a toy in years gone by. In the last century they used the nuts for a game, perhaps the forerunner of marbles, called 'Cobs' - hence the popular name 'Cob Nuts'.

Holly has a lot of superstitions surrounding it; cottage gardens would be enclosed by a holly hedge, as this was believed to keep out evil influences; it was a protection against the evil eye, storms and fire. Some people still believe it is unlucky to cut down a holly hedge or even a holly tree.

The oak tree has a wide range of magical powers - merely to carry an acorn preserved youth. Willows were the emblems of grief and lost love - hence the term 'Wearing the willow'. Yew trees were very commonly planted in churchyards and this is because the yew is the symbol of everlasting life - at one time, its branches were used to line newly dug graves.

The first Sunday in April is Daffodil Sunday, an invention of the Victorians who liked to make excuses for going out walking and invented special days for doing just that. This was the day to pick daffodils from Victorian gardens and take them to the local hospital for the sick.

It is four hundred years since the daffodil first arrived in Britain from Constantinople in the reign of Good Queen Bess. Two thousand years ago, poets in Greece found inspiration in the daffodil for their poems, myths and legends. From one of the myths originated the name 'narcissus', the vain, handsome Greek youth who fell in love with his own image reflected in a forest pool. He was held fast by his own beauty and gradually pined away and died. Those who sought him found only the flower, which today still bears his name. Although daffodils and narcissi appear to be two separate flowers; the narcissus being white-petalled and heavily scented while the daffodil has the single yellow trumpet, in fact they are identical, differing only in name.

There are now many hundreds of varieties of daffodil, and they are the main export of the Scilly Isles. The first consignments arrived in London in February many years ago, packed in a few hat boxes. With the British love of flowers, the demand for daffodils is great and today we anticipate the arrival of the first spring flowers in January. Every year brings an increase in the number of daffodil growers in Britain, and it seems incredible that some bulbs can cost over £50 each.

When tulip bulbs were first introduced into Europe, they were much prized as vegetables, often being pickled and used as a table delicacy. The tulip was discovered four centuries ago by the Austrian Ambassador to Turkey - himself a great flower lover - tulips were first seen blooming in the gardens of Sulieman the Magnificent. Their name is derived from the Turkish 'dulhban' or turban, an apt description of this magnificent flower. With skill, the Ambassador contrived to take some excellent specimens of both bulbs and seed back to Vienna, from which our modern tulips are derived. Early flowers, resulting from a greenish double flower were followed later by the red and yellow specimens. A Dutch botanist, Clusius, who lived in Vienna, later returned to Leyden with a precious parcel that he guarded jealously. Fortunately for us, some months later, thieves broke into his garden shed at dead of night and dug up all the bulbs. The stolen bulbs were sold to gardeners living in seventeen provinces of Holland, and this was believed to be the start of the great Dutch tulip growing industry. It is said that the first tulip came to England from Vienna in 1578, but this date varies according to which reference book we read. At times, it was rumoured that a bulb could reach the sum of £370. I remember visiting the Chelsea Flower Show years ago, when the first pink tulips were on show, and the bulbs of these cost nearly £100 each. Nowadays the tulip growers of Spalding in Lincolnshire despatch millions of boxes of their blooms each season and the highlight of each spring must be the mile-long parade of tulip-decorated floats that used to cover a four mile route. This is a colourful and glorious spectacle of over a million flowers, and thousands of visitors flock to the area to see the Tulip Queen.

The other day I wanted some elastic and I thought to myself 'Where do I shop for that now?' I remember our little village shop where we could buy just about everything we needed. There would be boxes full of bandages, lace, cards of wool of all colours for mending stockings and so on. There would be corn plasters, boxes of pencils, writing paper and birthday cards. A line was strung across the shop hung with tea-cloths, towels, handkerchiefs and men's wool stockings. Even it you could not see what you wanted, there would be some fumbling under the counter and the goods were produced. If they were not available, the shopkeeper would try and get whatever you wanted within the week. The shelves were filled with jams, packets of soda and Persil - sugar and cheese were nearby. Never mind the hygiene certificates we must have today, with shops having to provide two sinks and so on. In my days of working in the village shop when I first left school, you went into the shopkeeper's living quarters to wash your hands. I often smile to myself when I think what the shopkeeper's wife used to say to me, 'Now dear, you won't handle the sausages at certain times of the month, will you, as they might go off'. I wonder what workers in the supermarkets of today would think of that one! How I used to hate it when a customer would come in for cheese or bacon and then ask for a gallon of paraffin. The smell on your hands was the devil to get off, and to this day I have never liked paraffin.

The cellar of the shop was a dark masterpiece of storage; methylated spirits and turps were stored next to the sunlight and primrose soaps, Rinso, Persil and soda were also packed into the corner. Then came the Butler margarine and lard, all in 56lb boxes, bars of salt came in 28lb blocks which had to be sawn into $1/4$ stone blocks with a zinc saw. Further on were Duplex lamp glasses and flowerpots of all sizes. Next were boxes of dried fruit, currants, sultanas and raisins, which had to be cleaned by rubbing through a sieve and picking out the stalks and stones. The dates came in a large box and had to be broken open with a crowbar. In the centre of the cellar were crates of cheese which had to be skinned. On trestles were Scribbans cake; lemon, sultana and Genoa, and from the ceiling hung the sides of bacon.

There was something special about the village shop; it was a place where people met and you could hear the latest news and gossip. Notices of coming events in the village hall would be pinned up and it was also the centre for leaving magazines or picking up tickets. Even the dry-cleaning and laundry van would call to pick up or leave items for collection there. Another convenience of the shop was that it would open again after tea, and a lot of people would gather outside, waiting for the shopkeeper to re-open. He would stay open until 9.30 or 10.00 at night.

One villager told me that he remembered going into the village shop with a group of other boys to buy a quarter pound of sweets. If the shopkeeper's wife could not get the right weight, she would bite the sweet in half - how about that for hygiene! A lot of goods were put on tick in those days and one of my brother's mates would always put down items on his mother's bill until one day his father caught him coming out of the shop with bags of sweets. His father took off his belt and gave the boy a rum hiding and that put paid to putting any more sweets on tick.

Wet days in April are a good time to tidy the tool shed. The tools come out of the shed, and I wonder aloud if there is any need to keep so many 'crooms'. My brother comments that they are good working men's tools for the garden and such implements are not seen today. You will not find anything like them in the shops today; the croom was one of the most primitive and at the same time the most useful implement that was used on farms. Nor was it only used on farms, but for a number of rural industries. There were three types which I remember being used, one with five teeth made of heavy wrought-iron, probably for breaking down the ground, it was very heavy and I think any land worker would have been tired if he had used it all day. The two-tined iron muck croom is not in use today, but years ago, muck spreading was an annual event in East Anglia. The large croom with five tines was mainly used to clean weeds from the river after they were cut in June. The weeds were then stacked and used for fertiliser - nothing was wasted.

The iron dibbler, or dibber as it is sometimes called, is something we never use today. Some three feet long, this was used before the seed drill appeared and was the only means of sowing. Dibbers were used by a man holding one in each hand and walking backwards across the field. Children followed him, putting four seeds into each hole and chanting

'Four seeds in a hole
One for the rook, One for the crow,
One to rot and one to grow'

A straw twister was another tool that has been in my shed for years. They were used for making bonds for binding straw or hay into bales. Then I have a thistling hook which I think my father used many years ago. Thistles were extracted from the crops with this tool before they seeded. A lot of boot leather was worn out by farm workers walking up and down the fields weeding and tending the crops - nowadays, sprayers nearly half a mile long do the work in an hour or so.

Many of these old-fashioned tools are on display in local agricultural museums, such as forks, once made so strong and in different sizes; some had two tines while others had three or four. Those with two tines were probably used for heaving the heavy shocks of corn onto the waggons or stacks.

When travelling around the area, I love to visit village churches. There are a lot of curiosities in our English churches - sightseers rarely miss the important cathedrals but many old churches have curious histories or objects connected with them, which are well worth seeing. Most of these wonderful temples were built in the Middle Ages, on sites that had often been held sacred long before Christianity arrived in the area.

Many of our early churches were built entirely of wood and one example can still be seen at Greenstead in Essex. Hundreds of our parish churches contain masterpieces of carpentry and stone work and the skill of the craftsmen of years gone by often strikes you as you enter a church. There are wonderful timber roofs and intricate carvings on the choir stalls and pew ends of grapes and animal figures.

Near Walpole in north-east Suffolk is an old chapel which has been a Meeting

House for a Non-conformist Congregation since 1649. This was one of the earliest independent chapels in the country. It doesn't look like a house of worship, in fact you could drive by and think it was a farm house. Once you step inside, it feels like you are going back in time. Originally the structure was a typical timber-framed Suffolk farmhouse with walls of wattle and daub, it was then enlarged and converted into a Meeting House. Today the galleried and box-pewed interior vividly conveys the setting and atmosphere of the 17th and 18th century dissenting worship. The pulpit is extravagant, with an immense hexagonal canopy with ogee domed top and a ball finial suspended from the rafters. Two tall, round arched windows on each side of the pulpit light the chapel.

Another interesting church in our area is St Peter's Church in Theberton. This is a large church with a thatched roof and circular tower. Around the parapet base there are four gargoyles which drain the rain water from the tower roof. There are some very fine stained-glass windows, and inside the porch is the remains of a German Zeppelin which was brought down nearby in 1917. Some of its crew were buried in the churchyard extension until the 1970's when their remains were removed to a German cemetery in Staffordshire.

The lych gate of St Mary & St Peter's Church in Kelsale is one of the finest in Suffolk. lych gates were not built purely for decoration as one might imagine, but for a very definite purpose. In former days it was in the lych gate that coffins were rested before being taken into the church for the first part of the funeral service. In some of the older lych gates the original lych stone or coffin rest is still retained, but there are not many left now as most were taken away in the eighteenth century. The word 'lych' is derived from the German 'Leiche' which means corpse.

I recently visited the church in Wenhaston as for years I had heard about the 'doom' painting. Painted about 1520 and measuring some 17ft by 8ft, it originally filled the upper part of the chancel arch and formed a background to the rood. Later, when the rood figures and cross were removed, the doom was whitewashed over and left in place. There it remained until 1892 when the chancel arch was rebuilt as part of the restoration. The whitewashed doom was cast into the churchyard as it was only thought fit for burning. A providential downpour in the night loosened some of the whitewash and it was recognised for what it was. Carefully cleaned and restored, it a wonderful painting, and the doom scenes are fascinating.

At St Mary's church in Bawdsey, I was pleased to see Edith Cavell's tablet on the wall, commemorating her work as a nurse - I used to go to London every year to attend a service held in her memory. In 1842 some adventurous lads let off fireworks from the top of the church tower, and the unfortunate result was almost total destruction of the church. There were certainly some mischievous lads about in those days! The church was rebuilt the following year.

All Saints' Church in Ramsholt is unusual in Suffolk in having a round tower. Standing in this churchyard, looking towards the river, one feels great peace and contentment. The church still has box pews and a two-decker pulpit. They also have excellent Waller headstones dating from 1744, just outside the porch on the left.

Watching the rooks at this time of year reminds me of the old saying, 'Old-fashioned hall, dull Aunts and croaking rooks'. There are sufficient of these clerical-looking birds to allow both town and country men to become well acquainted with their musical caws. Rooks do a lot of good by eating hosts of insects such as wireworms, cockchafers and leather-jackets which destroy crops. At one time the rook was dubbed by a naturalist as a corn-eating bird, but one has only to look at the beak with its distinguishing white patch at the base, to see that it is a 'dibber'. It is certainly not made primarily for grain eating - if you watch rooks in a big field, where one part is being sown and another turned over, the flocks will follow the ploughs, picking up the insects and grubs exposed and ignore the drills altogether.

For most of the year, rooks feed on insects and worms, but if for reasons of drought or frost they are unable to dig, they turn to cereals, legumes, fruit, root crops and anything else they can thieve for a livelihood. The rook is friendly and quite fearless of man for a quarter of the year and for the remainder is exceedingly shy and cunning. For three months they are in and around the rookery, leading an altogether domestic life and afterwards, the birds may be seen in flocks, hunting and exploring the fields, both ploughed and grass lands. Often they are so starved in bad weather that a sudden gust of wind will lift them off their feet and blow them like scattered leaves, over the hedge - they are but bones and feathers.

Rooks are said to be great weather forecasters. When they fall about in the sky as if they have been shot, it's a sure sign of rain - they fly in tumbling motions, a curious sight. If they fly low across the land, this also foretells rain. If they sit around their home area, or come back in the middle of the day instead of in the evening, or if they call late and loud, it is a sign of a storm coming. They build low when the spring is to be rough and high if March is to 'go out like a lamb', but for preference rooks build in the swaying top-most branches of lofty trees. Nobody knows why a whole colony of well-established rooks will sometimes suddenly desert a rookery, never again to return, even leaving their young to die in the nests. This is a very bad sign, and being superstitious like most country people, I would expect something unpleasant to happen very soon afterwards.

The rooks of fifty years ago were undoubtedly aristocrats in tastes and tendencies and almost always built rookeries near the bigger country houses. Now they seem more democratic and adventurous; as the rookeries become smaller, the birds are less self-contained and tend to wander further afield. Tennyson once said 'Blowing about the skies, without their deep-throated caws, our fields and meadows would sound silent'. Rooks show their intelligence in appearing to know the difference between a gun and a walking stick, and a Sunday from a Monday!

25 April is St Mark's Day - he wrote the second gospel and was supposed to have founded the city of Venice. His day was once the day for divination, especially about marriage, sickness and death. One of these ceremonies, waiting in churches at midnight, in barns or watching your uneaten supper were supposed to produce the ghost of a loved one.

The first cuckoo of the year tells us that spring has arrived, although hearing it for the first time before 6 April is supposed to be unlucky. It is also unlucky to hear it for the first time on 28 April or on Midsummer Day, 5 July. If you hear the cuckoo from your right, this is lucky but if it comes from the left or from behind you, this is unlucky. One should never hear the cuckoo for the first time when lying in bed for this portends poverty and illness. If you turn the coins in your pocket as soon as you hear the first cuckoo, this will bring you luck.

REMEDIES

Even today, many of the old remedies are still used in many country homes. Near to Easter it was thought that Sacramental bread and wine had healing properties, as had bread baked on Good Friday. Some of this bread was crumbled into many quack remedies. 'Thank goodness' said a farmer when it rained on Ascension Day in 1870, 'my old dutch (woman) will be able to get some holy water', for water caught 'straight from heaven' in a clean vessel on that day was an excellent remedy for cuts and sore eyes. Water collected from church roofs and from springs and wells of holy repute, was keenly sought after. In the New Forest, holed stones made potent by exposure to the rays of the full moon for three consecutive nights, were worn by the sick.

The ring finger is healing, but the forefinger, or poison finger, must never be used to apply ointments. Another remedy was the use of the house-leek as a charm against house fires and it was also used to make a soothing lotion for burns or inflamed insect bites. It was also good for bringing out bruising. This plant was always to be seen growing on the roof of the 'little house' down the yard or on the back'us, and it was considered lucky to have it growing there.

Rheumatism, arthritis and similar complaints particularly afflicted agricultural workers living in damp, ill-heated cottages. Fenmen believed that an eelskin garter, tied below the knee, prevented rheumatism from rising higher and elsewhere in England and in America, a snakeskin was similarly used as a remedy against cramp.

There were many wild herbs and flowers that we used as remedies. Blackberry leaves were boiled then strained, and honey added to make a tonic, which was taken to cure coughs. Cowslips and primroses were also used to make a tonic, and dandelion leaves were good for gout when the leaves were added to salads. 'Cut finger' was our name for periwinkle, as we bound these around cut or scratched fingers. Another cure for cuts was the dust from a mature puff ball. The elder bush has a number of uses; grown near the cottage door, it was said to guard against lightning. My father would use branches from this tree to stick his peas, as this was supposed to keep mildew away, and when he planted the celery in trenches, he would cover the soil with elder twigs as he said it would keep the celery fly away. He would put little sprays of elder in the horse's harness to keep the flies away from its eyes.

Handy Hints

* Alcohol stains on woolly material can be removed by washing with plenty of cool, dissolved soap containing a little ammonia. Brush this into the material and then rinse thoroughly with tepid water.

* Coffee stains on material can be removed so long as they have not been boiled. Soak each stain well with glycerine, brushing it into the material and then leave it for two or three hours. After this, pour on a little dissolved soap and brush the stains out. Wash, rinse and iron as usual

* Creosote can be removed from cotton material with methylated spirit. The methylated spirit will dissolve the creosote. The best method is to soak the stain in the methylated spirit and then wash with a cool, thick solution of dissolved soap
* Iron mould stains can often be removed with the juice from a stick of stewed rhubarb. Do not put any sugar with it, but use while hot. Leave the stain in the juice for some minutes until it fades. If a stronger remedy is required, a teaspoonful each of cream of tartar and citric acid, mixed with a teaspoonful of hot water will remove the stains
* Sea water stains can generally be removed with brushing. If they do not come out in this way, washing may be needed. Sea water often destroys the colour, and if this has happened, the only remedy is re-dyeing
* Tapestry chairs can be cleaned by beating and then rubbing plenty of dry bicarbonate of soda into the material. Leave it for a few hours and then brush hard with a very stiff brush and clean with the vacuum cleaner
* Tar stains can be removed by dipping them in a saucer containing some eucalyptus oil. Squeeze the garment well until the tar stain disappears. When clean, remove the oil with a non-flammable liquid dry-cleaner by dabbing with cotton wool, putting a piece of blotting paper under the stain

RECIPES

This is the time of year when ingredients for salads begin to come to perfection. As children we collected many plants and herbs for use as medicine and food. We picked the tips of willow herb, which when cooked could be eaten like asparagus. Wood sorrel was used as a green sauce. This herb was mashed and mixed with vinegar and sugar and served with meat, but you would have to collect it early in the day, before it closed up. The tips of stinging nettles were also collected and used as a vegetable, and the leaves of dandelion which are rich in vitamins B and C, can be added to salads. As an alternative to spinach, the herb 'fat hen' was gathered.
The dog rose provides the hips for rose hip syrup and we used to pick bowls full of wild strawberries, which grew on the outskirts of the woods. We would

September

SEPTEMBER

September always seems to me to be the month of warning that autumn will soon make its sweeping entry and the scene is set for the brilliant colours of gold and rust. The promise of autumn is here; the nights are beginning to get dark, and the fruits of a million plants glitter in the hedgerows like so many jewels in a crown. In the morning, the cool air greets the sun and a crown of dewdrops sparkle from every spider's web. There is a smell in the evening breeze of open fires as gardeners begin to burn the rubbish - it's time for clearing up and thinking about another year. Above all, the earth gives forth a fruity scent, that only comes at this time of the year before the winter rains wash away the fertility and warmth of the past summer.

Insects are responding as the year's clock winds down. Wasps blunder over the blackberries gorging on the ripe fruit, their toil is almost over and the tiredness of autumn is with them. Soon they will die, worn out with all the frantic activity of the summer months. A dearth of wild flowers on the lanes and verges drives butterflies to our gardens in the daytime. They are especially fond of the flowers of the sedum and rotting fruit, such as plums, which attract tortoiseshells, peacocks and painted ladies. At night many fine moths come to the nectar of the petunias still in bloom. Towards the end of the month many species hibernate and we shall see no more of them until the spring comes again. On warm September evenings when we like to sit in the garden, the mosquitoes and midges start to bite, and we have to move indoors. However, this doesn't last long as the first cool autumn night will see the end of all but a few that survive the winter in hibernation. Swallows will start to congregate on roof-tops, TV aerials and telegraph wires, keeping up their continuous twittering and forever changing places, like a game of musical chairs. Soon they will be preparing for their departure overseas.

This is a busy season for the housewife and as I think of them, I like to jot down all the jobs that should have been done by now and those that need to be finished before winter sets in. I pick seed heads of clematis and look for bulrushes that can be sprayed with hair spray, likewise pampas grass, to stop them becoming too fluffy. Then I must go round the garden and pick the poppy seed heads, mombretia and crocosmia, they look so pretty in the winter, arranged with dried flowers. There are cuttings to be taken of favourite plants and bulbs to be planted for indoor display in early spring. Then I go out into the fields and lanes collecting nice, fat rose hips and sloes for wine making and crab apples and quince for making jelly - and then have to hunt around for 1lb jam jars.

Everywhere the wild creatures are beginning to stock up their larders. Dormice are fattening on the ripe fruit and hedgehogs start the process of laying down a store of fat under their skin. The birds have a field day with the elderberries, while blackberries seem to be the general food of many mammals, birds and insects. Hips of the wild rose, haws from the hawthorn and berries of the rowan are ripe, and summer birds linger to enjoy the bounty. Acorns fall on hot days or when the gales thresh the oak boughs, and as soon as they reach moist ground, they split open ready to germinate and are greedily eaten by pheasants, wood pigeons and small mammals. Squirrels will take their share and jays also collect them. Jays are nearly as clever at burying and finding acorns as the squirrel. They prefer sloping meadowland and will carry the food some distance before they hide it, pushing it into the ground. Many a countryside oak must owe its existence to the forgetfulness of jays and squirrels! There is a saying about squirrels and their nuts: 'When he eats them in the tree, Weather as warm as can be, but when he gets a large supply on the ground, expect a cold winter.'

Walnuts will also be ready this month. The walnut has been grown as an orchard tree since Saxon times and was a great favourite with the Romans. On his marriage, the roman bridegroom would scatter walnuts among the children as he walked to his new home with his bride, a custom that signified that he had left his childhood behind. Years ago, a favourite spot to plant the walnut tree was by the pigsty, where it would get plenty of organic material to make it fertile.

There is an old saying that if the tree never produced nuts, it should be beaten in March when the sap was rising and this practice gave rise to the saying; 'A woman, a dog and a walnut tree, The more you beat them the better they be'. If the nut trees produced well, it meant lots of boy children. All winter it stands bare and neglected and in the spring, no delicate pink or white blossoms bedeck its branches. During summer, the hard, unpromising, green shells gleam in the sun and we hardly glance at them but come autumn, our walnut tree comes into its own. In July, before the woody shells have hardened, walnuts may be pickled, but by the end of September, the nuts will be ready to pick. The leaves will soon be turning brown and the hard green shells will have withered and burst and the gathering of walnuts becomes a ritual.

The dye of the walnut has been used for generations for the colouring of hair and one can well understand this, as when shelling the outer skin of the walnut, the hands are stained for days.

St Giles' Day is 1 September and there is a saying that St Giles finishes the walnuts. St Giles was a Greek of noble birth, born in Athens in the eighth century and brought up as a Christian. One story tells how he saved some sailors, in peril of being dashed upon rocks, by his prayers. St Giles was a popular saint in medieval times, and important trading fairs were held on his feast day in Winchester and Oxford. Some school children near Oxford still have a day off school to attend the traditional St Giles' Fair, which takes place in the street named after him. St Giles made friends with all the animals of the forest and, on the front of Norwich Cathedral, you will see St Giles with a deer leaping up to greet him.

Country people look for the Harvest Moon more than any other moons. Her brightness is exceptional and often puts all but the most brilliant of stars out of business. Farmers would find her a useful lamp for harvesting after dark. In addition, in the old days she was used as a barometer and even now, before watching the 'weather forecast' on TV, it is worth remembering the following:

'If the moon show a silver shield
Be not afraid to reap your field,
But if she rises haloed round
Soon we'll tread on deluged ground'

As harvest is coming to an end, many villages will be thinking about the Harvest Supper in their village halls. In the old days, when the last load of corn had been carted and stacked, the farmers would clear their barns and a meal would be provided by their wives, for the workers and their families. This meal was known as 'Horkey', and many people would eat nothing at home on that great day. A pig would be killed and there would be plenty of meat and plenty of home-brewed beer and cider. The men would raise their glasses of beer and shout 'largess' meaning the harvest is in. The farmer's wife and helpers would have decorated the barn with flowers and branches and food would fill the long tables.

Thomas Tusser says:

'In Harvest-time, harvest-folk, servants and all
Should make, all together, good cheer in the Hall,
Once ended thy Harvest, let none be beguiled
Please such as did help thee, man, woman and child.'

After all was eaten, the supper tables were cleared and a quantity of hazel nuts, gathered by the men, placed on the tables. The man nearest the head of the table would begin by making a speech proposing the health of the Master and Mistress, and then each man had to either sing a song or tell a story.

Horkey was the predecessor of the modern harvest supper, and the word originates long before the Christian era. In Suffolk, until early in the last century, a pair of horns, painted and adorned with flowers were often borne around the table at the Horkey supper, and placed on the head of the Harvest Lord, to the accompaniment of a coarse song. The title of Harvest Queen, given to the second reaper, recalled the old custom of making a straw puppet, which was believed to be the spirit of the harvest. This had to be kept alive, to ensure good crops for the following year. The roughly made puppet was eventually replaced by intricately woven corn dollies shaped to resemble bells, horseshoes, umbrellas, whips and other objects, and these were used to decorate the church for the harvest thanksgiving services.

Today one rarely hears of a harvest supper being held in a barn but in village halls willing helpers provide wonderful spreads. It is more likely to be ham

194

and salad with a baked potato followed by apple pie and cream but whatever one has to eat, it is nice to get together and to appreciate the food we have. We then have the Harvest Festival services at which we used to see the churches decorated with flowers, corn, vegetables and fruit. Years ago, it was called Harvest Thanksgiving and the congregation received Holy Communion with bread made from the brand new corn. How lovely it is to go into a church decorated with samples of the harvest - there is a special smell as soon as you open the door. There are little bundles of corn tied to the pews, and the windowsills are full of apples and vegetables. Golden Rod, Michaelmas Daisies and sprays of rose hips, Chrysanthemums and Old Man's Beard, all add to the festive atmosphere. The children from the village school are brought in to the church especially to see the harvest arrangements and they bring their gifts, which are laid around the font. When I was a Sunday school teacher, I used to get the children to scratch their names in young marrows; as the marrow grows, so does their name, and you would be surprised at how well the name stands out. Most children like to have a small garden patch, and their marrows can be their gift for harvest. Other gifts I got the children to bring were a glass of water and a lump of coal, as well as the bread and grapes to put on the altar. Only small things, but just enough to make us think how much we take for granted. As we sing 'We plough the fields and scatter', perhaps we shall remember the starving millions in other parts of the world. Arriving home with the strains of the last hymn, 'Now thank we all our God', ringing in our ears, we can look back and see that the fruits of the earth have again been gathered in and know that we shall eat well and be warm in our beds through the coming winter - and have enough to share with others.

Harvest is the time to think about all the different varieties of bread that have been the staple diet of many nations since time began. Early in history, man began to record the things that were of the greatest importance to him and there is considerable evidence of the use of corn from the very earliest days of recorded history. Wheat has always been the most expensive member of the corn family in this country and hence, white bread has been held in high regard. Another reason for this is that in pre-Reformation days, the bread for church mass was made from the best wheat flour. Many country people still believe that bread and cakes made on Good Friday will never go mouldy. Names of bread in other countries can be very different from our own - Dodge bread is the name for corn bread in the USA, and a recipe for 'Batter' comes from Richmond, Virginia. This was probably an emergency bread made by the ingenious housewives who emigrated from England in the 17th century. Corn and other grains have often been in short supply in years gone by, crops might fail or war might damage them, and then famine bread was made. Women were forced to add beans, peas and even common buckwheat to boost her meagre store of grain to feed her family during hard times. Pumpernickel is a black bread made in Germany from coarse rye flour. The acid taste of the rye is said to be quite pleasant when the bread is thickly coated with butter.

Many counties of England have their own special type of bread. Good Friday Caraway bread is popular in Somerset, Cut Rounds seem to belong to Devonshire, while Oxfordshire is known for its Lardy cakes. Wales is known for its Currant Bread and in Ireland, Soda Bread has been eaten for many years. There are many, far more interesting loaves than the wrapped, sliced ones we buy today in such vast quantities.

The hedgehog is a 'gentleman of the countryside'. He has an insatiable curiosity, a unique method of defence and, surprisingly, a fair turn of speed. Put a hedgehog down in a shed and he will investigate every article, smelling it carefully. His method of defence is well-known, but it is not always known that it is an amazingly well developed muscle that envelopes the crown of his head and body that enables him to roll himself into a tight ball. A vet once told me that it is this muscle that gives him such a bulky appearance, and the misleading impression that he is a portly old gentleman, incapable of moving fast. In fact, he can run fast and swim too. His eyesight is not good, and he hears rather than sees, approaching danger. Furthermore, he is sensitive to vibrations along the surface of the ground.

The hedgehog is most useful in the garden and will clear it of snails and slugs. He can soon become tame and will stay in the garden for weeks at a time if you put out food such as cat's meat and water, or even a little milk for him. Weather lore says that hedgehogs conceal themselves in their holes before a change of wind from north-east to south.

The hard fruit season is now in full swing. Apple trees are bent over with fruit, it is such a pity that our fruit farmers can't always sell their fruit because the size is wrong, and so many of our orchards have been pulled out. The apple has a long history and is believed to have derived from South Western Asia, where the mix of the native Malus species could have given fruits of a size and quality attractive to man. The first steps towards growing apple trees may have begun in the Middle East, or South Eastern Europe, with the techniques involved being spread by the Greeks and Romans. As Christianity moved westward and religious orders formed settled communities, the apple followed.

In the early days, much fruit was grown from seed, but apples do not breed true from seed, and as time went on, good apples were propagated by grafting a number of special types - some have survived to this day. Today in England, only East Malling continues to breed new varieties by crossing known parents at Long Ashton, using a technique known as mutation selection in which mutations are induced by submitting plant material to radiation.

There is nothing like a good old English apple, and we are fortunate in East Anglia to have so many varieties to choose from. Look out first for the Worcester Pearmain, crisp and red, then we have Discovery, Katy and James Grieves, which are followed by Russets, Coxes Orange Pippin, Laxtons, Spartan and Idared. One that has made a hit in latter years is Jonagold and Red Jonagold, which is a modern apple, crisp, juicy and full of flavour - it will also keep well into the new year. Some of the older varieties are not so easy to find these days, Blenheim, Lord Lambourne and the old-fashioned, moss-brown russets, wrinkled like the faces of ancient peasants, will be as sweet and brown in March as they are at Christmas.

'Was not the Island of Apple Tree the resting place of the Blessed,
Where fall not rain nor hail nor any snow?'

Some apples and pears will be ready to pick in early September, others will be ripe by the end of the month. Gathering apples is a wide-awake affair, a heavy job fraught with excitement. The best apples, rosy and unblemished, always

197

hang at the top of the tree, and poised on top of the ladder or scrambling among the branches, one wonders if they are worth the risk of a broken limb. Shaking the tree is a last resort for the apples would be damaged and would not keep. A knowledgeable fruit farmer once told me that the test of whether an apple or pear is ready to be picked is to lift each sound ripe fruit up in your hand, if it comes away easily from the twig with a slight pull, it is ripe and ready to pick. Do not attempt to pull hard, as fruit that is still firmly attached to the twig is not quite ready and should be left to mature. Apples and pears keep better if each fruit is wrapped in paper and then laid on shelves or in boxes or trays in a cool, airy place.

Fruit picking was the main money earner for the women of the villages, and mums pushing prams with food packed up for the day. It was hard work with bags hanging round your neck for picking the fruit into. Once the bag was full, you undid the bottom and let the apples fall out into big boxes; this had to be done very carefully so that the fruit was not bruised. The Orchards were full of the village women and with their children playing, everybody was happy. The money earned bought school clothes for the children for the start of the new school year.

The big fruit farmers are controlled by the Fruit Growers Association, which tells them when to pick their fruit. This depends on when the fruit store has room for the fruit to come in, so many fruit farmers have the fruit stored, then it comes out later in the year to be sold in our shops and supermarkets. So look for the 'Buy British apples' sign, and help our fruit farmers.

There is a lot of magic about the apple; one belief is that before eating an apple, it should be rubbed to remove any evil spirits that might be inside. Another old superstition is that rubbing an apple on a baby's tongue will ensure that the child has a good singing voice. The apple tree was one of the Celtic holy trees and was considered the tree of life.

'Who sets an apple, may live to see its end.
Who sets a pear, may set it for a friend.'

Now that the harvest has been taken in, the plough will soon be turning the soil over. Years ago this would have been a special time for the horsemen as drawing matches were held around the countryside. The modern matches are called 'Furrow-drawing Matches' as they are held to discover the ploughman who can draw or plough the straightest furrow. Suffolk seems to be the only county to make a distinction between a furrow-drawing match and a ploughing match. In the furrow-drawing, a single furrow is drawn and the ploughman who has the straightest is the winner, whereas in a ploughing match, a whole stretch, perhaps twelve furrows, has to be ploughed before the work is judged and the prize given. One of the prizes years ago was a brass kettle. It was a prize to be treasured as they were well made of good-quality brass, and it was a boost to the ploughman who won it.

I still love to see the heavy horses working, and every September the Southern Counties Horse Ploughing Association put on a ploughing match and furrow-drawing competition in conjunction with the Suffolk Horse Society. The Suffolk Punches were wonderful horses, they never broke down and you could always trust them to do a good day's work. They worked hard as did the men behind the plough who used a lot of skill and, walking up and down the fields, covered about an acre per day

In September, older folk's thoughts go back to the outbreak of the Second World War. I was only four years old then, and I remember my mother getting us out of bed in the early hours of the morning to dive for cover as the 'doodle-bugs' were overhead. When the sound cut out these unmanned bombs would drop from the sky. With the rationing, country folk had more chance of getting a reasonably nourishing diet. We could grow our own vegetables and catch the odd rabbit or pheasant. People who worked on the land got extra rations at harvest time, which were very acceptable. Rations consisted of one or two eggs per week, 2oz each of cheese, butter and tea plus a few ounces of meat - not many people had cooked breakfasts. Elderberries and dried beetroot were used as fruit in cakes. Dried milk was mixed up thick and used to spread on a cake to look like icing when there were birthdays, nothing was wasted. Ministry of Food leaflets were always being given out such as 'How to use stale crusts'.

In the country, there were Pig Clubs, where you could buy pig meal and then, when the time came to kill the pig, half the carcase had to be sent to the butchers and you kept the rest. This must have been a great day, to have liver, offal and fat to render down to make lard and dripping.

Sugar had to go a long way and this is when a lot of people gave up having sugar in their cups of tea. Saccharin tablets were used - four tablets equalled one ounce of sugar. The sugar ration was often saved to make jam as saccharin could not be used, but bottling was a way of using up fruit, with a syrup using saccharin. Honey was not rationed, so jam was made with half honey and half sugar. Golden syrup was another sweetener, and my father put this in his cups of tea.

Vegetables were a big stand-by, and this is where 'Dig for Victory' came in. Runner beans were salted down in seven-pound stone jars, dried apple rings were made and looked like chamois leather when finished but, after soaking, they soon came back up to full-flavoured apples again. Tea leaves were used and dried to make tea two or three times more. Butter and margarine were mixed together to make them go further and the wrappings were scraped and scraped to get the last little bit. These wrappers were then used for greasing cake tins, pudding basins and so on. I have included two wartime recipes in this month's recipe section.

Many people have said that rationing was no bad thing as it taught them to be careful. There was a shortage of all materials; underclothes were made out of used parachutes, if you could get hold of one, and most ladies were pleased to get this fine silk, while grey army blankets and striped winceyette sheets were used to make pyjamas and sleeping suits. Sugar bags were made into curtains and floor covering was made of roof felting, painted red or green and polished when dry.

This is the time of year when spiders, like many other creatures, begin to look for some warm place to make their home during the winter months. I smile to myself when I hear people shriek out when they see a spider in the bath or running across the floor. They are such harmless creatures but there are many superstitions about them. One of the best-known sayings is, 'If you want to live and thrive, let the spider run alive'. If you find a small spider in your hair or on your clothes, this is known as a money-spider and indicates that money will be coming to you. If you see the spider spinning her web, someone will give you a gift of new clothes. You must never kill a spider or you will suffer misfortune. A spider's web rubbed on small wounds will heal them. Stormy weather is forecast by the filaments on which the spider's web is suspended; if a storm is coming, you will notice that the spider shortens the hanging thread, and after the storm has passed, it will let the thread out again.

September is still the traditional month of oysters - the first month with an 'r' in it. Julius Caesar, like so many other Romans, was very fond of oysters and there is a story that he invaded our coasts because of the oyster beds - known to be some of the best. Colchester has an oyster ceremony in September which marks the opening of the oyster fishing season. There is a ceremony of drinking a royal toast with thimbles full of gin and eating pinches of gingerbread.

September is the season for hop picking in Kent. Picture a small pine cone composed of green leaves and you will have some idea of what a hop looks like. They grow in spectacular clusters on a bine to a height of four times that of a field grape vine. A herbaceous perennial, the hop is native to Europe and has been cultivated in England since the days of William the Conqueror. The hop was first mentioned by the roman writer Pliny, as one of the garden plants of the romans, who apparently ate the young shoots as we eat asparagus.
The hop belongs to the nettle family and is related to the hemp and mulberry. In its lupulus glands it carries valuable oil of a distinguishing aroma and resins and these resins are responsible for the hop's reputation as an aid to sleep and to transmit their bitter taste and preservative properties to beer. Many people buy pillows stuffed with hops, which will help them to have a deep and dreamless sleep. The hop has medicinal qualities but for considerable periods its use was not favoured and in brewing was frowned upon by Henry III because it was thought to spoil the taste of beer and even to endanger people's lives. In about 1552 however, hop growing became firmly established on a field scale for use in brewing beer. I am told that there is nothing like a pint of well-kept English bitter as a thirst quencher and a drink that cheers and refreshes.
Hops need a warm, sheltered place and skilled cultivation to grow them. Once

planted, they live for many years, but are a most laborious crop to produce as there is something to be done every month of the year. They need a rich soil and much manuring and hoeing. It takes three years for the hops to reach perfection. At one time, men walked on stilts to tie the hop strings up to their wire cages eighteen feet up in the air, and later to 'twiddle' the hop bines round their strings. The art of stilt-walking was handed down from father to son for generations. When the plump and aromatic cones of the female flowers are firm and crisp to the touch, they are ready for picking.

Today the bines are cut down and carried to a shed where the hops are removed from the bines by machine, but in the old days of hand-picking, the pickers used to be organised into small parties, each having a 'bin' to pick into. Once the hops were picked and measured into pokes, they were taken to the oast houses to be dried. Men worked day and night for five or six weeks drying the hops. After drying, the hops were swept into a 'pocket' suspended below a hole in the drying room floor, and pressed down so that as many as possible were pressed into each pocket which must reach a certain weight.

When September came around years ago, many thousands of people travelled down from the east end of London to the hop gardens of Kent for a spell of hop-picking. My late aunt used to tell me how they would look forward to travelling down to Kent on the special trains. Whole families went back every year to the same farms where they stayed in 'hopper huts' and, after working in the fields all day, would build fires in the evenings and enjoy singing songs and telling stories. Today, hops are picked and processed by machine and, as with many other crops, far fewer people are required to harvest the crop.

We often use the green trailing hops we find in the hedgerows to decorate our churches for the Harvest Festival.

September is the time for Michaelmas Daisies and what a picture they make in a vase, with a few stems of Golden Rod. Sadly, we don't see as many Michaelmas Daisies in gardens nowadays, mainly because they do suffer from mildew. The name comes from the fact that they are often flowering on Michaelmas Day, 29 September. The Michaelmas Daisy is a native of America while the Golden Rod comes from Canada where it grows wild. Golden Rod is said to possess many magical powers, one being that it is an effective divining rod with the power to pinpoint water.

Hydrangea flowers can be dried in September; just wait until the flowers have begun to change colour before cutting them from the bush, then place the flowers in a bowl tall enough to support them. Pour in about 2-3 inches of water, then keep an eye on them and as soon as you notice all the water has been used up, take them out and hang them up to dry in an airy shed.

Michaelmas Day falls on 29 September - St Michael the Archangel is the patron saint of soldiers and horses. This is one of the Quarter Days of the year and one of the most significant dates on the country calendar. It was traditionally the day when farm tenancies changed, when rents fell due and when many people started new jobs or left service. Michaelmas came to be associated in the minds of many country people with financial troubles as it was the time when unsuccessful tenant-farmers moved out and new tenants arrived. Landlords held a rent audit and provided a feast for all their tenants. Although the custom has generally died out, it still survives on some large estates. Today the celebration is more likely to be held in the local pub than in the Great Hall of the mansion. Most farm tenancies ran out at Michaelmas and a few weeks before, the local papers advertised dispersal sales for farmers who were giving up farming. Fairs were held for the dispersal of livestock and the great sheep sales were held then. At the height of agricultural prosperity, up to 100,000 sheep were sold annually. In the late eighteenth century, sheep were fetching about 12 shillings each and it is said that £300,000 changed hands at the sheep sales - more than the ordinary farmers today are getting!

Michaelmas was also the day when jobs were changed. If, as the year drew to an end, the farmer made no move to renew the farm worker's or maid's engagement, or they wished to go elsewhere, then it was to the hiring fair that both parties went. About the early 1900s, when jobs were hard to come by, men would walk miles looking for work. It must have been hard too for those waiting to be chosen for work. Once an agreement had been made with a farmer, the newly hired worker received a 'fastpenny' as an earnest of wages to come. Hiring at the fairs in many districts lasted until the outbreak of the First World War.

Many country people used to keep geese and the tradition was that a goose was given to the landlord on Michaelmas Day, and also eaten by the cottagers on that day:

'Whosoever eats goose on Michaelmas Day
Shall never lack money his debts for to pay.'

The fatted and roasted goose had been appreciated as a succulent dish for festive occasions since early civilisation. It is more difficult to date the Michaelmas Goose exactly, but it is said that Elizabeth I partook of goose while waiting for news of the Armada, and ever afterwards ate goose on Michaelmas Day.

The goose was good for so many things, the quills of the feathers were used for making pens, the grease was rubbed on the chest for coughs and colds and the feather beds were made from the soft down feathers. Geese we also used as guards as they are as good as any dog at letting you know if anyone is about. There is a saying that wild and domestic geese make good weather forecasters. When they seem to be unsettled, and bathe themselves a lot, rain is on the way, but if they preen themselves it means wind is coming. If they are noisy, it is generally a sign of stormy weather coming.

At one time, goose rearing on a large scale in England was more or less confined to the swampy areas of the eastern counties. Norwich was so famous for its geese that a Norwich goose was renowned as the hallmark of succulence and fatness. These wet, low-lying lands have largely been drained and made suitable for corn growing so that the rearing of geese has been far more widely distributed. With combine harvesters and modern machinery, stubble is more thoroughly gleaned than of old, but geese are 'good doers' and given a free run after the harvest, rapidly put on weight.

In recent years selective breeding has meant that the domestic goose has been greatly developed in size so that you can buy one to suit your family. One tip I have been given is that you should always roast a goose breast downwards in the pan. This helps the fat to run out, while keeping the breast moist and tender.

Although the full season is nearing its end, in the woods and lanes deep in rural England the ground is strewn with many kinds of wild fruits and nuts. The blackberry is one of the most useful and has its roots deep in our history folklore and has been eaten for a very long time. Our forbears were careful not to pick them after Michaelmas when the devil had the unpleasant habit of spitting on them, and in Sussex, people used to believe that anyone who ate a blackberry after that date would die or lose a relative before the year was out. The fruits vary a lot in size and flavour, which is not surprising when one considers that there are nearly four hundred varieties of wild blackberry in Britain. The rooted stems sometimes stretch along the ground for several feet before becoming rooted into the earth, and countrymen complain that they are dangerous because people trip over them when walking on the country footpaths. In Norfolk, it was the custom for children with whooping cough to be dragged three times under a bramble stem whose ends were both growing in the ground, the treatment to be repeated after three days.

The old herbalists considered unripe blackberries to be good for sore mouths and scurvy. While still red, the berries were gathered, dried and powdered and then carried in ship's medicine chests for use against scurvy and sea dysentery.

August is often a sultry, hot and thundery month and we used to say that summer thunderstorms could be dangerous, especially if they were dry ones. Even so, the odds of being struck are estimated as only about 2,400,000 to one - the chances of being hit are lessened even more if you do not run to shelter under isolated trees that stand alone in the middle of a field. Some trees are more prone to lightning than others - the elm, ash, poplar and pine in particular, but the oak is supposed to be the worst of the lot. Other places to try and avoid if caught out in a storm, are streams, rivers and ponds - the vertical human frame may act as a conductor if it features prominently in a flat landscape. Do not be afraid of getting a good soaking, for being thoroughly wet will add to your safety. If the flashes are very bad, lie down flat, don't run about.

'Beware of the ash, it counts the flash,
Beware of the oak, it draws the stroke
But the blessed thorn will keep from storm'

The belief about covering up cutlery, silver and metal objects, also mirrors is quite an old custom and many people still believe in this superstition. You are not supposed to hold on to anything attached to wires, such as the telephone, and keep away from the fireplace, for a chimney lined with soot, forms a good conductor of lightning. If you are out in the open, don't stay put on a tractor seat, don't put up your umbrella and if you happen to be playing golf, walk away from your clubs. Of course, the noise of thunder announces that the danger is past. You can tell how far away the storm is by counting the seconds between the flash of lightning and the peal of thunder - this will tell you the distance in miles from the centre of the storm.

Windmills

Windmills were introduced into Britain in the twelfth century, and because of our flat and windy position here on the east coast, many were built in East Anglia. Most were post mills in which the whole contraption, made of wood and usually weather-boarded, was mounted on a large wooden post and turned into the wind when ready for work. In East Anglia, these mills were used for pumping water before being adapted to the grinding of corn. Different types of windmills were developed as time went on, some with six or more sails and built on artificial mounds to gain a little extra breeze. Some windmills stood by isolated farmsteads near villages and others were close to small towns. Driving around the fens, you will still see windmills working to pump water from drainage ditches.

When visiting Holland, I was delighted to see the many windmills there. Some of these are composite mills; these have ladder steps from the ground to where the revolving part meets the top of the low stone tower. Holland is proud of her many stately windmills and many steps have been taken to preserve them from decay. The towers are kept freshly whitewashed or creosoted. During the Second World War the windmills were used to give codes to British pilots by the position of their sails for warning about the position of the enemy or for dropping food parcels.

There has been a revival of interest in windmill power over the last decades but it will be a long time before it is widely used again, if ever, in our power-hungry world as windmills are expensive to run and maintain

'To let the cat out of the bag' is a well-known saying, yet not many people know of its origin. Rather than selling their suckling pig at market, it was once a practice amongst some dishonest country folk to substitute a cat for the pig and take it to market in a securely tied bag. If anyone was foolish enough to buy the animal without examination, all well and good, but if the sack was opened, then 'the cat was let out of the bag', and the trick exposed. Nowadays the phrase refers to the disclosure of any piece of secret information. Another name for the sack was a 'poke', and it was from this same practice that the phrase 'a pig in a poke' derived, meaning a blind bargain.

A London doctor, having a few days in a Suffolk village, was enjoying the peace and quiet and asked an old fellow what the death rate was in the area. Having thought for a moment, the old boy scratched his head and said, 'Well, I don't really know, as near as I can get it, its about one a piece all round'.

REMEDIES

Years ago people would walk miles to hear about charms or magic. One common one was for sciatica, in which a knuckle bone of a leg of mutton or a raw potato carried in the trouser pocket or round the neck was supposed to be a cure.

Whooping Cough

In Norfolk, when a child was seized with whooping cough, a common house spider was caught, tied up in a piece of muslin and pinned over the mantlepiece. So long as the spider lived, the cough would continue, but when it died, the cough would disappear in a short time. Another way was to tie a bag of live spiders around the child's neck until the cough subsided. On the Suffolk-Norfolk border, a hole was dug in a meadow and the child was placed in the hole with head bent downwards. The turf that had been cut out of the hole was placed over the child and he remained in the hole until he coughed. It was thought that if the charm was done in the evening with only the mother or father to witness it, then the child would soon recover.

RECIPES

Apples

What would we do without our good English Bramley apples? I always look forward to the Bramleys, which are so versatile for making pies, puddings, cakes, chutney, sauces, preserves and even apple ale. I used to enjoy watching my mother making apple rings to dry, for use during the winter months.

Bramble Dessert

2lb cooking apples
12 oz blackberries
4oz granulated sugar
8oz fresh breadcrumbs
4oz soft light brown sugar
4oz butter

Peel and core the apples, slice and put in a pan with the blackberries and a little sugar. A very little water may be added. Stew gently until soft. While the fruit is cooling, mix the breadcrumbs with the brown sugar, melt the butter in a pan and add to the breadcrumb mixture stirring well. When this mixture has cooled, layer the fruit and then the breadcrumb mixture alternately in a glass serving dish. Finish with a layer of crumbs. Chill for two hours. Decorate with cream before serving.

Apple Crunch

This is a quick and delicious sweet to make.

1lb apple puree
3 slices of bread
2oz butter
4 tsp desiccated coconut
4 tsp Demerara sugar

Fill a shallow, oven-proof dish with the apple puree. Cut the bread into cubes. Melt the butter in a pan, add the cubes and stir to coat. Add the sugar and coconut and stir well, then pile on top of the apple mixture and grill until crisp and brown. Serve with cream.

Two Wartime Recipes
Parsley Pudding

8oz Self-raising flour
2oz grated raw potato
2oz finely chopped suet
Cold water to mix
A little finely chopped, cooked meat
8 dessertspoons finely chopped parsley
Salt and pepper

Mix together the flour, grated potato and suet with enough cold water to make a stiff dough. Knead lightly and roll out into a neat oval. Place the meat on the pastry with the parsley, salt and pepper, fold over and enclose in greaseproof paper. Steam for 1½ to 2 hours. Serve with gravy

Sweet Pudding
2 cups of flour
1 cup sultanas and currants mixed
1 small piece of cooking fat
1 cup grated carrot
1 tbsp sugar or honey
1 tsp baking powder
1 tsp bicarbonate of soda
A little milk to mix

Simply mix all the ingredients together thoroughly, place in a greased pudding basin and cover with greaseproof paper. Steam for two hours and serve with or without sweet sauce or custard.

Passion Fruit is a lovely climbing plant, so-called because its several parts symbolise the passion of our Lord. Two types of this plant produce edible fruit - Edulis and Quandrangularis, and both jam and wine can be made from the yellow fruits.

Passion Fruit Jam
Take the red pips out of the fruit and pulp it in a food processor, then to 1lb of pulp add the juice of one lemon and 1lb sugar. Boil together and test for setting in the normal way.

Passion Fruit Wine
4lb passion fruit
1 small tin concentrated grape juice
Juice of ½ a lemon
Yeast and nutrient
6 pints of water
Cut up the fruit and add boiling water then leave covered for about four

days, after which time strain through muslin on to the sugar and grape juice. Add yeast and nutrient and stir until dissolved. Keep closely covered in a warm place for 3-4 days, then pour into a fermenting bottle. Try to keep for a year before drinking.

Marrow Jam

5^1/$_2$lb marrow
5^1/$_2$lb sugar
Salt
3 lemons
^{1}/$_2$lb crystallised ginger

Cut up the marrow, place in a bowl and sprinkle with ^{1}/$_2$ teaspoon salt. Leave for 12 hours then strain off the salty water. Put the sugar on the marrow and allow to stand for another 12 hours. Cut the lemons and the ginger into small pieces, add to the marrow and boil together until the marrow is quite transparent.
You can use pineapple instead of the ginger if you wish.

Fruit Cheese

Now that the rush of making jams and freezing fruit and vegetables is coming to an end, don't forget to make fruit cheese if you still have a lot of fruit on your hands. Damsons are particularly suitable for this preserve. You will need a considerable quantity of fruit because it reduces a lot in the process.
Cook the fruit without water in a covered earthenware dish in a very slow oven until it is quite soft. Pulp through a fine sieve into a pan, and for each pound of pulp, allow three quarters to one pound of sugar. Heat gently until the mixture is thick and all the sugar dissolved, then boil it until it reaches a thick, creamy consistency, with no excess liquid. To test whether the process is complete, draw a line along the bottom of the pan, if a clean line is left, the cheese is ready to be packed into jars.

Hedgerow Cheese

Blackberries must be picked before the end of September, when the devil is said to spit on them. These plus elderberries, crab apples and sloes can be used to make a delicious variation on jam. You can put any hedgerow fruits together in the pan using 1lb mixed fruit to every 11b of crab apples.

Wash and roughly chop the crab apples and place in a large pan, wash and remove elderberries from stalks, wash and pick over sloes and blackberries. Place in a large pan and add 1 pint of water for every 3lb fruit. Simmer until all fruit is soft, sieve softened fruit and measure pulp. To every 1 pint of pulp, add 1lb sugar, boil to setting point and skim. Pot and cover in the usual way. This has a thicker, more old-fashioned consistency than jam but it is a good stand-by if you are short of fruit to make jam.

Red Plum Chutney

This chutney goes well with curry, it is fresh and fruity with a hint of sharpness.

> 2lb Red plums
> 1lb cooking apples
> 1lb onions
> 12 peppercorns
> 12oz seedless raisins
> 8oz Demerara sugar
> 2 level tsp ground ginger
> 1 level tsp mixed spice
> 1 pint pickling vinegar

Halve the plums, stone, peel and quarter them and roughly chop the cooking apples. Skin and chop the onions and tie the peppercorns in a muslin bag. Place all the ingredients in a medium-sized pan and bring slowly to the boil. Simmer for about 1¼ hours or until the chutney is of a thick, mushy consistency, stirring occasionally.

This makes about three pounds

Marrow Pie

This is an old dish that my mother used to make, and I made it when we first married. It is a useful way to use up old marrows that have gone yellow. We used to peel the marrow, cut it up into cubes and leave it in a bowl overnight with sugar. Next morning we would add large raisins to the marrow and put this into a pie dish. Sometimes we would add a few slices of apple and grated lemon rind. This was then covered with pastry and baked in the oven until cooked. Many cooks used to make this as it was a cheap pie to make and when the harvest suppers came, this pie took pride of place on the table.

Pickled Onions

There's nothing better than pickled onions with cold meat, and now is the time to pickle them.

4lb pickling onions (shallots)
1lb salt
5 pints water
Spiced vinegar
Cinnamon stick or a few cloves (optional)

Put the onions in a bowl and cover them with boiling water. After about 10 minutes, drain the onions well and peel off the skins - this way they will come off easily without making you cry. Cut off the roots and crown carefully - try not to take off too much or the onions will break up. Dissolve the salt in 5 pints of water, put in the onions, cover with a plate and leave to soak in the brine for 2 days. Drain well, put the onions in clean jars and cover with the cold spiced vinegar. If you want sweet pickled onions, add 6oz sugar to the vinegar, and for extra flavour add a piece of cinnamon stick or a few cloves. Seal with plastic-lined lids to avoid corrosion by the vinegar.

Pickled Red Cabbage

Red cabbage is ready in September and is one of the easiest to pickle. All you need is a good firm cabbage, cut very thin and placed in a large bowl or dish. Sprinkle with salt and leave overnight. Prepare vinegar by boiling with mixed pickling spice, 1oz to the quart of vinegar, tied in a muslin bag, and one or two pieces of root ginger. Strain the cabbage and pack it tightly into jars, pour over the hot, strained vinegar and seal while still hot. Leave at least six weeks before using.

October

OCTOBER

October is one of my favourite times, although a good many people I know give up their interest in nature this month, 'We've had it' they say with a sigh, but the more practical observer knows that there is still a great deal of interest all around. This is the month when we see the most dramatic changes in the countryside, as the leaves fall and the newly ploughed earth replaces corn and vegetables. The autumn tints are beautiful and as the summer dresses are being thrown off and the garb of winter is being donned, I like to remember that for every leaf that falls, a new bud is formed. Those who study nature throughout the year, by day and by night, look forward with joy and hope when they see the autumn leaves falling to the ground. There is a feast of colours to be seen before the winter fast, for in October we are living on stolen time when every balmy day may be the last. The tractors are turning over the brown earth, followed by masses of seagulls swooping in their wake for worms and other morsels.

The late Autumn is the time when most of the wild creatures become gluttons in one way or another and it is remarkable how much some of them consume. By doing so, they put on extra layers of fat which is useful not only because it helps them to withstand the cold weather, but also because it is an additional defence against lean times ahead

October is the month for spiders. On still mornings, with just enough movement of air, one can see thousands of these little creatures being carried off, they know not where. When their home-made rope touches twig or grass blade, they find their new home, for all aspects of field or hedgerow are the same to them and chance determines their fate. A spider's web is a beautiful thing on a foggy morning. Some spiders have a way of straying into houses and have the misfortune to fall into baths - or do thy climb into the overflow pipes?

In autumn the spindle tree comes into its own as the inconspicuous pale green flowers of May and June turn into soft pastel-pink fruits. By October, it is one of the loveliest sights of the season; its purple-bronze leaves are turning to yellow and red and among these the fruits dance on slender stalks. The smooth, waxy capsules deepen to a brilliant pink, quite unlike the colour of any other autumn fruits, and are in wonderful contrast to the smooth green twigs and grey branches of the tree. When ripe, the fruit splits open to reveal four hard seeds, each wrapped in a thin, papery coat of brilliant orange. The fruits themselves bear a resemblance to a priest's hat and they linger on the twigs long after the leaves have fallen, letting us enjoy the beauty of the spindle tree for many autumn days.

The rowan (Mountain Ash) is a much-favoured tree, planted in great numbers along the sides of our roads. They are a beautiful sight at this time of year - the brilliant orange berries are unmistakable and can be gathered to make a good jelly.

As the light fails on sombre October evenings, one frequently hears the hoot and shriek of the owls as they sail forth on profitable hunts. With the cover becoming less each day, it is not so easy for small creatures and birds to move safely while finding night retreats. Owls doze lazily through the day but with the coming of darkness, their whole demeanour changes as, wide-eyed, they quarter the woods and fields, methodically hunting by sight and sound. Most big-eared owls, such as the barn and tawny owls, make no bones about swallowing a mouse, vole or even a young rat whole, jerking it back and down the gullet without ceremony. When I suffer from indigestion, I often envy the owl his ability to cast up indigestible food in the convenient form of a pellet, like some rude tramp spitting a damson stone over the hedge into someone's garden.

October is a restless month, the wind blows the rooks about, making them use bad language; jays shriek like witches, while wood pigeons seem always to be bustling about on business of great importance and hares take on their winter coats. I love to hear the call of the cock pheasant, but with the undergrowth becoming thinner there is less cover for the birds. By day and night there is much movement in the bird world with many hectic comings and goings. Swallows and martins set off on their long migratory flights to Africa, while ducks, geese, fieldfares and redwings arrive to winter with us.

With the harvest behind us, Christmas begins to occupy our thoughts and there are many things that can be collected and used for decorations later. While out on country walks, look out for the sloes in the hedgerows for making into sloe wine or sloe gin - always a welcome addition for Christmas. Save the poppy heads from the garden, these can be painted later on, and pampas grass heads can be very attractive in winter decorations. If the grass head has been left until it is fluffy, don't despair, just spray the heads with hair lacquer and this will hold the fluffy feathers in place. These and many other dried flowers and seed heads can be used to advantage for decorations at Christmas.

Watch out for wasps at this time of year. They are feeling uncomfortable with the weather getting colder and this makes them lethargic. In this stupefied state, they crawl about and are dangerous for they are too weak to get out of the way and it is easy to put a hand on one by mistake. If it becomes warmer their strength returns for a time and they have their hours of delight still eating the over-ripe fruit.

The large, black and orange bumblebees we now see will be the queens, all ready to take a well-earned rest sleeping throughout the winter. Having mated, they will hibernate until next spring when they produce their eggs. Sites that may seem ideal for a winter's sleep, may not be so good once the bad weather arrives. Many bumblebees never make it through to the following spring, but now they are content, sitting on a wall and preening themselves on warm, sunny days.

On dull, wet days all is quiet, but when the sun does break through the clouds and the rain pauses, the small tortoiseshell soon appears on the Michaelmas daisies, together with bees and hoverflies. On the rotting apples near the nettle patch are Red Admirals, dry and fresh in brilliant red, black and white. The butterflies enjoy these last hours of sunshine, but when the clouds cast shadows, they vanish again.

October is the month when animals 'come home' - rats and mice leave the fields and make their way to warmer places, where straw is stored in barns and sheds. One year I left my shallots in a wooden tray in my garden shed, and when I wanted to plant them out in April, they had disappeared. Later I found them at the back of the shed behind a bale of straw, partly eaten. So look out, if you want to store vegetables in boxes of dry sand, make sure that you have them in a vermin-free place. Rats have been known to gnaw through plastic boxes and consume the contents.

The hedgehog can be seen emerging from beneath a rubbish heap, with its mouth full of leaves. It toddles to an old tree stump where, beneath the roots, it will make its winter home.

There is always something cosy about lighting a fire as the evenings draw in and nothing better for warmth and comfort than a real wood fire. I use kindling (small pieces of wood) for starting the fire - this is a harvest that is constantly renewed by high winds or gales and is always worth collecting. I have a large box in the shed into which my brother is always putting odd pieces of wood, telling me that I will be glad of it during the winter months. Years ago you would have seen the odd car standing in a lay-by and passengers returning with arms full of dry beech branches to be taken home and used on the fire. As children, it was our job to gather kindling every Saturday, this was known as 'brumping' or 'sticking'. We used to make hand-carts out of old pram wheels and an orange box to carry the sticks home. Oak and ash sticks were preferred, and we always knew where to find the best ones. We also collected fir cones, which make very good fire-lighters, and were always pleased if we found a tree had been cut down as there were pieces of wood, 'chips', lying around where the tree had been.

After the harvest was all done, many farm workers used to ask the farmer if they could have a hedge to cut for the winter fuel. Ash and blackthorn were the best for heat. You would often see large fires burning at night on the edge of the harvest fields. Men would work well into the evenings to finish the hedge. Neat stacks of wood would be on the headlands, and then the farmer's tractor and trailer would be borrowed to cart the wood home. This was stacked in the yard, and I can remember my father sawing the wood up by moonlight. There was a lot of hard work to wood cutting, 'three warms' we used to say, cutting it down, sawing and splitting and then the warmth from the grate gives the final heat.

I know a lot of people in Suffolk still have open fires, and I am reminded of a wood jingle given to me years ago by an old country woman.

'Beech wood fires are bright and clear

October

If the logs are kept a year
Chestnut's only good they say
If for long it's laid away.
But ash wood new or ash wood old
Is fit for a queen with a crown of gold.

Birch and fir logs burn too fast
Blaze up bright, but do not last,
It is by the Irish said
Hawthorn bakes the sweetest bread.
Elm wood burns like churchyard mould
E'en the very flames are cold.
But ash wood green or ash wood brown
Is fit for a queen with a golden crown.'

Gone are the days when faggots of wood were used to heat the old brick ovens and short pieces of wood were also used to heat the cooking range. This was such a contrast to the modern cookers with their fans, controls and ceramic tops. Even the old Aga cookers that used to be heated by coke are now run on oil. In my mother's kitchen, there was an old oil stove standing on top of the oven, there were no temperature gauges or controls and yet she used to turn out the most lovely cakes and puddings. The oil stove was fed by gravity from a glass container fixed to the end of the stove. Some stoves had two burners, some three, and it was lovely to hear the 'blob, blob' of the oil and to watch the blue flame burning in the funnels. You had to watch that the stove did not stand in a draught or air, or there would be smuts and black cobwebs everywhere.

St Luke's 'little summer' starts on 18 October; so called because there is often a fine, dry spell of weather in mid-October. This was also a day for choosing a husband. In York the day was called 'Whip Dog Day', when children ran around the streets with small whips chasing away dogs. Many important fairs were held on St Luke's Day, it is the final burst of summer and the signal for all sorts of creatures to be out and about in a last forage for winter stores before the cold weather starts in earnest.

The cabbage must be one of the most under-rated and over-exposed vegetables on the market in Britain. It has been called the 'doctor of the poor, the medicine that is the Gift of Heaven', and with considerable justification. Our cabbage has many virtues, being used in days gone by as a cure for varicose ulcers, burns, wounds, carbuncles, rheumatic pains, sciatica and even lumbago, applying the cabbage leaves to the affected part. For hoarseness and persistent coughs, drink as much as you wish for a concentrated decoction: Boil five to six leaves to a litre of water for at least half an hour and sweeten with honey. In the eighteenth century, red cabbage syrup was used to relieve the chest, known as Boermave Syrup. Leaves of a red cabbage were pounded and then squeezed in a cloth to extract the juice. This was then weighed and half its weight of honey was added and together cooked over a gentle heat, skimming as necessary until a syrup consistency was reached. To heal blisters, cook cabbage leaves in milk, leave until cold and then apply to the affected area. Kipling wrote, 'Anything green that grew out of the mould, was an excellent herb to our fathers of old'. The cultivated cabbage originates from the wild variety that is a native of British and European seashores, and has been eaten since Roman times. Culpeper says, 'Cabbages are extremely windy, whether you take them as meat or medicine'.

All too often cabbage appears as a pale-green soggy mess on our plates - so many people spoil the cabbage by over cooking. Ideally it should be shredded and cooked quickly with only a very little water. Try using two bay leaves in the water when cooking to prevent the smell going all through the house.

October is the time for conkers and, with their dark mahogany, polished and shining cases, are one of the loveliest nuts. I always know when it's conker time as there is a wonderful horse chestnut tree near our village hall and when you see the ground scattered with sticks and pieces of wood under the tree you know the boys have been trying to knock the nuts to the ground. I think it is as true of conkers as it is of human beings, that the biggest are not necessarily the most tough. Now and then you might find a conker the size of a bantam's egg, yet once you had skewered him and threaded him on the knotted string, at his very first encounter - bang! - his brown skin would split and his white innards would be scattered all over the ground. At the other extreme, the small ones are equally useless.

When we were children, the boys' pockets would be bulging at this time of year, conkers were a great playtime amusement. We tried to make our conkers harder by pickling them in vinegar or even trying to bake them in the oven. Mother would get so cross as very often we forgot them and there would be a loud bang as the conkers split into hundreds of bits.

Now is the time when children love to take a stick and go nutting for sweet chestnuts, hoping they will find the balls of prickly green cases to be split open with a knife to reveal the prized nut inside. There is a country tale that the nightingales like to come back to the chestnut year after year. The nuts are good to eat and wonderful roasted at an open fire. We found that they were easy to skin if slit at the pointed end with a knife and placed in the oven on a baking sheet; after about ten minutes, the skin could be whipped off with little trouble. The Italians know much more about chestnuts, they serve them as a vegetable covered with a rich sauce and as a soup. Mrs Beeton says that chestnuts make a good forcemeat stuffing for roast turkey.

As children we loved to collect other nuts at this time of year, even acorns, which fitted so neatly, like eggs into the egg cup of the beautifully chased and patterned olive green chalice. We used to collect acorns in the war years to be taken and used for animal feeds, but after the war, we never found a use for them. We also collected the hazel nuts with the green elf-caps, rough beech-mast with its three-sided kernel and walnuts that we made into little sailing boats, half a shell with a matchstick mast and a paper sail that we launched in the bath and puffed along.

I wonder do children still enjoy such simple pleasures? Do they squeeze the base of the snapdragon flower to make it open its mouth? Do they pop the half-opened fuschia buds and the white globules on the snowberry bush that make such a satisfying noise? Do they hold buttercups to each other's chins and say 'Do you like butter'? (If the yellow was reflected on your chin, as it always was in the sunshine, then you 'liked butter'.) Do they place ladybirds on the palms of their hands and say 'Ladybird, ladybird fly away home, Your house is on fire and your children all gone'? Do they still make leaf skeletons that are later pressed and stuck in a book? Or 'photograph' a fern frond by placing it against the printing paper in a frame and exposing it to the sun? I hope a new generation of children hasn't forgotten these simple games, which their grandparents will tell them they used to play when they were young.

The cereal harvest is now over but the sugar beet harvest is just beginning. Sugar beet grows like a big parsnip topped with a bunch of fleshy green leaves. I use a lot of sugar in the course of a year for making jam and preserves and I always marvel when buying a bag of sugar at how it comes up from the soil in one long root and yet we buy it all ground up in granules. Perhaps in contemplating how this wonder comes about, we may keep calm when stuck behind a large lorry carrying a load of sugar beet to the factory!

I am sure that many young people do not realise the hard work many of us used to do to get the sugar beet. When I was first married in the early 1950s, we used to work on acres, chopping out the sugar beet on piecework. The farmer gave us so many rows, marked out with sticks at each end of the rows. If you hoed well the first time, it paid off as the second hoeing did not pay so well. My husband used to go along and 'chop out' the beet, then I used to go on my hands and knees and single the beet out behind, six inches apart. There was an art in chopping sugar beet out, now it is all done by precision drill.

Sometimes, if there was space between some sugar beet seedlings, we used to have packets of swede seeds in our pockets and now and again we would plant a few seeds. We had some lovely swedes from the fields, much better than we could grow in the garden.

Then in October, the time came for lifting and topping the sugar beet. We walked down the rows, pulling the sugar beet and knocking off the soil from the roots after the tractor and machine had lifted the roots.

Then, with a sugar beet topper - a blade with a hook in the end - we cut the green tops off. Some mornings it would be so frosty that you would not know if you had cut your finger as your hands were so numb with cold. Some days it would be damp and foggy, it's no wonder so many farm workers suffered with bad backs and rheumatism in later life. We used to have old hessian sacks tied around our waists with a bit of binder twine. This would be heavy with wet mud, sometimes clinging to the sugar beet. The beet had to be clean with not too much green top left on it.

October

The sugar beet was then left in heaps in the fields, where they would be collected and carted to the side of the farmyard or field, often a concrete pad was laid for this purpose. Then the lorry would come from the factory, and was loaded by hand with large sugar beet forks with little steel balls on the end of the tines to prevent the beet being damaged. The farmers were sent permits so that they knew when to send their beet to the factory. Sometimes there was free loading and no permits required, so if you were lucky, you could get your beet in before the bad weather. Sometimes my husband loaded lorries with sugar beet on Boxing Day.

They were hard-working days, but we had a laugh, went home at the end of the day tired, and cooked a meal, often filling up the copper to heat, so that we could have some hot water to have a good wash.

A friend once told me about sugar beet pudding. Her father used to boil some up in the old copper until he got a syrup out of them, rather like maple syrup. The syrup was then put in the bottom of a pudding dish with a suet pudding mixture on top. After the pudding was boiled, it was turned out and the syrup ran down the sides of the pudding.

One's own garden is a good place for the study and application of weather lore. Spiders working on their webs, or using long frame lines indicate good weather. Pond weed sinks before rain. The leaves of many trees, including lime, sycamore, plane and poplar show more of their undersides when rain is imminent and may tremble in advance of thunder. On a summer evening, steaming watercress beds, ponds or lakes show that the next day will be hot.

Copious dew, particularly if it forms on stones as well as on vegetation, is associated with settled warm weather. It is a bad omen however, if down flies off colts-foot, dandelion or thistles when there is no wind, as very soon it will become quite stormy.

Birds are a short-term weather guide. There is a reliable saying:

Swallows high, staying dry,
Swallow low, wet 'twill blow'

This makes good sense, for the insects upon which the swallows feed are found at much higher levels during fine weather than when it is less settled.

225

With the darker days and longer evenings, my mind goes back to the Sunday teas of my childhood. Father would dig up sticks of celery on the Saturday and this would be washed and then served with cheddar cheese and apples, whilst we children toasted bread by the fire. This was the regular pattern for Sunday teas all through the winter. Mother used to do bake-ups on the coal cooking range. She would not be too happy if the wind was blowing in the wrong direction on these days as this would upset the draught to the stove. Either the food took longer to cook or it would be burned by the fierce heat. Like most, my mother never used recipe books and the flour, sugar and dried fruit were measured out by the handful; so much of the cooking was done by faith and guesswork but rarely did the cakes turn out less than delicious.

Father too was part of baking days as he had to supply plenty of kindling wood and if the coal in the shed was getting low, logs would have to be cut up and used on the range. Mother did not like using wood on the range as it always 'furred up the flues' - they would become choked with soot. Every few weeks, mother would take the range to pieces and, with a brush on a long wire handle, she would sweep all round the overn, removing the soot from the sides and from the plates. This was a very dirty job and was always done before we children got up in the morning but it was amazing how much hotter the oven became after this messy task was completed. When I was first married, I used to cook on a range and I had to go through the same performance as mother - it was a job that I never liked, but it had to be done. What a luxury just to turn on the gas or electric ovens of today.

Pears can be delicious, and I remember that my mother used to peel the hard, cooking variety - Orange Pears - put them into a large dish with a little golden syrup, then put them into the cooking range, leaving them all day. When taken from the oven, they were a delicate pink colour. Conference pears are long, slender and tapering and are best bought firm, although they will soon soften and be fit to eat. Doyen de Comice is larger and oval-shaped and is often called the "queen of pears" - the flavour and texture are truly outstanding.

The fruits of the passion flower are now ripe, they have a slight perfume and resemble apricots. At one time, the fruit was eaten with wine and sugar, but I have found that the flavour is not strong enough for wine making. This lovely climber is an emblem of Christ's crucifixion with its strange flower construction. The five-fingered leaves represented the hands of the crowd, or in some versions they were symbolic of the spear which pierced Jesus' side. The five stamens were the five wounds, the three stigmas were the nails of the cross, the anthers were the hammers, while the pistil was the flogging column. The threads of the corona were the crown of thorns or the halo of His glory and the coiled tendrils were symbols of the flogging cords. Ten disciples, excluding Peter and Judas, were represented by the five sepals and five petals and the white of the flower symbolised purity and the blue heaven.

Calendula Officinalis, better known as common pot marigold pops up all summer with its pretty orange or yellow blooms; the genus name calends reflects the fact that it seems to be in bloom every month of the year. In some country areas the marigold was known as the 'Husbandman's Dial' because the flower head turns its face to the sun as the day progresses, acting as a sort of primitive clock. Marigold also has a reputation as a powerful aphrodisiac, and was also believed to cure jaundice fever and skin irritations. The yellow dye extracted from the petals was once used in the dairy to colour cheese.

Now the nights are drawing in, many ladies will be getting out their knitting needles to finish off presents for Christmas. When we were children, my father would say, 'Put your ganseys on as it's cold out broad' - meaning put your jumpers on.

Knitting is an ancient craft and many traditions have developed since its birth some 2,000 years ago. One of these was the knitting of ganseys by fishermen's wives, which took place in many parts of Britain. Gansey knitting developed on the Norfolk coast and it was in the sixteenth century that the purl stitch was first used to produce patterns. Most of the wives knitted ganseys for their loved ones, some were knitted with rings of pattern on the sleeves, the number of rings denoting the number of children in the fisherman's family. Other patterns were given names that had the ring of the sea about them and signified things the fishermen came across in his working life. There was a pattern known as 'hailstones', a double moss stitch and lightning was a zig-zag pattern. There was 'coil of rope' (cables), diamonds for the mesh of the nets and rope ladders. Patterns were never written down but were handed down from mother to daughter - rarely was the same pattern knitted twice. A true gansey is knitted in one piece, having no seams and using a good 5-ply wool known as 'Seaman's Iron'. It must be knitted with five long double-pointed steel needles, four of which are used to hold the stitches whilst the remaining one is used to work with. The sleeves must be knitted downwards from the shoulder and cast off at the cuff so that any repairs may be made simply by pulling out the worn wool and knitting down again.

Pomanders are lovely, sweet-smelling things to make - they make nice gifts or can be put on your sales table. You will need a large, fat, firm orange or a large Bramley Seedling apple - apples shrink more than oranges. You will also need about 18 inches of half-inch wide tape, a few needlework pins, a wooden cocktail stick, 2oz cloves, 1 teaspoon dried orris root powder, 1 teaspoon powdered cinnamon, a small curtain hook and 24 inches of half-inch wide satin ribbon.

Mark the apple or orange into four equal sections, then cut the tape in half. Place one piece around the apple or orange from the top, right around and back to join up, pinning it in place as you go. Then use the second piece of tape to cross the first so that you have four quarters. Press the cloves into the skin in a line, closely working a section at a time, use the cocktail stick if necessary to make the holes for the cloves. Keeping the rows even, fill in the section towards the centre until it is completely covered with cloves, and cover the other three sections in the same way. Place the orris root and cinnamon in a paper bag, put the studded apple or orange in the mixture and close the bag tightly, pressing it around the fruit and shaking.

Pomanders must be dried fairly slowly, either on a mantlepiece above the fire or on a sunny windowsill, or even in an airing cupboard - but do leave the door open if your airing cupboard is very hot. During the first few days, the juice leaks from the fruit so it is wise to place it on newspaper. Pomanders take about two weeks to dry and when they are ready, the skins of the oranges will have shrunk slightly, turned dark brown and become completely hard. After two weeks, unwrap the pomander, remove the tape, which by now is looking very grubby, and press the hook into the top. Pin the ribbon in place of the tape and tie a bow on top. If you wish, you could place small dried flowers in the rows to mark the sections instead of the ribbon. Pomanders retain their scent for several years. Hang them over the hooks of dress hangers and place in the wardrobe. They are said to keep moths away from the clothes, but apart from this they make the cupboard or wardrobe smell absolutely gorgeous.

At the end of October, we change the clocks as summer time ends. Children will have to stay indoors, and evenings will seem longer for them. Some evenings, when I was a child, if we were lucky, mother might let us stay up for an extra hour and help her to cut old clothes into strips for rug making. Once we had cut the lengths, they then had to be cut into two-inch by one-inch strips. Mother would put these into a hessian sack with a sharp rug needle. The was a good way of using up old clothes. Most cottages had one of these rag rugs by the fire. They were so warm to sit on and we sat as near the fire as possible as it was the only heating in the house. Then we would get chilblains and our toes would become inflamed and sore from sitting so close to the fire. Mother used to get Snowfire tablet or cream and rub our toes with it. Sometimes she used Lion ointment.

Hallowe'en is the great festival when it was believed that the dead rose from their graves and when witches and ghosts and all dreaded beings were at their most active, carrying out mischief and performing their magic. Despite this, Hallowe'en is really the time when children play harmless pranks. Children also like to make lanterns from pumpkins with grotesque faces cut into them, and a torch or candle inside makes them glow, so that the faces appear to be alive with witch-like features. Apples are important in Hallowe'en lore, particularly in America. A girl can take several apple pips, give each the name of potential suitor, place them near the fire, and see which is the first to pop. This will be the name of her suitor. This was also the night for testing the faithfulness of lovers. Any girl can find out whether or not her boyfriend is living up to his name, by putting a nut into the fire and drawing a conclusion from whether it burns quietly or bursts. On the other hand, if she has two lovers and she wants to know which one to encourage, she has only to stick an apple pip on each of her cheeks and stand there patiently until one of the pips falls off. If she does not have a boyfriend, let her go into the garden at midnight on Hallowe'en and as the clock strikes twelve, pluck nine sage leaves, one at every stroke up to the ninth. Then if she is to be married, she will see the face of her future husband. Should her nerve fail her, she can make the whole thing into a dream by cutting a sprig of yew from a churchyard in which she has never been before, and sleeping with it under her pillow.

Another way to see the face of her future husband was to take an apple and a lighted candle into her darkened room, stand before a mirror and cut the apple into pieces. One piece would be thrown over her right shoulder, while the other pieces would be eaten, during which time she would be combing her hair. At midnight, if she looked into the mirror, she would see an "image" reflected there, but on no account was she to look behind her, or she would conjure up all manner of evil spirits.

A group of young people might gather on Hallowe'en Night, tie apples to pieces of string and then whirl them about. The first apple to fall down indicates which person is to be married first. Or each of the group can contribute an apple to the tub full of water, and then "bob for apples". With hands held behind their back, each contestant has to seize an apple with their teeth, tight enough to lift it out, and the best way to do this, if one didn't mind a ducking, was to pin the apple against the bottom of the tub. The person whose apple he or she managed to catch was their future mate.

REMEDIES

Now the colder days are with us, it's time to think about some old remedies for keeping a cold away. A favourite country remedy used to be to eat a few pieces of mouldy apple. Several apples were peeled, cored and sliced thinly in rings and then strung from the attic rafters. When they had acquired a ripe coating of mould, they would be ready. A few slices chewed slowly were believed to cure the most obstinate sore throat.

To prevent a cold, set some sprouting onions in vases so that they just touch the water - the way hyacinths are sometimes grown. Place one of these in every room in the house and the onions are supposed to draw away the germs. Or you could keep a plate of sliced onions beneath the bed, although I would rather have apples than onions under the bed - I dread to think of the smell in the bedroom!

Some remedies are more pleasant; bake a lemon until it is tender, then eat the hot pulp and juice with honey immediately before going to bed. Lemons remain fresh for quite a long time if they are kept in an airtight jar and then warmed before use to get all the juice out.

There are many remedies for cramp, a thing I often suffer from in the night. One was to carry a mutton bone in one's pocket, another was to wear 'cramp rings' - bracelets made out of old coffin handles. In many country areas today, people still make a practice of carrying a potato on their person, in the belief that it will prevent either cramp or rheumatism. Another saying was to put corks under your pillow to stop cramp occurring in the middle of the night, or you can tie periwinkle stems around the leg or arm that is most likely to be affected.

RECIPES

This is the month when we see changes in the meals we serve as we start to think about root vegetables - the good old stew or soup. Almost any vegetable can be put into a stew and there is no need for a lot of meat if you have plenty of root vegetables. Parsley and celery give a special touch to any hot-pot dish. The first pheasant will soon arrive in the butcher's shops. If you are lucky enough to obtain a brace (pair), they do need to hang for five to six days in a cool place to develop the flavour. I like to braise them; I lay streaky bacon across the breast and cook them in some good home-made red wine. You can tell the age of the birds by the spurs on the back of the legs - the bigger the spur, the older the bird.

Rosehip and Crab-apple Jelly

Rosehips area valuable source of vitamin C and during the last war, volunteers were given the task of collecting them in order to make bottles of syrup. Two and a half bottles of the syrup were made in one year. Hips should not be picked until October when the first frost has softened them.

> 5lb crab-apples
> 2lb rose hips
> 3 pints water
> 1lb sugar per pint of fruit juice

Wash and slice the crab-apples and cook in $1^1/_2$ pints of water until they are soft. Mince the rosehips and cook in $1^1/_2$ pints of water for 10 minutes. When both are cool, strain the two mixtures together and leave overnight. Don't squeeze the pulp as this will result in cloudy jelly.

Measure the juice and allow 1lb sugar to each pint. Boil rapidly until the jelly sets when tested. Pour into jars and seal.

Rose Hip Honey

> 1lb Rose hips
> $^3/_4$lb cooking apples
> Sugar

Put the hips in a pan and cover with water. Bring to the boil and simmer until tender. Cool and then strain through a jelly bag overnight. Next day, pulp the apples in a little water, add the hip juice and return to the pan. Add 1lb sugar to each pint of fruit juice then cook until it sets. When this stage is reached, put into hot jars. Always use a wooden spoon for this recipe or the jam will become very dark in colour.

Quince Jelly

Try to get hold of real quinces, which are large fruits, rather like a pear in shape - they smell wonderful. Failing this you can use the fruit of the chaenomeles, better known as the Ornamental Quince.

>   4lb quince
>   Sugar
>   2 lemons
>   5 pints water

Wipe the fruit, cut up and put into a preserving pan with the water, which should barely cover them. Peel the lemons, cut the peel thinly and add to the fruit together with the strained juice. Simmer long and slowly, about one and a half hours. Strain through a jelly bag and leave to drip overnight. Never squeeze the jelly bag, if you do it will make your jelly clouded. Measure the juice into the pan and add 1lb of sugar to 1 pint of juice. Stir until setting point is reached. Skim, pot and seal.

This jelly is delicious served with cold meats and with hot roast chicken. A couple of spoonfuls added to an apple pie also gives a super flavour.

Sloe Gin

The very thought of the rich, ruby drink warms my heart, but as a friend once said, 'If only bottles of gin grew on trees too'.

>   1lb sloes
>   6oz white sugar
>   1 bottle of gin

The sloes are better for a touch of frost, but rather than wait for the first frost, you can place the sloes in the freezer for a few days before starting. Then defrost the sloes, prick them all over and place in a large jar, pour the sugar and a few drops of almond essence over them, top up with gin and cover. Shake the jar daily for three months, then strain, bottle and seal and it will be nicely ready for Christmas. After you have strained the gin off the sloes, put them back into the jar and top up with a bottle of sherry. You will be surprised at what a boost this gives it.

The same method can be used to make blackberry whisky and cherry brandy, both of which will be ready by Christmas if you shake the jar every day.

When you have taken the sloes or blackberries out of your liqueurs, buy some good chocolate, and melt it in a bowl over warm water. Strain the fruit from your liqueur and put the fruits into the chocolate and mix gently. Spoon small amounts of the mixture into small sweet paper cases, place on a tray and put into the fridge until they set hard. This method can also be used with the cherries from cherry brandy.

Swiss Chard

This is a form of Seakale Beet and has a very high food value, being rich in calcium, protein, iron and vitamins A, B1, B2 and C. There is no waste from this vegetable as both the leaves and stems can be cooked and enjoyed. Trim the mid-ribs free of all the leaf, chop the ribs into three-inch pieces, cook like celery or asparagus and serve with butter. The leaves are cooked like spinach, no water in the pan, cook in their own liquid. The cooked leaves make a delicious light supper dish served on toast, topped with a poached egg or grated cheese. Swiss Chard is not often seen at the greengrocer's shop, so it is worth planting a row of seeds now under cloches.

Hazelnut Loaf

4oz hazelnuts
2-3oz mixed dried fruit
4oz soft brown sugar
4oz margarine
10oz self-raising flour
pinch of salt
2 small eggs, beaten
About ¼ pint milk

Roast the nuts for about 20 minutes in a moderate oven, then remove the skins by rubbing them between the hands. Chop the nuts roughly and put on one side. Rub the margarine into the flour, add the sugar and other ingredients, including the nuts. Add the eggs and mix to make a fairly dry dough by adding the milk slowly. Place in a well-greased loaf tin and bake in a pre-heated oven for 45 minutes until golden brown. This is delicious cut in thick slices and spread with butter.

Apple Batter

4oz plain flour
$^1/_4$tsp salt
1 egg
$^1/_2$ pint milk
1lb apples - peeled, cored and sliced
2 tbsp lard or vegetable shortening

Make the batter as for a Yorkshire pudding and let it stand for about one hour. Melt the fat in a shallow tin, place the apples in the tin, then pour over the batter. Bake in a fairly hot oven - 200C or Gas Mark 5 - for about three quarters of an hour.

Pickled Nasturtium Seeds

Nasturtium seeds when pickled, are a good substitute for capers and may be used in sauces.

Pick the seeds on a dry day, wash and dry them and place in a solution of brine in which 2oz salt is used to 1 pint water. Leave the seeds to soak in the brine for 24 hours, then drain and rinse well. The nasturtium seeds are then packed into small jars and covered with cold, spiced vinegar before being sealed.

Carrot, Apple and Celery Chutney

2lb carrots
1lb cooking apples
$^1/_2$lb onions
2lb ripe tomatoes
1 head of celery
12oz white sugar
1 pint spiced white malt vinegar
1tbsp salt
$^1/_4$tsp cayenne pepper
2 tsp paprika pepper

Clean and grate the carrots. Skin the tomatoes and chop. Peel and core the apples and chop. Wash and slice the celery. Peel and chop the onions. Place all the vegetables into a pan and heat gently with the salt, cayenne and paprika pepper and half of the spiced vinegar. Stir well, bring to the boil and cook uncovered until thickened. Dissolve the sugar in the remaining spiced vinegar, add to the pan and cook, stirring occasionally until thickened. Pour into clean, hot jars and seal.

Apple and Pork Loaf

1lb minced pork
4oz rolled oats
1lb cooking apples
3tbsp water
1 large egg
1tsp mixed herbs (sage & parsley)
$1/2$tsp Tabasco sauce

Preheat the oven to 180°C, Gas Mark 4. Stew the apples in the water and sieve when soft. Place all the ingredients in a bowl and mix well together. Press the mixture into a 2lb loaf tin and bake for 1$1/4$ hours.
May be served hot with a tomato sauce or cold with salad.

Now is the time for roasting or baking potatoes in their jackets, and in spite of what people say, microwave baked potatoes are not the same. Start them off in the microwave to save time by all means, but to get that nice crisp skin, they must be baked in the oven. What can be better than the smell of a piping hot potato straight from the oven, when you come in from working outside, one guaranteed to make you feel hungry. Better still - cut the baked potato and put butter or grated cheese on it then pop it under the grill for a few minutes - delicious!

Scottish Potato Soup

2 onions
2 potatoes
2 turnips
2 carrots
2 celery stalks
Salt and pepper
Parsley
Knob of dripping

Heat the dripping in a saucepan, lightly brown the onion and other vegetables. Add 1 pint of stock or water and a beef stock cube, and salt and pepper and simmer until the vegetables are cooked. Sieve or blend in a liquidiser, return to the pan, add 1/2 pint milk and reheat. Serve decorated with chopped parsley and with nice crusty bread. This is very filling and warming.

Hallowe'en Chutney

3lb pumpkin, peeled and chopped
1lb cooking apples
1/2lb sultanas
1/2lb onions, chopped
1/2lb demerara sugar
1 1/2 pints malt vinegar
4oz fresh root ginger, grated
Pinch of salt
1 red or green pepper, sliced
1 tsp nutmeg

Put pumpkin in a pan, cover with salt and leave overnight. Next day, drain and rinse in cold water. Place all the ingredients in a preserving pan, and cook until a chutney consistency is reached.

Apple Charlotte

This was a pudding my mother used to make, which was cheap, but delicious. Grease a bowl and put in a layer of peeled and sliced apples, then a dusting of brown sugar and a knob of margarine. Cover this with breadcrumbs, and continue building up these layers until the top of the bowl is reached, finishing with a layer of breadcrumbs. Cook in a moderate oven for about one hour.

NOVEMBER

The countryside draws into itself frostily but sweetly, and the year distils into the first of the winter months. For true country lovers however, the death of the summer and the slow passing of autumn have a certain balm. The damp, short days leave us in no doubt that we are on the edge of winter. Just how keen the frosty blade will be when it touches us, we do not yet know. Morning mists rise slowly from the fields and, ghostlike, reveal the rural scene below, rising upwards to mix and mingle with the grey clouds above.

The varied colours of the autumn leaves have almost gone from the trees as November gales bring down the last of the leaves, and we are left with naked curves, shapes and a network of branches etched against the leaden, grey skies, letting in a flood of light. The woods suddenly take on a feeling of lightness in strange contrast to the low ceiling of the clouds in the sky.

Old Man's Beard, which we call 'Traveller's Joy', silvers the wayside with its long trails. This plant was discovered by John Gerard in 1597 and is also called 'smoking cane', 'gypsy's tobacco' and 'boy's bacca', because the stems can be smoked like a cigarette.

In the evening sunlight, smoke from the bonfires rises with the mist and, in their blue and gold, fire, water and air combine and change with every moment. From bonfires in gardens and by hedge sides rise columns of smoke and, where the flames have blazed up, are left white flakes of ash. There is great satisfaction in having a bonfire. I was once told that it rejoices the heart of the beholder to have a good clear up and a bonfire.

Although there is still food in the country, the easier pickings have gone and it is necessary for small mammals to search a little harder. They become a little more adventurous this month as they scour the countryside - they need to search almost continuously for food. We will also hear the eerie calls of the first mating foxes. At one time they would only come out at night but nowadays they don't worry, they will feed and kill during the day, especially in areas where there is little disturbance.

241

Acorns, which used in past times to be fed to the pigs, are now falling. Years ago when they fall in the meadows, they were a threat to the cattle as they often swallow them whole and the little sharp crowns were liable to penetrate the wall of the cow's stomach, with fatal consequences. Pigs crunch them up and so are able to eat them without any problems. Wood pigeons, in spite of the small size of their gullets, swallow them whole. Many a time I have dressed pigeons and pheasants and found whole acorns crammed into their gullets. I'm not sure how they digest these, presumably the large seeds pass direct to the gizzard where strong muscles break and grind them together with small stones and grit.

November 1 is All Saint's Day (or All Hallows Day), and November 2 is All Souls Day and both days are devoted to the dead. In days gone by, there used to be much bell-ringing and bonfire lighting on these days. In both northern and southern counties 'souling' was carried out and this meant that begging took place. Small cakes, fruit or sweetmeats were almost universal and most begging was done by children who sang funny verses. On All Saints' Day, Hallow buns were made at Fareham in Hampshire and at Petersfield, these buns were also known as Holland Cakes.

November 5 is Guy Fawkes' Night, but in the past it was known as bell-ringing night - it was also Cake Day, but the emphasis was definitely on fire and frolic. Most children still like to celebrate with bonfires and the making of guys, though those who take round their guys or stand with them on street corners seldom chant the old rhymes. One of the rhymes we used to chant was:

'Remember, remember the fifth of November
Gunpowder, treason and plot,
It sure would be treason if for any reason
The day should be forgot.

Up to 1914 children in Walpole St Peter in Norfolk used to parade round the village with blackened faces, carrying hobby lanterns made of mangolds with eyes and mouths cut into them through which lighted candles shone. As they walked they sang:

242

November

'Please remember the fifth of November,
Poor old Guy, when he went to war he got a black eye,
With a hole in his stocking and a hole in his shoe,
Please can you give us a copper or two.'
The traditions have changed a great deal and nowadays it is more sensible for parties or groups to be held with one person letting off the fireworks as there have been so many bad accidents over the years. It is no longer considered safe to let children out at night, or even in the daytime, asking for a few coppers for their Guys, so all the more reason to have an organised party.

On November 5, the ancient rite of turning the Devil's Stone was always faithfully observed in the little north-Devon village of Shebbear. The stone, a large boulder, not of the usual rock formation found in the district, lies outside the lychgate of the church, shaded by a large tree. It is said that it was dropped by the devil himself and that if it was not turned on this particular night, misfortune would strike the inhabitants of Shebbear. Accordingly, shortly before midnight, a loud and discordant peal was rung on the church bells, to exorcise the evil one. The bell-ringers then marched outside, escorted by torch bearers, and duly turned the great stone over. The ceremony ended with a joyful peal of thanksgiving and a well-earned and hearty meal for everyone.

The Medlar tree is not often seen today, but it is during this month that the fruit becomes ripe for eating or sucking - I think that perhaps sucking is the best word for it. I remember as a child, that there used to be a tree near my home and we enjoyed a medlar, sitting on the bank and sucking the fruit. Sadly, this tree was blown down years ago. At one time, there were several trees in every country parish and I think this was a tree of past ages. The medlar (Mespilus) has quite an interesting history, in fact it creates something of a mystery in the arboreal field. A small tree, it originally came from Persia or Greece, where it was cultivated for its fruit. Then suddenly, in the sixteenth century, the tree appeared in England. A medlar is not fit to eat until it is 'rotten', and amongst wild fruits, it is unique in many ways.

If the weather is right, November brings in splendid fish, notably the herring and its relative, the sprat. Down the North Sea Coast, through the straits and westward down the Channel was where the shoals used to be on the move and were caught by fishermen. Sadly, as on old fisherman told me, this has changed and now they can only fish where they are told. Then, a good fishing season meant a lot to them and it used to produce a cheap meal. These days, no fish is cheap, through no fault of the fishermen who risk their lives every time they go out to sea. They must get very frustrated at times by all the rules and regulations.

Herring is not used so much nowadays, perhaps because it contains so many bones. The truth is that if they were scarce and dear, we would treat them as a delicacy, like smoked trout. It is worth remembering that herring caught inshore, which have not been on ice, always have a better flavour. When we were children, we used to look forward to the fish man coming round. The fish was plump and we never minded if there were a few bones. Sometimes we would get one in our throat, and mother would give us a piece of dry bread to eat - this soon got rid of the bone. We used to fight as to who was going to have the soft herring roes - they were a Saturday night treat, with toast made by the open fire. Fried sprats served with mashed potato also made a splendid meal to keep out the November cold.

The kipper is another fish people don't seem to eat so much nowadays. Once known as 'the bachelor's breakfast', it needs no more cooking apparatus than a jug of boiling water. Somehow I don't think the modern-day bachelor would stop to cook a kipper for his breakfast today, their breakfast is coffee and a little cereal and then off to work.

At this season of the year in the country it was time for pig killing. I have memories of delicious foods, for when a pig was killed there were so many by-products, like brawn (pork cheese), pork pies, pasties, sausages, chitterling pie, pigs trotters, pigs haslet and pig's fry. A good neighbourly custom, for both farm and cottage, was a present of a portion of the pig's fry. It was sent on a dish to the cottage wife, who would then return the empty dish unwashed and sprinkled with salt. The unwashed dish implied the hope that farm platters would never be empty, whilst the salt was a good luck offering for success in the curing of hams and bacon.

244

November

The weather can be very changeable at this time of the year, and the period between 6 and 13 November is often called Buchan's cold spell. This was named after Dr Alexander Buchan who was Secretary of the Scottish Meteorological Society. In 1967 he wrote that we would get six cold and three warm periods during the year. His fame came about by sheer chance - when nine Buchan periods were nearly all correct, his name became a household word.

Martinmas, falls on November 11 - the feast of St Martin - and was formerly one of the great feasts of the church. It was a great day for drinking health and for eating Martinmas goose. Although the day has pre-christian origins, it was claimed as a feast day by Pope Martin I in the seventh century. For generations, Martinmas was an important day for the payment of rents and the beginning and ending of tenancies and engagements. It is still one of the Scottish term-days when farm labourers are normally engaged by the year and is sometimes known as 'Pack-Rag Day' because the servants packed their possessions and left the farms to find employment elsewhere.

St Martin's Day often falls in the midst of a spell of warm weather - the air is light and the sunshine delicately beautiful. This is known as St Martin's Summer and is a pleasant, tranquil memory of the summer that has gone. As the white mist of the chill November morning thins and departs from the familiar hedgerows and lanes, there is something glorious in the splendour of the trees reaching out to the bright, soft Martinmas sun.

After 1918, Martinmas took on a new significance as Armistice Day, the anniversary of the end of World War One. The millions who died in the war are remembered on November 11, not only by countless services in churches, cathedrals and at outdoor memorials, but also in the two minutes' silence observed at eleven o'clock in the morning - the hour at which the Armistice was signed. Today, the services are held on the nearest Sunday to November 11 - Remembrance Sunday, when the dead of both wars are honoured together. The poppy is the flower we all associate with Remembrance Sunday, but the cornflower also has a role to play - it was the emblem of the Ypres League which was started in the early 1920's and disbanded after the Second World War. Around the end of October each year, they used to hold a 'Smoking

Concert' at the Caxton Hall in London and on the following Sunday, placed a wreath of cornflowers on the Cenotaph. It was also the traditional flower of Harrow School and is still frequently worn by old Harrovians at special events, such as Ascot. It has become a badge of recognition and this ordinary little flower inspires great affection among the 'old boys'. At one time, the blue cornflower was sold together with the red poppies for Armistice Day, in memory of the French soldiers who died in two world wars.

In the midst of all the destruction and terrible carnage, poppies were growing in their thousands. The flowers were noticed by a Colonel John McCrae, who wrote about them in what became one of the most famous poems of the First World War:

'In Flanders field the poppies blow
Between the crosses row on row
That mark our place, and in the sky
The larks still bravely singing fly,
Scarce heard amid the guns below. . . .'

When the poem was published in 1915, an American lady was so moved she began to wear a poppy on Remembrance Day at the end of the war. The Royal British Legion took up the idea and the first poppy day was held in Britain on November 11, 1921. The poppies we all wear today are made by ex-servicemen in factories. This is organised by the Royal British Legion who do a wonderful job. So when we wear our poppies with pride in memory of the millions of fallen comrades, we say 'No, we haven't forgotten, No, we'll never forget'.

As the nights get colder, and the air is cooler, the winter fogs start and linger all day. November is the month for fog and when I was a child, it always seemed to be the most dismal month of the year. Fogs were so common - real 'pea soupers'. Bonfire smoke can't get away and seems to move sideways, making it difficult and causing bronchial sufferers real distress. Apart from the annoyance and danger to mankind, fog also has some effect on nature, especially on birds, who won't feed in the darkness prolonged by fog.

For centuries, country men have believed that the moon can exercise an influence on the growth of plants and even to affect livestock. Nor is this belief to be lightly dismissed as another countryside fallacy, for experiments in connection with what is called moon-sowing have had interesting, if not conclusive, results. I have been reading that, years ago, astrologers believed the moon exerted an influence on the rise of the sap in plants and some still believe seed sowing and crop gathering will produce the best results when conducted under the appropriate phase of the moon. The idea in moon-sowing is to plant on a waxing moon which ensures better growth than planting on a waning moon. Experiments carried out on lettuces and cabbages showed that those planted two days before the full moon had more vigorous growth, larger and firmer heads and were nearly three times as heavy as those planted at other times. In addition, their yield was greater; as much as 30 per cent increase in the crop being recorded. An identical result was achieved when growing beans.

Herbalists of mediaeval times wrote at length on the correct time to gather various medicinal plants, with emphasis on the fact that the virtues of remedial herbs were at their best only when gathered on the appropriate day of the month. The study of animal, as well as plant life indicates that the moon has more effect on living things of the earth than was generally conceded previously. I have been told that the moon has an effect on broody hens and occasionally, a hen will bring out her chicks a day or two earlier than the usual twenty-one days and this has been attributed to the influence of the moon. Experiments done in the past have shown that more eggs will hatch if set when the moon is new so that it will be full a week before hatching time arrives - chicks resulting from such hatchings are said to be stronger and more vigorous and to grow more quickly. It is also claimed that chicks hatched when there is no moon are not good layers.

In France it was believed unwise to make wine when the moon was waning.

Whatever the weather, the farming season never stops, not even in November, and when this month arrives, much of the urgent types of harvesting will have waned. The grain harvest, with all its problems, is now only a memory, the potato harvest is all but finished and the kindly fruits of the good earth are safely stored away. The back of the sugar beet lifting is broken, and most of the winter corn has been sown, and now much of it shows pale green over the countryside, while every day the persistent plough creeps up and down, slowly changing the face of the countryside.

November 20 is St Edmund's Day; he was the patron saint of gardeners and farm workers, but not much is known about him. November 22 is St Cecilia's Day, the patron saint of music and musicians and, towards the end of the month, the festivals are devoted to the pursuits of smithing and lacemaking. St Clements Day on November 23 is almost a forgotten saint's day. St Clement was a Christian martyr who died in the fourth century. He is the patron saint of blacksmiths, and years ago, his feast day was a popular event in the calendar year. On this day, blacksmiths would parade around the countryside carrying an effigy of St Clement, which they called 'Old Clem'. Money was collected, toasts were made and a good meal was had by the blacksmiths.

Our late blacksmith, Mr Hector Moore, looked as if he had done his tramping in his workshop over the years, shoeing many thousands of horses. His well-worn face and hands tell the tale of a lifetime of hard work. In 53 years, he has never had a day in bed because of illness although he said, 'I have felt like it at times'. I laughed and asked if the smoke and fumes affected his chest and he replied, 'Blast no, I smoke as well and it has not killed me yet.' Men like him are scarce - he has a wonderful way with the horses. I watched Hector shoe a six-year-old stallion that was a bit frisky. 'He will be alright,' said Hector, 'I was like him once, full of life, but as he gets older he will calm down like us old uns'.

One of the greatest mysteries of the countryside is the horseman's word. For years people who worked with horses, such as blacksmiths, grooms and ploughmen, have had complete power over their horses just by whispering certain words in his ears. The legend of the great secret has been known for years and there are many stories of uncontrollable horses being tamed by man's whispered word. I am sure that the stallion Hector was shoeing knew who was the boss as he tried to move around - Hector's word was final. As I watched the smoke coming from the horse's feet, I asked how much the job cost the owner of the horse and was told that it cost £20 plus VAT. 'That's cheap' I said, 'Yes,' said Hector, 'and you can always get a kick from the horse as well and if you are unlucky, a hernia. The owners don't think it is cheap as the horses need new shoes every six to eight weeks.'

There are many sayings about horses, for example that somebody has locked the stable door after the horse has bolted; you cannot judge a horse by its harness; a grunting horse seldom fails his master and you can lead a horse to water, but you can't make him drink.

I once met another old gent whose life had been spent looking after horses. He came from the West Country where farms were often miles from a village blacksmith. So he would go to the farms instead of waiting for the work to come to the smithy. As he travelled around the countryside with an old car and a trailer looking for work, he would watch out for a sign, and he said 'And I bet you would not know what the sign was, my gal'.

A townsman might not know that a horseshoe on a country door is always nailed heels up, for country folk believe that otherwise the luck it invokes runs out. Even if a townsman did know the country lore of the horseshoe, and happened to see one nailed heels down, he might think it an accident or that it had been hung in ignorance. But the journeying blacksmith would be on the look-out for a 'heels down' horseshoe on a gate. As soon as he saw one, he would know that his services were needed.

St Catherine's Day on November 25 was the great day for lace makers, who appeared to have confused her with Catherine of Aragon, a patron of their industry. The eve of St Catherine's Day was known as 'cutting off day' as at this time, lace makers cut off and sold the lace that they had made. On the Eve of St Catherine's Day, the lace makers used to prepare a 'Cathern Bowl'. Apples would be roasted before an open fire and then suspended by strings from the beams until the pulp fell into a bowl of cider, spiced with sugar and cinnamon, set beneath it. When all the apple pulp was successfully caught and mixed, it would be strained and offered to guests. Candles were lit and placed on the floor, and each girl would jump over them. If she put the flame out, then ill-luck would follow her for the rest of the year. The belief that flames can purify one's life, and that passing through fire can change your luck is an ancient one. St Catherines' Day was an annual holiday and lace makers would have set aside a small sum of money to provide cakes to be enjoyed on this day.

'Rise maids, rise
Bake your cattern pies.
Bake enough and bake no waste
And let the Bellman have a taste.'

One anniversary that is not listed on any calendar is for the third Sunday in November. This is called 'stir-up Sunday', supposedly from the collect for the day; 'Stir up, we beseech thee, O Lord, the wills of faithful people'. This was the traditional day for the making of Christmas puddings and schoolboys went round the houses singing,

'Stir up we beseech thee, the pudding in the pot,
And when we get home, we'll eat the lot!'
Traditionally the Christmas pudding contains thirteen ingredients, symbolising Christ and the twelve apostles. Every member of the family had to stir the pudding mixture and make a secret wish, and the mixture was stirred in an east-west direction in honour of the three kings.
The association of plum pudding with Christmas is a fairly modern one, only dating back to about 1836, but the pudding itself, like other boiled puddings, has been popular since 1617 when the pudding cloth was invented. Before that, so-called puddings were stuffings or spiced mixtures boiled in a pig's bladder, rather like a haggis.
Pudding making used to be a very lengthy business due not only to the number of ingredients used, but also to the number of puddings required. There had to be one for Christmas Day, one for New Year's Day and even a Christmas pudding for the birthday of each member of the family. All the puddings were made at the same time as they would easily keep for a whole year if necessary. It was a great deal of work, especially for the mothers of large families! In Norfolk, at Terrington St John near King's Lynn, it was customary for an extra pudding or two to be made for the coachman, so that he could give a piece to all the horses, cats and dogs, as it was supposed to bring good luck during the coming year. My recipe for Christmas pudding is in this month's recipe section.

250

I recently asked my brother to lend me his shetknife (penknife) and he remarked on whether many lads today carry a shetknife, a shilling and a piece of string in their pockets. We then went on to talk about the old meat skewer which had so many uses when we were children. We always used to bend them to make hooks for rabbit lockers or even as a handle for the shed door. We also used them for making holes in conkers. We always knew where to find a meat skewer because mother had a stone jar by the sink with half a dozen in it, as father would use them for all sorts of things in the shed or even to keep chicken gates closed.

We used to make use of so many bits and pieces; string was always wrapped around a flat piece of cardboard; paper bags were folded flat to be used again; margarine and butter wrappers were always used to grease the bun or cake tins and also to put on top of suet puddings before the cloths were tied on. Nowadays we throw so much away.

The Christmas season seems to get earlier and earlier each year. November is the month to make your puddings, cakes and mincemeat (see Recipes). The mince pie has changed a great deal since its earliest days. An Elizabethan recipe would be to shred the meat - mutton or beef, and suet together, season with cloves, mace, pepper, raisins and currants to make the pie. In 1650, Oliver Cromwell passed an Act of Parliament authorising the imprisonment of anyone found guilty of eating a currant pie - they were thought to be far too rich and indulgent, and hinted at paganism.

Later it was discovered that suet, spices and fruit, which now included apples as well as dried fruit, could be mixed with brandy as long as 3-4 months in advance and stored in stone jars, provided the shredded meat was not added until just before the pies were made. From this, it was only a short step to omitting the meat altogether - this was already being done during Lent, and hence we have the modern-day mince pie.

There are still a lot of legends about the mince pie, even in this day and age. One is that they should still be eaten between Christmas Day and the twelfth day in order to ensure a lucky year. When visiting friends, if you are offered a mince pie, you should make a wish. The mince pie was originally oval in shape to represent the manger in which Jesus was laid, and contained three spices, a reminder of the gifts from the three kings. What a nice story to tell young children - maybe the shops would like to sell oval-shaped cooking tins, rather than round, so that this little story may not be forgotten.

As children, we loved to play on the rag rug in front of the fire on winter evenings. It was always said that the fire was the heart of the home. We were not allowed to sit up late, and sometimes had to be in bed before father came in at 6pm, but then we would take our comics to bed and read by the light of our small night-lights. Mother would let us have one of these a week for a treat, just to read in bed and after half an hour or so, she would come in and take them out of the bedroom. Later on, at school, we would swap our Tiny Tots and Beano for Dandy, Film Fun, Radio Fun, Girls' Own, The Champion, Rover and Knockout - all well-known comics at the time.

My father read the Daily Herald and mother the Red Letter magazine and in addition, every so often, my father was given a bundle of magazines by the wife of the farmer where he worked. These were Punch, Picture Post, Life and Woman's Journal and we used to look forward to looking at the pictures and wondering at all the wonderful places we saw in them.

During the winter, our bedrooms were not heated and we had to keep under the covers so as to keep warm. At this time of year my mother would go round with old newspapers and a knife, and push the paper into all the spaces around the windows to keep out the draughts - even the keyholes were stuffed with paper. Heavy sacks were hung up at doors to help keep the cold out. Some of the tied cottages we lived in were damp and we often had chesty colds. The fumes from my mother's 'Valor' oil cooking stove did not help. We were given 'Veno's Cough Cure' and had our chests rubbed with 'Vick Vapour Rub' and camphorated oil. The worst thing was when we had to put on our coats to go down the path to the outside toilet. There must have been many a child scared half to death while sitting on the wooden seat. Every little noise made us think that someone was coming, or worse, that a rat or mouse was about - it was not very nice.

Andermas, as St Andrew's Day was often called, was a great Scottish feast day and holiday. Boys would go hunting rabbits and haggis was made - whisky was always the chief drink.

RECIPES

November is the time to be thinking about Christmas preparations; the puddings and cakes should be made by mid-November and mincemeat soon afterwards.

Christmas Cake

Try this recipe, a mixture of pineapple, apricots and ginger with a little cherry brandy makes a delicious cake.

    18oz butter
    18oz caster sugar
    9 eggs
    18oz plain flour

4 level tsp ground cinnamon
5 tbsps cherry brandy
8oz seedless raisins
The following should all be chopped
    2oz glacé pineapple
    2oz crystallised ginger
    3oz angelica
    1oz blanched almonds
    8oz glacé cherries
    4oz walnuts
    2oz dried apricots

Cream together the butter and sugar, beat the eggs and add to the mixture a little at a time. Fold in the flour and cinnamon together and stir in the cherry brandy. Divide the mixture into three; add apricots, pineapple and crystallised ginger to the first mix; angelica, almonds and cherries to the second and walnuts and raisins to the third, mixing well.

To make the layers look different, add food colouring to the top two and a little treacle to the bottom layer. Put the three mixtures in one after the other into a well-greased and lined 9-inch cake tin and bake for 3½ to 4 hours at 150°C or Gas Mark 2.

Leave the cake to cool in the tin. When it is cold, wrap it in foil, keep in an airtight tin and decorate about a week before Christmas.

Mincemeat

As Delia Smith says in her cookery book, 'Once you have tasted home-made mincemeat, in mince pies, you'll never again be able to revert to the shop-bought product.'

    8oz raisins
    6oz mixed peel
    4oz apricots (soaked overnight)
    12oz sultanas
    4 oz blanched almonds, chopped
    12oz currants
    1½lb cooking apples, peeled and cored

6oz suet (try to get butcher's suet)
1lb brown sugar
Grated rind and juice of 1 lemon
Grated rind and juice of 1 orange
2tsp mixed spice
$1/2$tsp ground cinnamon
1tsp ground nutmeg
6 good tablespoons rum or sherry (let your hand shake a bit!)

Mince together the dried fruit and the apples and mix in the sugar, suet and spices, finally adding the sherry or rum. Pack into jars and cover.

Christmas Pudding

1lb sultanas
1lb raisins
1lb currants
1lb demerara or moist brown sugar
8oz peel
8oz suet
1lb fresh breadcrumbs
1lb plain flour
2 medium grated carrots
8oz almonds
$1/2$tsp salt
2tsp ground nutmeg
2tsp ground cinnamon
2tsp mixed spice
6 eggs
1 pint stout
2 medium grated apples

Chop the almonds then mix all the ingredients together. Don't forget to let all the family make a wish as they take their turn to stir the pudding. Place the mixture into four fairly large basins, cover with greased paper then tie on a cloth. I boil my puddings in my electric copper for four to five hours, the day after I have made them - this allows them to mature a bit. When they are cooked, I put fresh cloths on them then, on the day for which they are required, I steam them for another three hours.

Chestnut Stuffing

November is the month to gather chestnuts - there is an abundance at this time of year. One of its many uses is for stuffing the turkey. The chestnuts should be cooked, then peeled and ground in the food processor if you have one. The ground chestnuts can then be frozen and stored until needed at Christmas.

Chestnut Dessert

This recipe was given to me by a fellow WI member.

1lb chestnuts
1oz butter
3oz caster sugar
4oz bitter chocolate

Cook the chestnuts in boiling water until they are tender then remove the shells and skins and sieve them to make a puree. Cream together the butter and sugar then beat in the chestnut puree. Melt the chocolate gently in a heat-proof basin over a pan of hot water, add the chestnut mixture and blend well. Turn into a lightly oiled and bottom-lined tin and keep in a cool place until ready to serve with fresh cream and fruit - pears go well with this dish.

The colder weather makes us start to think about 'scare colds' - there are still some country folk who believe that a hot nightcap or scare-cold is a better way of preventing colds than being dosed with vitamin pills. Certainly it is a pleasant custom and one which we are glad to use. Mulled ale is the favourite of menfolk and is still found in some country pubs. An earthenware jug is filled with ale, then an iron beer heater, conical in shape with a curved handle, is pushed into the fire. Sugar and spice are added to the ale and when the heater is hot, it is plunged into the jug. Sometimes a wineglass full of brandy or rum is also added.

Mulled wine is generally preferred by the womenfolk, using homemade wines such as plum, damson, sloe and elder berry. Sugar, spice and a squeeze of lemon juice are added to the wine before it is mulled and the nightcap is poured, very hot, into wineglasses. Sloe gin is a nightcap not offered on ordinary occasions and is a favourite with visitors and friends.

Coffee Liqueur

This is a nice liqueur and is easy to make. Take a pint of brown rum, one pint of cold percolated coffee and sugar to taste. I should think it would keep colds at bay!

Milk Punch

> 2 pints rum
> 2 pints spring water
> $1/2$ pint tea
> $1/2$ pint boiling milk
> $1/2$lb sugar
> 2 oranges
> 6 lemons
> A little grated nutmeg

Peel the oranges and lemons finely, remove the pips from the pulp and put all into a jug with the rum, cover and leave for a day or two. Add the water, together with the sugar, tea and grated nutmeg. After mixing well, the boiling milk is stirred in and the punch allowed to stand for six hours. It is then strained and bottled ready for use. After a glass of this, we should all be fit!

Game

The hunting season for pheasants is from October 1 to February 1. A two-pound bird should serve two to three people. Put some bacon rashers over the breast when cooking pheasant or partridge, it helps to keep the meat succulent. The wood, or wild pigeon is another good meal, if you want to make pigeon pudding with a good suet crust, but I only use the breasts with bacon pieces or pork slices. It needs long, slow cooking. My mother used to make this pudding early in the morning. It would sit in a saucepan by the cooking range, slow boiling all day until we ate at tea-time.

Do save the carcass of any bird to boil up for soup, it is the base for any soup and it makes a good meal in itself, as you can add any vegetables and herbs. Once you have boiled the carcass up, let it stand to cool so that you can skim the fat off first before adding your bits and pieces.

This is also the time for a good, warming pea soup. In my mother's day, a pig's trotter, or some bacon bones would be put into a bowl and soaked overnight with hard green peas, and dried haricot beans. Any other vegetables that were left over went into the large saucepan and cooked slowly all day on the side of the kitchen range. The soup came out thick and hot, and served with dumplings filled us up for the day.

Marrow bones were also used to make a good soup, and would also cook slowly on the top of the range. Sometimes, marrow bones were served as a meal with a crust on top. The marrow was channelled out with marrow scoops, and these silver scoops are now popular with collectors.

Brawn

  1 pig's trotter
  $^1/_2$ pig's head
  Salt and pepper corns
  2 bay leaves
  Water to cover
  $^1/_2$ bottle homemade apple or white wine
  1 onion
  1 blade of mace
  1 sprig of thyme

Put all the scrubbed meat into a large pan and cover with unsalted water. Tie the herbs together in a muslin bag and add to the pan with the onion. Simmer until the meat falls from the bones - the slower it cooks the better. Strain the liquid well, return it to the heat and reduce by one-third, then add the wine and salt.

Meanwhile, pick the meat from the bones, cut into small pieces and add to the pan. Cook for 10 minutes, then turn into small bowls. Turn out when cold and set.

Curing pork

If you wish to cure a small pork joint, the following method is easy.

5 pints of water
3/4lb sea salt
3/4lb brown sugar
2oz saltpetre

Put the following into a muslin cloth or bag

1tsp juniper berries
1 small piece of nutmeg
1 bay leaf
6 cloves
2tsp peppercorns
A few sprigs of thyme

Place all the ingredients - except the pork - into a pan and bring to the boil. Boil for 15 minutes, skimming off the froth and then let the pan stand until quite cold. Take out the cloth containing the spices. Pour the liquid into a crock or bucket, then put in the joint of meat. Cover with a lid and leave for three days. Remove joints required for immediate use, like boiled salt pork. This brine cure certainly gives the meat a nice pink colour and flavour.

Fish

A nice, freshly cooked fish is as good as a steak any day, and there are several ways to check that the fish is fresh, firstly the eye should be clean and bulging, shiny and bright - this is the most important test. Then lift the gills of the fish and check that they are red and clean-looking, never brown and pale. If the fish is fresh, the flesh should be elastic and firm rather than soggy and soft; the scales should be tight and bright, not falling off and lastly, the fish should smell fresh and clean, not fishy.

The manner in which fish is cooked is largely influenced by the flavour of the particular variety. For instance, salmon is naturally so succulent that it could almost cook itself, while white fish is very different, and we have so often to provide a flavour. Just like meat, fish is best cooked on the bone and this is why chefs use the bones and head to make a good stock for sauces. Bones only need to be simmered for 20 to 30 minutes, but remember that fish stock will not keep as long as meat stock.

Oily fish such as salmon, mackerel, sprats and herrings are all rich in oil - 12-20 per cent fat - and not always easily digested because the oil is distributed throughout their flesh. This is why they are darker in colour, while the white fish fat is largely stored in the liver which we discard. White fish can be used in dozens of different recipes and with many different sauces, such as parsley sauce with baked cod. On the other hand, oily fish such as salmon and mackerel make very good cold dishes.

December

S.E.Burrows
2000

DECEMBER

Glittering white, crisp frosts, shadowy landscape, lit by a low sun scarcely rising above the tallest tree top. This is the welcome moment of rest for man and beast, between fat autumn plenty and lean spring unease. No matter if Christmas is white or green, December's weather is real winter - there's no dodging that one. When the sun sets at 4pm and the smoky mists enfold the countryside, you feel that cold, clammy shiver between your shoulder blades and a good fire is very welcome once you get indoors.

The woods shower down the last of autumn's golden dress. The lightened boughs lift and bend to the whine of cold winds. Every movement of bird and mammal is clearly heard through bare aisles, which conduct their calls and cries to the watcher walking in the woods, and tracks show clearly in mud, frost and snow.

As the month goes by, the days and nights get colder, and I always put out food and water for the birds. When I am baking potatoes, I like to put an extra one in the oven, so that the birds can have a treat. So many of our birds have disappeared, I just hope that as the weather gets colder, they will come back.

This month moves towards the shortest day on December 21. We do not think of it as the beginning of the winter, although we always expect hard weather after Christmas, but the shortest day for us and for most country folk, really does mean the turn of the year. After it we look forward, not back. The shortest day marks the end of a cycle of work and rest. Growth, the promise of spring, longer days and fresh life all begin after the turn of the year.

How soon the seasons come around - I call it 'the rush month'. Cards to be sent, shopping to be done and logs to be ordered. The rush is on for Christmas shopping. I can't believe it when lights are switched on in big towns and late-night shopping is on, the suddeness of it always takes me by surprise! It's so sad when everyone is worrying about how much they have to spend for Christmas, and it's a real headache for parents (and grandmothers) to know what presents to get.

As the pot plants come into the shops and I see the Poinsettia, the famous legend comes to my mind. It was Christmas Eve and music was playing in the village streets of Mexico. A little girl who was poor became sad as she watched all the villagers pass her by on their way to the church with their presents for the Christ child. She had no present but ran into the house and picked up a cup, thinking she would take that as it was so beautiful. As she ran to catch up with the others, she fell and broke the cup, which made her feel even more sad as she now had nothing to give. As she sat by the roadside, she noticed a plant and thought she would take that, for even the humblest offering, if given with love, was worthwhile. She knelt and placed her gift on the altar and as she left the church her flower seemed to become brighter - it was turning to a bright red colour, and this humble offering then became known as the Flower of Nativity. Although the English countryside looks in many ways the same as it did twenty or more years ago, a new conception of farming has replaced the old. No longer is there the rule-of-thumb and often seemingly haphazard relationship between the men who work on the land and the source of their livelihood. Instead there are farmers who have turned into businessmen.

The struggle with nature is always a crude business. The farmer of past times was by the nature of his tasks more personally involved, helping the men on Christmas morning to feed the farm stock, giving them a drop of 'hard stuff' in their cup of tea. Today he becomes more and more the servant of he big companies who sell him machines and fertilisers.

As a result of these conditions and the pressure selling of the big firms, he loses much of the freedom that was his. The soil must produce larger crops, hens must lay more eggs, cows must produce more milk. Both vegetable and animal life are subjected to the struggle for higher yields

Years ago, the first or second week in December would be the season for turkey plucking. We would start at 8am, have an hour for lunch and finish at 4pm. Then we would go home and cook the family meal, after which we would go back to the turkey plucking from 6 to 8pm. I don't know how our poor backs and fingers used to stand up to this work.

Then a few days before Christmas we would go and dress the birds, which was another back-aching task. At 12pm the table would be cleared up and the farmer's wife would give us a nice hot turkey roast. Plates were pushed aside and we would carry on pulling sinews out of the birds' legs, and then finish dressing them. All hard work, but we were happy.

The robin is the most popular bird in England. It is identified with the Christmas season in many ways, and because of this is very often shown on our Christmas cards. When Christ was born in Bethlehem on the first Christmas, a robin sang in welcome from its perch above the manger. The legend adds that the robin was rewarded with a sweeter singing voice, which is particularly noticeable near Christmas. In reality the robin's song is more pronounced at this time of the year in readiness for the breeding season.
An old rhyme emphasises the sacredness of the robin:

'Robins and wrens are God Almighty's shirt and collar,
Martins and swallows are the next two birds that follow'

The robin is the bird of God and the bearer of good tidings. The story goes that the robin plucked a thorn from Christ's crown in pity, and in doing so, wounded his own breast. Our Lord blessed the bird and endowed him with everlasting life. Another version tells that a tiny bird of dusky hue timidly approached the cross and with its wings, wiped away the tears that flowed from the Saviour's eyes, whilst with its beak, it plucked out the thorns from His brow. A drop of blood fell on the robin and tinged its dull feathers with scarlet. It has always been considered unlucky to kill a robin, or to tamper with its nest, so highly is it held in man's esteem.

'The robin, aye the redbreast
The robin and the wren
If ye take out the nest,
Ye'll never thrive again.
The robin, aye the redbreast
The martin and the swallow
If you touch one of the eggs,
Bad luck is sure to follow.'

The robin first appeared on a Christmas card in 1862. The first Christmas cards were merely gentlemen's address cards, to which an appropriate seasonal greeting was added. Later these cards were decorated with robins and holly. An early design was a picture of a robin harnessed to a cart loaded with mistletoe and holly. Robins, humanised by dressing them in clothes were also popular. The most famous Christmas card was one given to Queen Mary by her mother, which had a whistle concealed in it. When the card was pressed, it gave an imitation of a robin's song. Many Christmas cards show three or four robins perched together on a holly branch. This is completely out of character with the real robin, which has its own individual territory and chases away all others except its mate.

The robin is still the most popular bird in England, and wherever English people have travelled throughout the world, they have found a bird with red markings they can affectionately call 'robin'. Today robins will feature prominently on our cards, sending out the same message and greeting, as they did on that first Christmas.

Getting the Christmas cards written and posted is one of the jobs I always tell myself I will get done early, but I never do. Cards are now an essential part of the Christmas festivities, and are looked upon as one of the old customs. However, they are little more than a hundred years old, and were unknown before Victorian times. In the eighteenth and early nineteenth centuries it was a pleasant thought but by no means a custom, to send complimentary verses, often of the senders' own composition to particular friends at Christmas.

The origin of the card is generally attributed to Henry Cole, who had a thousand cards printed to sell in his art shop in 1843. Costing one shilling - a lot of money in those days, they were not a great success at first, but in 1870, when the Christmas festival had arrived in earnest, cards finally became established. The introduction and development of cheaper postage helped in this.

Many of the early Christmas cards were works of art and sold for up to five guineas each, but when the wars came and mass production brought the price down, millions of people could afford to send them. How nice it was for mothers to send their sons a card and to receive one back - many becoming most treasured possessions. The designs have changed considerably in the course of a century, ranging from simple sprigs of holly and mistletoe with homely family scenes to some that today seem to bear little relevance to Christmas.

December 13 is St Lucy's Day and in the old calendar this was the shortest day. 'Lucy light, the shortest day and the longest night'. Nowadays, we celebrate St Thomas' Day on December 21 as being the shortest day and the turning point of the year. Thomas was known as the 'doubting disciple' of the bible, the apostle who refused to believe that Christ had risen from the dead until he could touch the wounds made during the crucifixion. It is said that ghosts are given their freedom on the Eve of St Thomas, and for some, St Thomas' Eve was considered to be very holy and no work was done at all. In many areas, young, unmarried girls used to place a sprig of evergreen under their pillows when they went to bed on this night in the expectation of dreaming of their future husbands. Gardeners used to plant broad beans on this day and as many were superstitious, none would like to see a white bean coming up on the row as this would foretell a death in the family.

A lot of mums, dads, grandparents and aunties will be going to schools or churches to see children in their nativity plays. How lovely it is to see the children perform these little stories - some may forget their lines or a few tears will flow, but many of us will have a lump in the throat or even a tear, as we watch the little ones. There's a smile when behind the curtains you hear that 'little John wants to be a King instead of a shepherd' and 'little Jane doesn't want to be Mary', or 'someone has taken her baby.' These things don't matter, they manage to get the story across and we feel so proud of them.
It's hair-raising for the teachers, but in the end, all turns out well. It would be a sad place without the children's concerts.
It is commonly believed that the custom of the crib was started by St Francis of Assisi who, at Greccio in 1224 prepared a crib with hay and had a real ox and ass standing beside it. This was evidently something new in that district as a few days before Christmas, St Francis gave instructions to a friend as to what should be done on the holy night. On that night, people from nearby religious

houses came, carrying torches and singing hymns of praise to worship the infant Jesus. Even today, in some churches where midnight mass is celebrated, a figure depicting the infant Jesus is carried in procession - - -

Once the children break up for the Christmas holidays, they can help with making Christmas decorations for the home or the church. On the continent and in America, it is common practice to hang a garland upon the front door to welcome friends and relatives at Christmas and it is now becoming popular in Britain.

To make a festive garland you will need a wire coat-hanger, some fine chicken mesh wire, moss, holly, fir-cones and ribbon. First, open up the coat-hanger and make it into a round frame, place the moss on the frame and secure it with the chicken wire (I have used a large potato cut in half when I can't find moss), then stick the holly and cones into the moss. Tie the ribbon in a large bow over the curved hook of the hanger and the garland is complete.

It's surprising how useful the potato can be when making decorations; when making a holly ball, wire the potato to a length of ribbon, sharpen the ends of the holly, push these all round the potato, remembering to put smaller pieces between the larger ones so as to hide the potato. Hang the ball from a beam or lintel in the ceiling and the juice from the potato will keep the holly fresh until Twelfth Night.

The Vikings are reputed to have brought over to this country, the custom of burning a Yule log, but this has now passed out of fashion, although many people still have a Yule log as a table decoration. Find a log, about 12 to 18 inches in diameter - silver birch looks pretty. Plane one side flat, or nail two small pieces of wood about two inches long, across the base of the log to make a flat stand. Next, drill three holes along the top and insert coloured candles. Make a number of holes along the log with a gimlet and these are then filled with twigs of evergreen and berries. Beech husks and cones can be wired or glued on to the log and the effect can be completed by winding a trail of ivy around the log and sprinkling it with glitter dust.

Dried plants, grasses, seed heads, old man's beard trails, rose hips and bracken can all be brushed with a little gum, sprinkled with glitter and mixed among the darker greens. The poppy heads saved from the summer can now be painted with silver or gold paint, and greenery can look surprisingly effective painted with a little white paint. Even the seed heads of mombretia can look pretty when painted - you don't have to buy expensive flowers to make a nice arrangement. A Chinese lantern (Physalis Solanaceae), taken from the stem, opened up and wired on to a false stem looks very attractive in a green decoration.

When we were children, we made paper chains using flour and water as glue, although cheap, these did look pretty. Mother used to get cross if we knocked the basin over and this floury mess went on the mat. At one time we could not get the coloured strips to make the chains, and one year we used newspapers. Later, we bought bright red and green crepe paper and cut it into strips and twisted it into chains. The candles, tinsel and little ornaments for the Christmas tree were treated with care as they had to last from year to year, and when the first coloured fairy lights came along for decoration, we thought it was real luxury.

There is a lovely Christmas story about decorations - 'The Web of Beauty'. Mary and Joseph and the Baby were travelling to Egypt to escape from Herod's soldiers. One night, when it was very cold and frost was on the ground, they stopped to rest in a cave. A spider was inside the cave and she wanted to bring a gift for the Baby. She had nothing, so she spun a web across the entrance of the cave to try and keep out the cold, and soon a hoar frost was glittering on the web. Later that night, the soldiers came by and saw the web across the cave entrance. 'No-one can be in there' said the commander, 'or the web would be broken'. So the soldiers went on their way and the Baby was safe. That is why we put tinsel on our Christmas trees, for the glittering tinsel stands for the spider's web that saved the Baby Jesus.

When we decorate our houses with evergreens, we are continuing a tradition that has its origins in pagan customs. Evergreens were always seen as the symbols of eternal life.

The yew is an intriguing species. It is planted in churchyards to protect the dead, and it was also said to protect the church from evil, keeping both the devil and evil spirits at bay. Sometimes yew leaves were scattered on a grave as the coffin was lowered, a practice which would also ensure everlasting life.

Evergreens bear fruit in the winter, and from early times they have been recognised symbols of strong life. So many people still have superstitions about holly and mistletoe and say that it should not be brought into the house before Christmas Eve. My mother used to be upset if we children brought holly in before Christmas. The holly, with its red berries is traditionally masculine and therefore lucky for men, whilst the smooth variegated holly and trailing ivy are the ladies' flowers.

In some parts of Europe the holly is still called 'Christ's Thorn', the legend being that the blood of our Lord dripped onto its berries and stained them red forever. Jesus Christ came to represent the Holly Lord and the word holly is a corruption of holy. Holly has thus become for us the traditional decoration at Christmas and we sing the old carol 'Of all the trees that are in the wood, the holly bears the crown.' It was first used as a decoration by the romans, who also had the custom of sending bouquets of holly, accompanied by New Year's gifts, to their friends as a sign of goodwill. Later it was used by the early Christians to decorate their churches, and so the custom has come down to us. There are several superstitions about the holly bush. Its nearness to a home was supposed to guard against lightning, and holly standing by the door or hung up over a picture was reckoned to be a protection against witches. For many years it was considered unlucky to fell a holly bush. Bunches of holly were used to 'thrash' chilblains to cure them, and holly berries were used to cure such troubles as gout, pleurisy, colic and cattarh.

Although it is an essentially lucky tree, it is still considered unlucky to bring holly into the house before Christmas Eve and it is essential to remove it before Twelfth Night. In the church however, we can leave the holly until Candlemas Day (February 2). To burn holly on the fire before the year is out is to court disaster, and to bring holly into the house is generally thought to be unwise.

The mistletoe, by long tradition, has never been allowed inside the church, since they say that this plant was overlooked by the gods because of its pagan and magical powers. It was valued by the Druids for its healing powers and in roman history, it was said to be an all-healing plant. Mistletoe was still known as 'all-heal' in later times, as it was commonly believed to cure many diseases. Some homes still keep a branch from one Christmas to the next, as a protection against evil. To kiss one's sweetheart under the mistletoe is to bring luck on the future of the relationship, and this is essentially a relic of the old fertility rites in pagan times. If a sprig of mistletoe was given to the cow who calved first, after New Year's Day, it was said to be lucky for the cow, and would also bring good health to the rest of the herd. If the mistletoe is hung over the door on December 21, there is a saying that it will act as a safeguard against frost during the coming year.

Laurel, bay, rosemary, box and pine have all been used as decoration from early times. Cypress was regarded as funeral greenery, but yew was used mainly for Easter decorations. When we gather our greenery for home or church at Christmas, it is interesting to think of all the mystery and folklore that surround them.

There are still some legends about Christmas that I love to hear and to tell, one being the legend of the Christmas tree. This little fir tree, twinkling with lights and festooned with gifts, is sometimes considered to be a modern institution, but this is far from true. The fir, with its fingered branches so suitable for the bearing of gifts, has a beautiful and moving legend that couples it with St Wilfred. It is said that while the famous missionary was chopping down an oak tree which had been hit by a storm, he looked at a young fir tree that stood unharmed behind it, raising green spires to the stars. Pointing to it, St Wilfred said to his followers: 'This little tree, a young child of the forest, shall be your holy tree tonight. It is the wood of peace, for your houses are made of wood, it is the symbol of endless life for its leaves are always green. See how it points upwards to heaven - let this be called the tree of the Christ Child. Gather about it, not in the wild wood, but in your homes; there it will shelter loving gifts and acts of kindness.'

When children break up for the Christmas holidays, parties are held in homes and village halls. When we were young children, the village party or Sunday School party was one of the events of the year. We counted the days until the party, and our eyes were bright as we entered the hall and saw the tables laid with sandwiches, pink and white iced buns with silver balls on top, jellies and blancmange.

We had to change our outdoor shoes for plimsolls so as not to damage the hall floor. After we had eaten all we could manage, we had games - musical chairs, blind man's buff, pinning the tail on the donkey, pass the parcel and so on. When the evening came to a close, it was time for the final treat, with either a magic lantern show or a conjurer. Father Christmas also came, and we each had an orange, an apple, maybe a few nuts and a little present as well.

It was such a treat for the children of years ago, and often we had to walk two or three miles home, or mother would let us sit on the carrier of her cycle while she pushed it along the country lanes with the owls calling out. We went to bed tired, but so happy - never mind if it was raining as we went home, our clothes were soon put on the airing horse to dry out by the fire. A hot cup of cocoa, then up to bed where we would lay dreaming of the next treat to look forward to, carol singing around the village and, if we were lucky, mother would take us to Ipswich on the 'bus to see a pantomime.

Each year at Christmas we sing:

'In Bethlehem was born the Holy Child
On hay and straw in the winter wild,
Oh, my heart is full of mirth at Jesus' birth

While other joyful songs have died out in the course of time and been lost to posterity, carols have survived and are as popular today as when they were first written.

Carols have a varied and interesting history. For nearly eight hundred years, Christmas was kept with nothing but rousing and boisterous songs that lacked all godliness. The carol was first sung by the Franciscans, - followers of St Francis of Assisi. At this early date in Christian history, the church gave little enlightenment to ordinary people. Only the learned could read the bible, and the church services were conducted in a language that no one but the priests and monks could understand. St Francis taught songs and told stories that could be understood by all. The carol was then born through these simple songs - the people were taught biblical stories and Christian ideas through them. The carol soon passed to other parts of the world, to Spain, France and Germany - but everywhere it went, it retained its childlike simplicity, its religious tendency and warmth.

December

In the reign of Elizabeth I, Christmas carols were sung throughout this country while in the reign of Charles I, poets wrote good carols. During the Reformation, with the controls of puritanism, all festive songs came into disfavour and carols almost disappeared altogether. Later, when the Methodist movement began, such well-known songs as 'While shepherds watched their flocks by night', 'Christians awake!' and 'Hark the herald angels sing' came into being. By the middle of the eighteenth century, thanks to enterprising publishers, the old carols were collected together with their proper tunes and people began to enjoy them once more.

Christmas Eve is both the best and the worst day, the day of cooking everything possible in advance, stuffings, apple sauce, brandy butter and the cold sweets; the arrival of guests who are staying in the house and the tying up of the last presents. If you still have an open fire there are plenty of logs to be brought in.

After all that, there is often a midnight Communion service, unless you have a young family when it is more convenient to go to church on Christmas morning. This is often the one time of the year when all the family are together and are able to go to the service.

In my younger days, when we came home from Midnight service, we often used to sit down to cold boiled ham, or even start the rabbit pie. This was looked upon as being more important than the Christmas bird.

In our house on Christmas Eve, our letters to Father Christmas were posted up the chimney, and our stockings were hung up, and we didn't forget to leave out a glass of home-made wine and a mince pie for Santa - before being packed off early to bed.

Thousands of parents tell their children the age-old story of Santa Claus and his sleigh with his team of reindeer - Dasher, Dancer, Prancer and Vixen, Comet, Cupid, Donner and Blitzen. Santa Claus has probably come to us from across the Atlantic, for the Dutch once took him to America. St Nicholas, the present-giving saint, is the patron saint of sailors, prisoners and boys, and the legends about him are nearly all concerned with his generosity to the young.

For the adults, there was work to be done on Christmas Eve, for the shops would be open until past eleven at night. Sometimes the menfolk didn't arrive home with their wages until early evening so much of the Christmas spending had to wait until then. The Christmas fare of turkeys, chickens and geese hung in rows outside the front of the shop and fathers would be working out their money to see how much they could spend.

Never speak ill of the animals on Christmas Eve - the lowly cattle and ass of the fields, present in the stable where Christ was born, or of pets warming themselves by the fireside, for legend says that animals can understand human voices until midnight, when the Christmas bells ring out.

In Ireland, visitors will see lights in the windows of the houses on Christmas Eve - candle lights, lighted trees, in fact all kinds of light, but these are not merely decorations. The practice of illuminating the window is based on the old custom to guide travellers, which originated from days when rules of hospitality were superior. On Christmas Eve, the light was placed in the window in remembrance of the Holy Family trudging from one inn to another, trying to find shelter. Every Irish home bids them welcome:

'A cup of milk
A wheaten cake
And a spark of fire
For the Traveller's sake

A door on the latch
A light in the pane
Lest the Travellers pass
In the wind and the rain.

For the food and fire
And candlelight
The Traveller's blessing
On us this night.'

At last the great day came with the children waking early to see what was in their stocking. There was always an orange in the toe, a few nuts, a sugar mouse, a chocolate watch and maybe the girls would have a small doll and the boys a hand-made wooden train. Families in the country would sit down to a special breakfast of rabbit pie with thick meat jelly. Then the family would go off to church. Afterwards the traditional Christmas dinner of chicken and plum pudding would be eaten, and perhaps this might be accompanied by some ginger wine or a glass of port.

It's a marvel to me how my mother used to cook a cockerel (no turkey in those days) with roast potatoes, in the small box-like oven over one burner and a saucepan with brussels sprouts and parsnips on the other side of the double oil-burner. Then there would be the plum pudding boiling away beside the fire on a bracket, called a trivet.

After dinner we went into the sitting room for games and roasted chestnuts on the grate. The oil lamp would give out a soft glow that reflected contented faces - only another 364 days before it would all happen again!

Today we buy food like nobody's business, as if there is not going to be a shop open two days after Christmas. I have seen people buy bread and cakes, as if there were going to be a shortage of food. We should all spare a thought for all the homeless people in the towns and cities, when passing up our plates for that second helping.

I always admire the people who give up their Christmas day with their family to cook for the lonely, old and poor. Many church groups like the Salvation Army will be busy; I've been told that they always get a full house for Christmas day. It means a lot of work, but what a wonderful thing to do, serving and helping others, when I am sure they could be with their own families. This thoughtfulness and kindness is the true spirit of Christmas, not stacking up the larder, or buying expensive presents.

There was a superstitious practice on Christmas Day of putting out twelve onions, representing the twelve months. Each onion had a pinch of salt on the top and if the salt had melted by Epiphany, the corresponding month was put down as sure to be wet while if the salt remained, the month would be dry.

It would not be Christmas without poultry. There are turkeys of all sizes to choose from and although they have held pride of place on our Christmas tables for a generation, the goose has its origins back down the ages. In many parts of Europe today, particularly in Germany and Poland, roast goose still remains the most popular Christmas fare.

The meat from the goose has the highest protein content of any poultry and is a good source of vitamins. There is also the option of buying a goose that is boned, stuffed and rolled ready for cooking - it is easy to carve and everyone gets a good helping of meat without the worry of bones. Often the first reaction is to the dark colour of the meat, more like a duck than turkey or chicken. You will get a basin full of fat, but I find this is invaluable for cooking, making exceptionally light pastry.

Goose grease has always been treasured by country people, and they had many uses for it. Well beaten into a cream with vinegar, lemon juice, finely chopped onion and chopped parsley it makes a tasty sandwich filling.

It was also kept in the medicine chest for relieving bronchitis or easing the 'tight chest' of a child, and for rubbing into hands to avoid cracks. It was used to massage the udders of cows to prevent chapping due to cold east winds and snow. Sheepdogs had the grease smeared between their pads to keep out the snow during a long working day. Finally, goose grease was good for polishing beaks, legs, hooves or trotters of animals before going into the show ring.

In the old days, the feathers were saved in order to make pillows and mattresses.

After you have eaten the turkey or goose, followed by Christmas pud and mince pies, will you still have room for a glass of port and a piece of stilton cheese?

I am sure many people will agree that a ripe, mature Stilton is a fine present to receive. To make a 14lb Stilton cheese will take 16-17 gallons of milk. This is first heated in huge metal troughs to separate the curds from the whey, then follows careful weighing, salting and putting into moulds where it stays for six days. It is then removed and wrapped, like a baby in a binder, for two days.

The cheese is left to mature slowly, acquiring its rich flavour, its good smell and its blue marking. Stilton is generally reckoned to be at its best at 14 to 16 weeks old - the maker's tips - keep cheese cool and covered with a cloth or wrapped in greaseproof paper.

For centuries, on Boxing Day, masters and householders gave gifts of money to those who served them and tradesmen rewarded loyal customers with free goods. Those collecting from house to house carried boxes and this is the probable origin of the term Boxing Day. From the 1830's onwards, this tradition began to be heavily criticised by the press, where it was claimed that the custom was abused by unscrupulous members of 'servant' class. On Boxing Day, householders were invaded by a small army of postmen, chimney sweeps, street sweepers and tradesmen requesting money. Failure to pay held the threat of reduced efficiency in the service that was provided in the following year. The new middle class fashion for charity-giving at Christmas now runs alongside the old tradition of giving presents to friends and relatives. The Bank Holiday Act of the 1870's extended the practise to more lowly clerks by giving formal recognition to the lengthening of the Christmas holiday, to include Boxing Day in banks, public offices and the Stock Exchange. After Boxing Day was given as a public holiday, it gave the two-day holiday and people had enough time to travel home to enjoy a brief family get-together and travel back again in time to begin work on December 27. How different in this day and age, when most people have the whole week off.

Boxing Day is now classed as a day for sport, when football matches are played, and often the local hunt meets for a day's pleasure.

Pantomimes have taken over from the concerts we used to enjoy at Christmas time, and many a village will be rehearsing their panto, giving up their time to entertain us. The Drama Clubs spring to life and begin rehearsing weeks before Christmas. There is nothing like the village panto. I know we always look forward to our village entertainment, the tickets are soon sold out. Whether it is Cinderella, Little Red Riding Hood, Aladdin or Jack and the Beanstalk - we all know we are in for a laugh.

It is all so different from our Sunday School treats when we were shown a magic lantern show of a pantomime and we thought it was so wonderful. We marvelled at the strange costumes, little did we think that one day we would see people in costume entertaining us live on the village hall stage at this festive time.

With the Christmas festival over, we have the New Year celebrations to look forward to.

Most people I know keep a diary for special dates, birthdays and so on, but how many keep a note of each day in a yearly diary? For years I have written down something about the weather and anything about nature and, looking back, I can see the changes in our climate. A few years ago we would have had very sharp frosts and cold biting winds. It's been a long time since we have had a bad winter and 'one must have a sharp winter to have a good summer.'

At the end of the year, I always find myself looking back and it is nice to look back over the years, so much has changed in the last fifty years, let alone a hundred. Many people think that we progress too fast and that we really gain very little and leave ourselves so little time to enjoy ourselves. There is a good deal of truth in this, but many such people might not be alive today had it not been for scientific progress.

The Victorians must have thought themselves well off, but it would surely be impossible for them to believe the strides and achievements we have made in our time - electricity, running water, bathrooms with flush toilets and warm houses.

In East Anglia, we are lucky in many ways, we have good schools, a low crime rate and beautiful countryside in which to live. There is a saying 'Count your blessings day by day' and I think if we try to remember that in the new year, it might just be a better world for all of us!

RECIPES

If you want an alternative to cranberry or apple sauce with your Christmas turkey or goose, try gooseberry - it has a nice tart flavour which is a perfect accompaniment:

> $^1/_2$lb gooseberries
>
> 1oz butter
>
> 1oz sugar

Simmer the gooseberries in a little water until soft. Push through a sieve and beat in the butter and sugar while still hot.

Cabbage

The cabbage must be one of the most under-rated vegetables, and with the Christmas season on the way, try and experiment with the Dutch cabbage, they make wonderful coleslaws.

Try shredding about $^3/_4$lb cabbage and add 6 tablespoons of preserved cranberries. Mixed together, they are just right to serve with cold turkey.

Another way is to mix $^3/_4$lb shredded cabbage with 5-6 teaspoons of grated horseradish and 6 tablespoons of cream or plain yoghurt.

Dutch Slaw

Coleslaw is derived from the Dutch words for cabbage and salad and this makes an interesting dish.

> 8oz chopped streaky bacon
>
> 1lb finely shredded cabbage
>
> 2oz chopped green pepper
>
> 1oz chopped celery
>
> 2 tbsps grated onion

Fry the bacon until it is crisp, and then mix all the ingredients together and serve with a good dressing.

Good French Dressing

¼ tsp dry mustard
¼ tsp freshly ground pepper
½ tsp salt
2fl oz fresh vinegar
½ tsp paprika
1 tsp sugar
6 fl oz vegetable oil.

Measure all the ingredients into a mixing bowl or glass jar. Beat with a fork or rotary beater. Always shake well before serving

Here are a few Christmas tips you may find helpful.

Celery: Do not store near turnips or cabbages as this taints the flavour

Parsley: This is used a lot at this time of the year. Be sure to use the stalks as they are good and will bring out the flavour. Parsley that has been frozen is good as when it comes out of the freezer, it is already broken up.

Lemons: These will keep for up to six weeks in a fridge if they are stored in a polythene bag. Always warm lemons before squeezing in order to get more juice.

Mincemeat: If you forgot to make your own mincemeat, or time is short, tip a jar of bought mixture into a bowl and add some grated lemon rind and some brandy or rum.

Milk: Ideal milk will whisk more easily if kept in the fridge for a few hours beforehand.

Jelly: To set a jelly quickly, simply dissolve the jelly in half the hot water required, then add enough ice cubes to make up the full amount of liquid.

Wine: freeze any wine left in the bottom of the bottle in ice-making trays. This will be ideal for using in casseroles at a later date.

Hot Punch

     1½ cups apple juice

     3tbsps sugar or honey

     3 x 1-inch strips of cinnamon

     12 cloves

     3 slices of lemon

     1 bottle red wine (Burgundy or even home-made wine)

Place the apple juice, honey or sugar, cinnamon, cloves and lemon in a saucepan. Bring to the boil and add the wine. Reheat but do not boil. Serve at once in a heated bowl.

Acknowledgments

Once again I would like to thank my many friends for their encouragement and assistance.

Firstly many thanks to Terry Hunt, the Editor of the East Anglian Daily Times for his kind Foreword.

To Miriam Clift for editing these pages and to Sonya Burrows for her wonderful illustrations for the cover and the inside sketches.

Again Iris Stebbings has been an inspiration while reading and correcting these pages.

Lastly a thanks to John Lucas for publishing this book.

watch for the little white flowers to appear and remember where they grew - we kept this a secret so that other children didn't know where the best patches could be found. Puff balls were another great find and if these were taken when young and tender, and sliced and fried with bacon, they made a tasty meal. Elder flowers and berries make delicious chutneys and wine.

Cowslip Wine

Cowslips are flowering now, and what a pity it is that nobody can make cowslip wine nowadays as the flowers are protected. This was a delicate and aromatic wine and a very fine drink. Baskets were taken to the meadows and, when fully out, the yellow flower was pulled from the green calyx and stalk. The flower was called the 'peep' and the following recipe was given to me by an old country lady.

> 8 pints 'peeps'
> 8 pints water
> Juice and grated rind of 2 lemons
> 3lb loaf sugar
> $^1/_2$ tsp wine yeast
> $^1/_2$ bottle brandy

Boil the sugar in the water for five minutes, then cool. Peel the lemons thinly and put into a large container with the juice of the fruit and the cowslip heads. Pour the liquid over and stir. Add the wine yeast mixed with a little of the lukewarm liquid and leave covered for five days. Stir daily.
Strain into fermentation jars, leave until fermentation ceases then rack, mature and bottle the wine and put it away in a dark, cool place for a year.

Candied Flowers

Another joy was to make candied flowers from wild flowers - used as decorations on birthday and christening cakes. Take 3 teaspoons of gum arabic in crystal form (this is important), then put this into a bottle and cover with 3 tablespoonsful of orange water. Leave for three days to dissolve, shaking it often. Use a small paintbrush to cover the petals of the flowers, the calyx and all the parts accurately. Then dredge lightly with caster sugar. Gently shake off the loose sugar and dry on paper in a hot cupboard, then store in a box.

Rhubarb and Ginger Jam

3lb young rhubarb
3lb sugar
3 lemons
1oz root ginger, tied in muslin
4oz crystallized ginger

Trim both ends of the rhubarb stalks but do not peel. Cut up into short pieces and layer with the sugar in a mixing bowl. Cover and leave overnight to draw the juice. When ready, pour into a pan with the root ginger and grated rind and strained juice of the lemons. Simmer until pulpy, stirring occasionally to prevent burning. Stir in the crystallized ginger, remove the root ginger and then boil until the jam thickens to a soft set. To obtain a stiffer set, add half a pint of thick apple or redcurrant juice.

Rhubarb and Orange Conserve

4oz tender rhubarb
3$^{1}/_{2}$lb sugar
6 medium-sized oranges
2 lemons
12oz raisins
4oz almonds, blanched, skinned and roughly chopped

Using the method above, cut up the rhubarb and cover with sugar overnight. Put in a pan with the grated rind of oranges and lemons and strained juice. Simmer and stir gently until it thickens, then stir in the raisins and almonds. Cook for a minute longer and, when set, pour into small, warm jars and seal.

May

MAY

Daffodils dying down and the annual seeds coming up; young leaves on the trees, young lambs in the fields. The feel of things growing everywhere, the smell of the countryside, the east wind in your face and mud on your boots. Spring is no longer in the air, it has come down to earth. May is the month of flowers and every lane is margined with the white beauty of cow parsley, or Queen Anne's Lace and stitchwort. The greater celandine has opened its yellow petals and may bloom until the swallow departs. Buttercups, dandelions, birds foot trefoil and gorse throw gold across the land. The woods are misted with bluebells, which change their sheen as they curtsey to the wind. Butterflies and bees gather together and meet on the wild crabtree. Sycamores display bronze tufts and mountain ash is coming into bloom. Lilac shows sprays of purple and the air around the village street vibrates with the screeches of the swifts. The cuckoo calls his monotonous notes and sheep and growing lambs are eating their way across the fields all day long. The Anglo-Saxons called this month 'Tri-milchi', the month when better weather and an extra flush of grass enabled the cows to be milked three times a day.

We all watch the weather forecast at this time of year, and, as fruit is setting, we do not like to see late frosts. The Scarlet Pimpernel is an attractive wild flower which used to be known as the 'poor man's weatherglass'. The flowers are only open from around 8am to 3pm and they remain closed all day on dull and wet days. It was also an important plant for herbalists because it was supposed to dispel melancholy and cure madness.

Hedgerows in May improve by the day, and if out walking, watch out for buttercups, cranesbill and deadly nightshade, which also have pretty flowers. The hawthorn comes into blossom and the white and pink flowers add a delightful splash of colour.

'Every shepherd tells his tale
Under the hawthorn in the dale'

In Suffolk, if you worked as a servant, on May Day you searched for a branch of flowering hawthorn, then, wearing a wreath of hawthorn you took this to the master of the house, where it was exchanged for a dish of cream. Years ago, to keep a house safe, it was the custom to collect a May branch and place it in the rafters on Palm Sunday or Ascension Day. Country folk used to ramble through the green woods on May Eve, blowing cow horns and calling to each other until dawn, returning home as the sun rose, laden with branches of May blossom to deck their houses to welcome summer. Maypoles are still part of life in some villages, made out of straight-growing branches of ash, pine or larch. The prettiest girl in the village was picked to be May Queen, and she would sit in a leafy arbour near the Maypole. In 1820, children with cow horns were dancing and singing at King's Lynn in Norfolk, carrying May garlands. Flora Thompson wrote about children in 1880, 'dressed as King and Queen, Lord and Lady and Maids of Honour', carrying willow wands, topped with the flamboyant yellow crown imperial, and garlands of leaves, wallflowers, bluebells and yellow cowslips from the mown grass, also carrying a wooden framework with a doll 'the Lady', within the frame. Muslin was draped over the frame and removed only after a donation was made. The procession then moved off to walk many miles around farms, cottages, rectories and 'big houses'.

Clearly the Morris Dancers' dress and garlands originated from this May Day ritual, and with the lighter evenings the Morris Dancers start to tour through our villages, leaping for joy as they dance. They usually dance in the yards of local public houses, giving a fine display. They are dressed in white shirts, decorated with ribbons and white trousers with bell pads tied below the knees, carrying coloured sticks and white handkerchiefs and accompanied by a concertina player. They leap and caper about, sometimes with a handkerchief in each hand and sometimes with sticks, to the rhythm of the music. There are over 80 Morris Clubs, which hold two or three large weekend gatherings each year, the best known being held at Thaxted in Essex. Each Club has its own regalia, coloured waistcoats, with broad crossed bands known as baldrics, and hats of many kinds, decorated with flowers and coloured ribbons. Whenever you see the dancers they are enjoying the dancing and literally 'leaping for joy'.

Now is the time to listen carefully for the nightingale. Like so many sweetnesses, it is only of short duration; except for the lone, unmated cock bird's call, which can be heard throughout the season, the nightingale's full song is heard only for six weeks, from April to the middle of June. Although country people are often sceptical if one suggests that nightingales sing just as well in the daytime, it is nevertheless true that there is no need to sit up at night to hear them in a natural countryside setting.

The Ancient Britons must have known the nightingale well enough, for its name is derived from two Saxons words meaning 'night' and 'to sing'. Perhaps the last week of May and the first week of June are the best times to hear the song. On a May evening the rooks rise in the fields homeward bound for the rookery where the squeakers await their last meal of the day. The blackbirds grow tired of singing and the robin sings a quiet little song before taking night shelter in a hedge. There is a significant hush and expectancy, then the nightingale sings out, and there is no finer or more mellow background to the song than an old English garden or a Suffolk wood. To write of nightingales without a quotation from Keats seems to savour of bravado, yet what better words than those of the countryman, godly Izaak Walton, when he wrote 'Lord what music hast thou provided for the Saints in Heaven, when thou affordest bad men such music on earth'.

I have been told that you should not cut hedges in May, there is an old saying, 'You should not cut hedges in the summer or the blackbird will put a curse on you'. It stands to reason that a blackbird does not want its nest cut down, when it has taken all the trouble to build it, nor does it want its larder removed when it has a brood to rear. Folklore often comes from such practical reasons as these.

Soon it will be time for the sheep to be sheared. Sheep shearing is hard work - shearers, with their backs bent, concentrating and working so quickly. Some men use hand shears, like a large pair of scissors, and cut off the fleece almost in one piece, but nowadays flocks are usually shorn with mechanical clippers by a gang of experienced men, who travel from farm to farm.

How quick and skilled are the shearers. Whether the fleece is machine or hand-clipped, by far the most important operation is the handling and wrapping of it. Merchants don't like fleeces bound up with twine, the correct method is to twist the neck wool into a sort of rope. In many cases, bits of stick, straw or stains can cause deductions for faults, which reduces the amount the merchants will pay. The weight of a fleece depends on the breed of sheep, but sometimes it can be as much as 15 pounds or more.

Another job not seen these days is singling the sugar beet crop - now it is precision drilled. When the sugar beet crop used to be sown, the seeds were packed in a small seed case, and the seedlings used to come up in a group. Then they were separated so that only the strongest remained, with plenty of space to grow. This separation was called 'singling', and was carried out by hand, using a hoe, and very hard work it was too. Sometimes it would be very hot with the sun beating down onto one's back. Years ago, men would go round in gangs and take on so many acres to work on. Walking backwards and forwards, as they 'took on the rows' of sugar beet, chopping as they went, it seemed as though the men had a rhythm. It would soon be noticed who were the good workers and who were not by the 'rubbish' that came up after hoeing. If a worker did not take on an acre, but just a few rows, they used a stick with their name on, or some mark to identify their piece of work. I have known farmers to ask a worker to go back and get more 'rubbish' out of the rows he had undertaken to work on. It was no good trying to 'get over the work', as the saying goes.

There are two kinds of teasel, wild and cultivated. The wild teasel is like the cultivated one in appearance but is of no use commercially for the bracts of the flowers, while they are prickly enough, are not hooked like those of the cultivated variety, fuller's teasel. Both varieties have the same tall, rigid, prickly stem, large spreading leaves and pale purplish flowers and both are familiarly known as teasers, the fuller's teasel because of its use in the teasing of the unprepared picker. Most of the commercial teasel crop is grown in Somerset but over the years the beds have been shrinking. Teasels are cut from second year plants sown in the spring - on Lady Day - and transplanted in the Autumn to be cut the following summer. The cutter wore thick gloves and used a short, curved knife with which he cut a handful of stalks at a time. Each stalk has one long upright stem in the middle. This is known as the King teasel, the finest and biggest head on the stalk, and the most useful. The largest heads that branch out from the centre are called middlings and the smallest are called scrubs.

After teasels were harvested, they were tied together in bunches of fifty heads and hung on poles called 'lugs', each pole carrying 1200 teasels. After 'lugging up' they were stored in barns to dry until they were in a fit state to be transported, packed in special 'teasel sheets'. When they arrived at the mill, the heads were graded and cleaned before being put into revolving drums which were then rotated in the opposite direction to the cloth. In this way, the strands were gently plucked, making the cloth smooth and level or 'combing up the nap'. The teasel is a nice plant to have in the garden, it is so useful in dried flower arrangements and the butterflies love it. But be careful - it will seed all over the place if you let it!

This is the time of year when chickens start to lay well, giving us an abundance of eggs. Gamekeepers would call on families where hens were kept to see if they had any 'setters' or broody hens. Any such would either be bought or just borrowed for a few weeks to sit on pheasant eggs. Then when the pheasant chicks were big enough to leave the old hen and fend for themselves, she would be returned. My mother used to set a hen down, and a day or two before the three weeks' incubation period was up she would test the eggs. She would take a bowl of warm water and put each egg in it in turn. We children would watch to see if the egg floated; if it did so, she would say that there was a chick in that egg, but if the egg went to the bottom of the bowl this was always a bad sign, that the egg was rotten. After the chicks were hatched, we loved to watch the hen come off the nest with her babies for the first time. Bantam hens make the best mothers and most people prefer them to ordinary hens.

A china egg was often put into nest boxes to deceive the hens and encourage them to lay in the huts and not around the open yards. There are other egg shaped objects with quite different uses which belong to the past. The wooden box-wood, or wooden mushrooms were used when darning socks, and there were eggs made of smooth marble used by needle women working on fine work. Polished granite in the shape of an egg was used as a comfort stone by women in labour to grip in their right hand. Water glass or Isinglass, is still used in some country cottages for preserving eggs and is still available from good, old-fashioned ironmongers and some chemists. A solution is made up and poured into a stoneware crock or a plastic bucket. The eggs to be preserved are wiped - never washed - and should be between one and three days old. My mother used to put the eggs in a wire basket and then drop them gently into the solution. They will keep for about nine months and are best used for cakes and puddings rather than boiled or fried.

I have been told that if an egg yolk never touches the shell, it will remain fresh for quite a long time. Before the War, some housewives had a 'fresh egg wheel' and this was based on the principle that if an egg was kept standing on its narrower end the yolk could rise and would be kept against the air cell at the wider end thus preventing direct contact with the porous shell. By keeping the wheel turned a quarter turn each day, the yolk did not touch the shell, but remained in the centre of the white. I still turn my egg boxes every day when I go into the larder. Eggs treated in this way will never up-end when boiling and will retain their excellent flavour.

The chickens were fed all the scraps, or 'chats' as we called them, from the table and potato peelings were boiled up on the cooking range in an old black cast-iron pan last thing at night. Next morning they would be mixed with a little meal and a teaspronful of Karswood Red Poultry Spice - this was to make the chickens lay. When the chickens were past their egg-laying days, they were killed and boiled. The meat, taken off the bones, was made into pies or eaten cold while the bones were used for soup, and what good soup this was. There is a superstition that if a hen lays a cock's egg - a small yolkless egg that can be either the first or the last the hen lays, it should be thrown over the roof of the house or ill luck would befall the hens.

May used to be the most superstitious month of all and more powerful in those parts of the country which were overrun by the Belgic people in the century that passed between the departure of Julius Caesar and the invasion under Claudius. People used to believe that the hawthorn was holy and to cut it was sacrilege, and there is an old country belief that the harvest yield may be foretold from the leafing of the ash and the oak. If the oak comes into leaf first, it is predicted that a dry, hot summer will follow and consequently there will be a bountiful harvest. If the ash is first to throw open its leaves, the prospects of a good harvest are endangered. True or not, in Hertford a gentleman kept records for over seventy years and found that this ancient belief proved itself to be true.

Anything to do with the oak tree ensured good luck, and you can find acorns carved in the woodwork of churches and old country houses. Manufacturers still make curtain rails with a carved acorn on the ends. If you were out walking when a thunderstorm began, it was considered the safest tree. Many people covered up all the mirrors in the house during a thunderstorm.

There are a lot of superstitions attached to spiders:

'A spider in the morning is a sign of sorrow,
A spider at noon brings worry for tomorrow.
A spider in the afternoon is a sign of a gift,
But a spider in the evening will all hopes uplift'

Spiders are believed to have spun a web to conceal the infant Jesus in the manger when Herod's messengers came to look for him. For this reason, it is unlucky to kill a spider or disturb its web. It is also said that watching a spider build its web inspired King Robert the Bruce of Scotland when he was held prisoner. For those in search of alternative remedies, it is claimed that a spider mixed with syrup will cure a fever, because the spider will eat the fever. Likewise, if you put a spider in a walnut shell and wear it around you neck, you will ward off the plague.

Peacock feathers are also surrounded by superstition. They were regarded as very bad luck as they have an eye at the end of each feather that watches you and causes terrible things to happen. This belief comes from a Greek legend about Argus, a hundred-eyed monster, who fell asleep on a spying mission and was turned into a peacock with all his eyes in his tail. Four hundred years ago, peacock feathers were given to liars and cheats to show they were untrustworthy. However, all is not bad news - in India, the peacock is considered to be lucky because it warns of approaching evil. It is also highly regarded in Japan and China where it is an indication of rank and a reward for achievement.

There is an old saying that when rooks build their nests high in the topmost branches, this means a good summer, but when they build low, it means a wet time. This is based on the myth that the rook can foresee storms or gales which would destroy nests high up in the trees. Some years, some of the birds build high and some lower down - I think this must mean we are in for a mixed summer.

Finding that country cottage must be a hopeless dream for the youngsters of today. The term country cottage can belong to a wide variety of properties, ranging from the derelict crofter-type to an extremely comfortable three-bedroomed cottage standing in one or two acres of land. Years ago it would have been the ambition of many a young couple to have a small cottage with just enough land to raise a few chickens or maybe two or three pigs or a goat and a garden for growing their own vegetables. It would not have had every amenity, these would have come later as it was very expensive to have the water connected let alone electricity. If you were lucky, you may have had your own generator, but modern sewerage disposal was out of the question. Those first-time cottages of years ago had a lean-to for a kitchen, with a hand-pump for pumping cold water into a stone sink and there would have been a copper in the corner for boiling the clothes. The sitting room would have had a cooking range, and a door leading off to the pantry - a small room with shelves all round in which to keep the china and food. Another door opened on to the staircase, often a very twisty affair - I don't know how they managed to get bedroom furniture up those staircases! The landing was used as the third bedroom and you had to go through one bedroom to get to the other. There was no bathroom or inside toilet - that was the 'little house' at the bottom of the garden. There would certainly have been problems with damp, I can remember my mother pulling up bindweed that had grown between the bricks near the front door, which was never opened as it had sacking pushed into the cracks to keep out the draughts. The damp used to creep up the walls and when we pulled the sofa from the wall, there would be bindweed growing up the walls and under the coconut matting.

I could not believe it when I was told years ago that there was once a tax on windows. Its hard to imagine a time when sunlight was denied to many people who refused to pay the Government a tax for the light from the heavens. The window tax was first introduced in the reign of William III in 1695. The tax was levied according to the number of windows a building possessed. If you had over ten windows then you had to pay tax. Some people felt so strongly against such a tax that they removed some of their windows in order to evade paying it. The spaces were filled in with brick and cement. Some left the sills intact, then painted an outline of the window frames upon the cement and plaster. Some even went so far as to paint in curtains upon these dummy windows. Rooms with dark musty corners were preferred to payment for something which the Lord gave freely. If you look around the area you will see houses with windows bricked in and painted to look like windows. One which comes to mind is Glemham Hall on the A12 road towards Farnham. I remember going to see the gardens there and being told that there were as many windows as there were weeks and months of the year.

It is always nice to see the first forced pink sticks of rhubarb coming into the shops. Rhubarb growing and forcing is a highly specialised industry and much is grown in the West Riding of Yorkshire and the Leeds area. At one time over 3,000 acres of land - about half the total rhubarb acreage of the country was in this area and many thought its success was due to the acid soil of the area. There is also a big acreage grown in Lancashire, Essex, Middlesex and Kent, where the rhubarb is grown naturally without forcing. The Chinese used it in herbal medicines and it is claimed to be one of the oldest cultivated plants. Records show that it was a root growing on the banks of the River Volga in Russia but we have to thank a Yorkshireman for this fruit. Born in 1564, Sir Matthew Lister was physician to Charles I and he brought seeds into England, presumably for medicinal purposes. The date it was first used in cooking was 1768, when it was baked in tarts, but when the first consignment reached the London markets, of the five bundles for sale, only three were sold. Although technically a vegetable, it is used as a fruit and by 1937, rhubarb ranked sixth in order of value and importance.

Today, so many tonnes of forced rhubarb are sent to city markets, but years ago every cottage gardener grew a patch of his own. It is important to lift a clump in November so as to get the frost on it and then put it in a box with straw under the greenhouse staging. You will soon get some nice young rhubarb, which is so good for crumbles, rhubarb wine and the first rhubarb turnover. My father always cut small pieces of rhubarb and put it into the holes before planting out his brassicas, this was said to cure clubroot. Rhubarb leaves can be boiled and used as a pesticide.

Before the days of accurate maps, beating the bounds, or boundaries, was an essential duty at Rogationtide. Instead of merely going from one field to another, the procession actually traced out the limits of its own parish and as each landmark was reached, these were beaten, probably with rods of willow stripped white. A short service of benediction for the crops and cattle was held but beating the actual boundaries was not enough, as later some dispute might arise over parish properties. So it was necessary to impress these rightful bounds on the minds and for the sake of the rising generation. To do this, at points along the way a boy would be hauled out of the procession and, to the great delight of his friends, was bumped against some old tree or stile, or even ducked in a pond or river. He usually had some small reward but his sacrifice was not as that demanded of the pre-Christian era dog or sheep which had to die at the boundary stone. Because life itself depended on the success of growing crops, the spirit of the corn or corn-god was immensely important in pagan rituals. Often the god was identified with an animal which was dedicated at the time of sowing. Great care was taken of these animals while the crops were growing, representing as they did the god-head. However, at harvest time they were killed, mainly to save them from old age, allowing the corn spirit to be transferred to a virile successor. We are a very small part of a long procession through the ages and only the land knows it all.

The Suffolk Show

So many people enjoy this two-day event whether they come from the town or the country. We are lucky to have the Suffolk Show ground which is now a park with well-established trees and shrubs. It is always advisable to put on good walking shoes as there are 260 acres of Show ground. I always think of the Flower Show as a 'mini Chelsea' with the flower arrangements growing more spectacular every year. It takes nearly all day just to walk round and take in the colours and skills of the displays.

The Show is the shop window of the farmers and country folk, and it is so nice for the children to see the different crafts - weaving, pottery and nature stands. The heavy horses, cattle, sheep and dog classes and the International show jumping course are said to be some of the best to be seen in the country. The heavy horse display is one of my favourite events, and takes me back to childhood days when may father was a farm horseman and used to lift my brother and me onto the horse's broad back to ride home for tea. It is said that the Suffolk horse looks his best when the sun shines on the all-chestnut coat, and an old saying is that Suffolk people are like the Suffolk Punches, when they put their shoulder to the collar, something has got to move. Our Suffolk horses achieved a lot of fame and glory during the First World War, for the work they did in hauling the great guns.

Years ago, farmers went to the Show on the first day and their workers on the second. Trade stand tickets were often given by the farmers, and this day was a great treat for farm workers and their families. In those days there was plenty to eat and beer was cheap. Many a worker had too much to drink as they could visit one tent after another drinking the free beer. In the old day nobody could afford to go away on holiday, so the Show was the most talked-about event of the year and everyone made sure they had a good time.

The ladies of the Women's Institute cook and sew exhibits which are shown in the Flower Show tent as well as baking for the WI market which is held in the adjoining tent. Here you can buy all sorts of goodies to take home and enjoy - plants, crafts, preserves, pies and cakes.

Admiring the flower arrangements at the Suffolk Show made me think of Constance Spry, who had a passion for flowers. It was her original flower arrangements that started a new trend in the modern world of presenting flowers. She was brought up in Dublin, and almost from the cradle was passionate about gardens and flowers. She won her first award whilst still at school with what she described as 'a little pink table arrangement'. When she grew up and married, she continued to garden and arrange flowers, but only in her spare time, and as an amateur. Most of her days were spent doing social work in London's East End, but the flower groups in her own home attracted so much attention that she was finally persuaded to open a shop. She started her first shop with three buckets and a deck chair, in a Victorian basement. Her first big contract was for Atkinsons, the perfumiers. Large urns, full of mixed flowers in strong, subtle colours, drew crowds to their Bond Street windows. Nobody had seen flowers arranged in such a way before. It was still the era of formal arrangements - tea roses in a vase, or Iceland Poppies sticking up in a black bowl. Mrs Spry's showers of flowers inter-mixed with such oddities as dead twigs or brussels sprouts were a shock, which soon turned to delight. So it went on until she had to get a larger shop. The Constance Spry classes in flower decoration soon spread throughout the country and her books on flowers and gardening were in great demand for many years. We have a lot to thank her for, and for bringing pleasure into our homes, churches and clubs.

The art of flower arranging is an important study in every girl's school in Japan, with the tradition going back as far as the sixth century, when Buddhist missionaries introduced it from China. At that time, China was known as the 'Flowery Kingdom'. They tried to preserve the floral arrangements brought to the temples as part of their religion is to prolong and maintain life. They believed that all the principal flowers had a spirit in heaven who was looking after their welfare. These flowers included the Lotus, the sacred flower of Buddha; Chrysanthemum, flower of long life; Pine, meaning most revered; and Bamboo which was just 'very popular'. The Chinese also had a goddess of the flowers called 'Hua Shen' and when it was her birthday, trees and shrubs were decorated with red paper. In Japan they still believe that flowers have souls and in Tokyo, a Buddhist ceremony is held annually for the repose of these souls. Then a miniature altar of flowers is set up and children, wearing golden crowns and carrying more blooms, dance before it. There are rules to oriental arrangements that many flower arrangers in Britain have learned. These rules are carefully calculated. 'Shin, Soe and Tai' mean heaven, man and earth. Heaven is the tallest, at least one and a half times the height of the vase, man comes next as the vase itself, while earth is represented by the water that feeds the flowers. The Japanese aim to make a flower picture and say that the flowers like to talk to each other.

29 May is Oak Apple Day and, as children, we only thought about oak apples as

those round, pink vegetable growths that first appear on twigs of oak. Not only do they feature in a fascinating life story of their own, but they have affected history and the lives of many people as well. Oak trees became symbolic to loyal supporters of King Charles II after he had hidden in an oak tree when fleeing from defeat at Worcester. When he returned to England from exile in Holland, he re-entered London on his birthday - 29 May 1660. The streets were crowded with cheering people waving twigs of oak, welcoming their King after nine long, miserable years. This was the first time his loyal subjects had been able to show their feelings. News soon spread that an oak tree had saved him and from then on, Oak Apple Day was to be celebrated each year. Four years later, Parliament declared the day to be one of thanksgiving and it was made a public holiday. King Charles founded the Royal Hospital at Chelsea and the Chelsea Pensioners still celebrate Oak Apple Day. One of my favourite wines is made from the young leaves of the oak tree.

Whitsunday falls on the seventh Sunday after Easter and 'Whit' is generally thought to mean white. Some think that this refers to the white garments worn by converts baptised on Whitsunday, while others that it refers to the old custom observed on this day of the rich giving milk to the poor. Whitsuntide was a time for feasting, frolics and games when Morris and country dancing was much in evidence. Whit Monday was the most popularly recognised day for the annual celebrations of the village clubs - we always looked forward to Framlingham Gala on this day.

Local readers may remember the Whitsunday Farthings - known as the 'Children's Whitsun Offering'. This was a scheme started by Bishop Whittingham in the 1950's as a means by which the children of the diocese could help the church. Children in each parish collected farthings to be given in offering on Whitsunday. It was a big thing for the children to try and get the most farthings - they would ask all the aunts and uncles on the Saturday before Whitsunday and it would be a rush to see who had collected the most. I have a leaflet on this subject, sent by a reader in which it states that 469,236 farthings were collected from 156 churches in the Diocese in 1957, a total of £488. 15s. 9d - a great deal of money in those days.

Some Country Oddments

Choose neither women nor linen by candlelight

Great men came from humble cottages

Many a one for land takes a fool by the hand

An estate in two parishes is bread in two wallets

The higher the bill, the lower the grass

It is unlucky to run past the churchyard

Never carry a spade through the house over your shoulder

A man of business should not break his word twice

He who waits for dead men's shoes will go barefoot a long time

A busy mill does not get grass grown

Some quick wits can digest before others can chew

He that repairs not a part will have all to build

Under water, famine; under snow, bread

If you chop your own wood, you will warm twice

REMEDIES

Old tales and legends have always been part of village life. No longer do people hang up a hag stone - a stone with a hole through it - in outhouses or sheds. As the name suggests, at one time it was thought to be a safeguard against witches and if a piece of iron was joined to the stone, this was better still as it was supposed to prevent any evil form entering your home. A stone with a hole in it hung on your bedrail was supposed to guard against nightmares and rheumatism and in some countries, a sacred stone worn around the neck was supposed to have miraculous powers.

Comfrey

Comfrey has many healing powers, and made into an ointment used to be a best-seller in our local WI Market in Woodbridge. Culpeper's Herbal says, 'Comfrey ointment had many uses other than for cuts and minor injuries . . .it's a herb from Saturn - I expect under the sign of Capricorn - cold, dry and earthy in quality. The root, boiled in water or wine, and the decoction, when drunk, helps all inward hurts, bruises, wounds and ulcers. A syrup made thereof is very effectual for all those inward griefs and hurts, and the distilled water for the same purpose also, and for outward wounds or sores in the fleshy or sinewy part of the body, whatsoever. A decoction of the leaves thereof is available to all the purposes, though not as effectual as the roots.' This wild herb would have been used a great deal years ago, but I would not experiment with taking a decoction. The ointment is safe - I have used it many times.

Not so long ago I was told, in all sincerity, that early gathered dew was good for sore eyes. It is also still used by some as a cure for skin trouble and if sniffed up the nose is supposed to cure giddiness. Dew has always had certain magical properties and for centuries has symbolised virginity. Dew gathered in May is supposed to be the most effective, especially that gathered from beneath an oak tree, and a girl who bathed her face in this dew would be beautiful all year round.

Warts

There are many old cures for warts. I was always told to rub a broad bean skin on the wart, also to rub a piece of raw meat on it too and then bury it in the soil. Another cure was to rub a snail or slug over the wart and then impale this on a blackthorn or other prickly bush - the wart would go as the snail wasted away. In East Anglian towns and villages there were many self-appointed wart charmers who, on being told the number of warts to be treated, simply stated the length of time in which they would disappear. Usually the charmer would not ask for a fee and would not allow 'please' or 'thank you' to be said to him. Sometimes he would 'buy' the wart for a penny, or would ask the patient to lend him some personal object, such as a handkerchief or a pen to keep during the period in which the wart or warts would vanish.

The bone of a hare's foot was considered a good remedy for the cure of warts. Another cure was to get a piece of lard with the skin on and rub the wart all over with the fat side, then nail the piece of lard upon a post with the fat towards the sun. After five weeks, the wart went away. I have also heard of rubbing the warts with a green elder stick then burying the stick to rot in muck.

The plant with the widest reputation for curing warts is the greater celandine. Other plant remedies included rubbing the wart with the juice of a radish, applying marigold flowers, milkwort or a cut bean. The broad bean shell was rubbed all over the wart and then secretly taken to be hidden under an ash tree while the following words were repeated:

As the bean shell rots away
So my wart shall soon decay.

Another old cure was to tie a horse hair tightly round a wart until it eventually dropped off. To avoid warts, hands should never be washed in water that has been used to wash or rinse eggs.

RECIPES

Warm days in May turn our thoughts to summer foods; salads, fruit and fresh vegetables. One of my favourites is the beetroot, but in this country we tend to overcook it and eat it when it is cold, drenched in vinegar. Raw beetroot is naturally sweet, and one of the reasons for using vinegar is to counteract this sweetness, another being to prevent mould forming. Raw beetroot can be used grated in salads or sandwiches, sliced with apples or cheese. To cook it is best to use young and tender beetroot which can be placed in boiling water and simmered, or cooked in a pressure cooker. Alternatively, if they are really small, they may be baked with a little fat, or casseroled and served as a hot vegetable.

Beetroot leaves may also be used as a vegetable and are quite pleasant to taste, being a relative of the spinach family. Wash them well and cook quickly in a small amount of water. The juices remaining after cooking the leaves may be taken as a drink, hot or cold, and are good for those suffering from arthritis, as is the juice of raw beetroot.

Asparagus

In the seventeenth century vegetable hawkers in London could be heard crying 'Ripe grass, who'll buy my sparrow grass, white onions, ripe potatoes and good green peas', sparrow grass being the first of the season's asparagus. To be at its best, asparagus must make quick growth and be cut when it is young, tender and succulent, then bundled quickly and carefully so that it is delivered to the door absolutely fresh and unwilted. It is one of the most delicious vegetables in springtime and is perfect to serve with the first trout of the season or with spring chicken. If boiled with milk, a delicious soup can be made and Asparagus Pie was a country favourite.

Take one large bundle of asparagus, a good cheese sauce and shortcrust pastry. Wash and boil the asparagus in salted water and, when tender, cut off tips and use remainder for soup. Have ready a round tin or plate lined with pastry, pack asparagus tips in closely, cover with sauce, place on a pastry lid and bake.

Lemon Barley Water

It is difficult to find a recipe for the old-fashioned Lemon Barley Water like mother used to make. Here is my own recipe:

    2 lemons
    4oz pearl barley
    2oz sugar
    2 pints boiling water

Wash the barley, then put into a saucepan, bring to the boil and simmer for 3-4 minutes.

Strain off the water and put the barley into a large jug together with the sugar, thinly peel the lemon rind onto the barley and sugar, pour over 2 pints of boiling water, stir to dissolve the sugar and leave until cold. Stir in the juice of the lemons, strain into a jug and add a little crushed ice before serving.

Elderflower Wine

Now that the hedgerows are full of blossom it is time to make some of the countryside's best home-made wines. The choice is wide as there is may blossom, gorse, oak leaf (using the young oak leaves), and, best of all, elderflower. Be sure that it is a nice, dry sunny day when you go out to gather the flowers.

>2 pints elderflower heads (not the green parts)
>1lb raisins
>Juice of 1 large grapefruit
>3lb sugar
>1oz wine yeast
>water

Tip the sugar into a large saucepan with all the water. Beat up the egg white and add, stirring well. Boil for half an hour then take from the heat and skim off any scum that has come to the top. Pour the elderflowers, grapefruit juice and raisins into a bucket and pour on the warm liquid. When cool, add the yeast, cover the bucket and leave for four days, stirring daily

After this, strain it into a demi-john, fix the air-lock and leave for six months

One tip - don't be over-generous with the elderflowers as this will make the wine cloudy or too smelly.

Elderflower Cordial

>24 heads of elderflower
>4 oranges
>3lb sugar
>1 lemon
>4 pints water
>2oz tartaric acid

Boil the water and leave to cool. While it is cooling, place the elderflowers, sugar, tartaric acid and the finely sliced oranges and lemon into a bowl. Pour the water over the other ingredients and leave for about 48 hours. Strain into bottles and use diluted.

Oak Leaf Wine

    8 pints young oak leaves
    2³/₄lb sugar
    8 oz washed sultanas or raisins (chopped)
    2 lemons
    2 oranges
    1 gallon water
    Wine yeast

Place the oak leaves in a bowl, pour boiling over them to cover and let them stand for 24 hours. Strain the leaves reserving the water and boil this with the sugar and the thin rinds of orange and lemon for 15 minutes. When cool, strain again, add yeast and nutrient and pour into a demi-john, leaving until fermentation ceases, when the wine should be racked.

This should produce a nice, medium-dry wine. A similar wine can be made using walnut leaves instead of oak

June

JUNE

The flowers and scents of June crown the year, and the music of June has a more moving beauty than other months. Perhaps because we know that the ecstasy of bird song will diminish as the month grows and that the songsters are fewer as the days grow longer. Blackbirds, thrushes and blackcaps are some of the warblers that sing on as tunefully as in May. The nightingale will not lose the throbbing sweetness of its first song until the month is near its end. The cuckoo still calls as clearly and as sweetly as he did at first, and everywhere the gently murmur of bees makes a soft accompaniment to June's song. A new note is heard too in gardens, hedges and woods, a twittering cheeping, this is the baby music of the fledglings as they flutter after their parents in the hope of food.

Butterflies are on the wing - look out for small tortoiseshells, red admirals and peacocks - they bring a dash of colour to our gardens. Out in the countryside common blues are all busy visiting the large array of summer flowers and by the streams, flags show a prominent yellow, water lilies open and wild orchids stand like toy soldiers. On the banks, ragged robin and lovely, wild foxgloves sway in the breeze, while the hedgerows play host to pink and white roses, red campions and knapweed.

June and July are the growing and ripening months, and the weather doesn't have to be dry for long before the gardeners and farmers begin to worry about their crops. We all hope for a steady, gentle rain and not a torrential downpour that flattens everything. There is no more welcome sound after weeks of dry weather than that of rain falling - the swifts tear across the sky, shrieking excitedly, and you can almost hear everything eagerly drinking it in. Then, after it is all over, the songbirds raise their voices in praise of the sparkling new world, and how sweet and fresh is the smell of the damp earth.

In June, the patchwork quilt covering the countryside shows up clearly with its gaudy colouring. The spring green may have faded a trifle, but the cultivated land contains almost every colour of the rainbow - crimson clovers, yellow charlock, fields of rape, purple uncut hay fields and all the rest. The quilt is now at its thickest and birds and small animals are largely hidden by the heavy summer growth.

Our longest days and fast growing make June a rewarding month. Wild flowers are everywhere and honeysuckle is out in both hedgerow and wood making a walk at dusk rewarding, smelling the perfume of this lovely flower. Walking through the grass, sticky cleavers or goose grass stick to your clothes. This was eaten by geese and their young and apparently prevented the birds from catching disease. The alternative name of 'cleavers' comes from the seeds which are covered with hooks and 'cleave' or stick to passing animals so that the seeds are spread further.

Driving through the countryside in June, it is lovely to see fields of red poppies. This flower is steeped in legend, in both Greek and Roman mythology, and even earlier, it was an important plant to the ancient Egyptians. These people put poppy seeds in the tombs of their dead, to ensure life after death. Poppy seeds of great antiquity, dating back some 3,000 years have been discovered in the tombs of the pharaohs.

After all our labours in the garden, we are now beginning to savour the fruits, and there is nothing quite like those first melting potatoes cooked with mint and served with butter. I can see my father now, bringing in a cupful of potatoes straight from the garden and saying, 'Here's a mess of potatoes for your dinner', and truly they were nice enough to be eaten alone.

Every year the total consumption of potatoes increases in Britain. In 1939, 210 pounds per head were eaten but this total was easily passed by Ireland where an average of 405 pounds were consumed. Potatoes have been the staple diet in Ireland for many years and there was terrible suffering and starvation when the Irish crop was blighted several years in succession - the 'Potato Famine'.

There are many hundreds of varieties to choose from and although they are a common vegetable, potatoes despite containing three-quarters of their weight in water, have a high vitamin C content and also contains iron, thiamine, protein, calcium, riboflavin and starch. The starch from potatoes is used to make a coarse spirit, Berlin spirit, by distillation. Yet, less than two hundred years ago, potatoes were shunned as a food by many people and they were grown more as a novelty. One English writer at the beginning of the eighteenth century wrote

'They are not fit for human consumption. It would be idle to consider them as an article of food when ninety-nine out of every hundred people will not touch them.'

Strange fears about potatoes also made them unpopular. One was that they caused fever and leprosy. Sir Walter Raleigh is mistakenly credited with introducing the potato into Europe. He planted potatoes on his Irish estates in 1586 but the vegetable was known long before then to the Spaniards and the credit is now given to the monk Hieronymus Carden. We have much to thank the monk for as it is still the working man's standby.

St Barnabas was a farm labourer, and his day was celebrated on 11 June by Barnaby fairs. Before the calendar changed in 1752, this was the longest day and was traditionally set aside for haymaking time. On this day it was customary to deck churches and houses with roses and sweet woodruff, these 'being made up into garlands or bundles and hung up in the houses in the heat of summer doth very well attemper the air cool and make fresh the place to the delight and comfort of such as are therin' - John Gerard(1633).

It was also known as 'Barnaby bright':

'Barnaby bright, Barnaby bright,
Longest day and shortest night'

In pagan times the great festival of the summer solstice was held in June and everywhere this was celebrated with huge fires on St John's Eve - the eve of midsummer day. Flowers and herbs appear frequently in June observances and usually in a magical way. Divination could be practised by plucking a piece of St John's Wort on midsummer night and noting its condition on the following morning; if it was fresh then all was well, but if it was wilted then this was an ill omen. The midsummer rose, plucked by a girl at midnight on St John's Eve and worn at church the next day would be full of charm. Rose leaves or rosemary, if scattered while running round the church in the moonlight, would bring a vision of the gentleman in full cry after her.

It is lovely to see the swifts back for the summer. They are aptly named for their flight is extremely rapid, and apparently tireless. You never see a swift perched on a wire or a roof, they are always flying on their endless search for insects. Their wings are long and beautifully shaped for speed - scythe-like. Occasionally you may see them clinging with their claws to the wall of a house, but if they ever land on the ground, they find it almost impossible to take off again. Their wings are not fashioned for raising them from the ground, and sometimes a grounded swift is attacked mercilessly by other birds. This may be because it is helpless, although swifts never attack other birds. Some country folk say that the swift is a bird of ill omen, which may be because of it's shrill, piercing screech. The screaming of a group of swifts above the roof tops in twilight, or in the silence before a thunderstorm is surprising, especially as they make this noise when so many other birds are silent. It is not hard to tell the difference between a swift and a swallow - the swift's plumage is a very dark brown, almost sooty in colour, and although the wings are long, the forked tail is short and stubby. Swifts invariably fly much higher than swallows, sometimes out of sight, but if ever in doubt, you will recognise the swift by the incredible speed of their flight and their uncanny screaming.

It is noticeable that there are fewer sparrows and starlings around sitting chattering on the roof-tops, and I believe the magpie is to blame for a lot of this shortage. I have seen this bird pulling baby birds out of nests - with the poor old mother birds trying to beat the magpie off. There are so many more of these birds about these days and it is nothing to see seven or eight magpies sitting in a field - a few years ago, this would have been unheard of and we would never have seen more than one or two together. They even come to the bird table to feed causing small birds to fly off. The magpie has a lot to answer for.

June is traditionally the month for weddings, but over the years customs have changed. Way back, weddings were called 'bridewains', and when a lad and his lass were too poor to give a reception, they sent invitations to all the folk in the villages around. Those who came brought presents and their own food and everyone had a merry day. In the afternoon, the bride would sit herself down with a pewter jug on her lap and coins of all descriptions would be dropped into it. A large, thin currant cake, marked in squares and called the 'bride cake' was produced but was not cut by the bride and groom as today; a clean, white linen cloth was spread over the bride's head and the bridegroom, standing behind her, broke the cake over her head. The attendants would then scramble for pieces of the cake, and there would be plenty of ale to wash it down. Then the fiddlers would play the music and dancing would begin, continuing until after nightfall. The newly wed pair would later leave, perched on a waggon loaded with goods for their new little house. These goods would have included a carved chest full of possessions, maybe a spinning wheel and often a wooden chair with the bride's new initials carved on one side of the back and the groom's on the other. I wonder what the young girls of today would say to the following advice, written in 1884

'How to Catch a Husband

First catch your love, hold him when you have him.

Don't let go of him to catch every new one that comes along.

Try to get pretty well acquainted with him before you take him for life.

Find out whether he earns enough to support you

Don't make up your mind that he is an angel

Don't palm yourself off on him as one either!

Don't let him spend his salary on you - that right should be reserved until after marriage.

Don't marry a man to oblige a third person in existence

It is your right to suit yourself in the matter,

But remember, at the same time, that love is blind

And a little friendly advice from one whose advice is worth having

May ensure you a lifetime of happiness or prevent one of misery.

In love affairs, always keep your eyes wide open

So that when the right man comes along, you may see him.

When you do see him, you will recognise him and the recognition will be mutual.'

We look for rain in June, but not for thunderstorms that often happen in early summer nor do we need the thunderbolts that sometimes come down. For years I have picked up these stone-shaped fossils and wondered what they were. In many chalk and limestone districts, thunderbolts would be lying around in quantity - these are lumps of iron pyrite that have two distinct forms. One is a round, rather amorphous lump while the other is long and bolt-like and when fractured, shows a crystalline metallic structure with a shiny brass appearance. There is no evidence that meteorites fall during a thunderstorm, or conversely, that a shower of them produce thunderstorms

In June there is no shortage of flowers for decorating our homes and churches. Years ago only the big houses had a shrubbery, since the cottage garden's main purpose was to provide the family with vegetables and there was seldom anything so space-consuming as a lawn. Room would usually be found for some flowers, mainly fragrant varieties like stocks, clove scented pinks and gillyflowers - known nowadays as wallflowers - and a climbing rose trained around the doorway frequently spilled over to festoon an entire wall and peep into an upstairs window. The individual blooms may not have been of exhibition standard, but they more than made up for that by their prodigious quantity.

House leeks were encouraged to grow among the tiles on a house or shed both for luck, and because their juice was helpful to anyone whose eyes were troublesome. The greater celandine usually found a place in the garden too, on account of its healing properties for minor wounds.

Conspicuous among the edible plants were the marrows and pumpkins, or 'millions' as they were usually called. These were often grown on a muck heap where their golden and green fruits grew to an immense size, promising an ample supply of million pies for the table during the autumn.

I love June evenings in the garden, with the blackbird singing its little heart out and the perfume of honeysuckle and lavender at their best. There can't be anyone who does not like the scent of lavender (Lavandula) or to whom it does not bring back memories of warm, scented summer gardens, or piles of fresh, clean linen in a drawer. We tend to think of it as one of the old English plants, familiar in the time of Shakespeare, but lavender seems to have originated in the mediterranean regions. There is a legend from that area that originally the lavender had no scent but the Virgin Mary dried the swaddling clothes of the infant Jesus on the nearby bushes and since then lavender has been blessed with its heavenly perfume. The Romans are reputed to have used lavender in their baths, and it is likely that they brought the plant with them to Britain in order to have a convenient supply.

Once called 'a comfort to the brain' by the sixteenth century herbalist, William Turner, lavender has long been used for medicinal purposes. Besides being used as a folk remedy for epilepsy, colic and stomach cramps, it was also used during World War One as an antiseptic swab for wounds. One early remedy for headaches called for fresh sprigs of lavender to be put in a quilted cap and worn on the head. I can remember my mother putting lavender water on a bandage and wrapping it round her head when she had a headache - if she had no lavender water then she substituted vinegar.

Lavender oil is used in fine perfumes and cosmetics, and the phrase 'Laid up in lavender' goes back to the time when laundresses laid sprigs of lavender between newly laundered linen to keep it smelling sweet while in the linen cupboard.

Lavender Faggots

Take nine strong stems of lavender, freshly cut from the garden (dried stems are too brittle), tie them tightly together with a long, narrow ribbon about four times the length of the stems, just under the flower heads. Now double back the stems and weave one end of the ribbon between them. Nine, being an uneven number, the warp of the stems should appear in alternate bands with the ribbon in cross threads, giving a pleasing effect. Once the ribbon has completely enclosed the flower heads inside the cage of stems, then take both ends of the ribbon, and make a neat bow to finish off.

Every garden should have a Rosemary bush (Rosmarinus Officinalis) - it is a cook's joy and has many uses. Distilled oil of Rosemary is still one of the chief ingredients of eau-de-cologne, and the water from simmered leaves produces an excellent hair tonic and acts as a freshener and purifier for the face. It is a native of mediterranean countries and does not grow wild in Britain, and it was the Romans who brought it to Britain. It likes a sheltered, sunny position, prefers light, sandy soil, and given a favourable spot, will spread into a shrubby bush. It also looks very nice in hanging baskets, and a rosemary basket makes a useful winter decoration to hang in cold greenhouses or conservatories. Rosemary usually flowers twice a year and every part of the plant is strongly aromatic, including the seeds, which grow in tight clusters when the flowers have faded. Sometimes called 'The dew of the sea', it is much-loved by bees. Like many old herbs, rosemary is steeped in folklore - one says that rosemary will only grow well where the house is ruled by a woman. The plant has been regarded by lovers as an emblem of faithfulness because of its power to strengthen the memory, and for the same reason, it is a symbol of friendship, being used often at both weddings and funerals.

Rosemary was one of the stewing herbs and was burnt for its scent as well as carried in bouquets to ward off the plague and fevers. It was also used in pot-pourri and herbal smoking mixtures. A tissane of rosemary will cure nervous headaches and has a beneficial effect on the brain. If taken constantly, it was said to improve bad memory.

It is easy to make bouquet garni, using dried rosemary, thyme and parsley a crumbled piece of bay leaf and perhaps a strip of dried orange peel. Place a saucer face down on some material - preferably muslin - and cut round it with scissors or pinking shears. Put the dry herbs in the centre, gather up the edges of the circle of material and simply tie them together with a piece of thread.

Southern wood or 'Lad's Love' as it was called is another charming plant with its pale green feathery foliage and rich pungent smell. Used in drawers and cupboards among the clothes it will keep the moths away as well as keeping the cupboard sweet and fresh for bedding.

Clean sprigs of marjoram, rosemary and eau-de-cologne mint together with the flowers of lavender give a most delightful fragrance.

For the relief of indigestion, simmer a few leaves of sage in a pint of water and drink a wineglass full after meals - this will not only help indigestion, but will also tone up the system. For sore throats, use the same infusion mixed with a little vinegar to gargle - this works wonders.

Blossoming out into creamy white flowers in June, the elder is a picture to behold. But it is an unlucky tree and has been described as the tree of the crucifixion - although there is no background or support for this idea. Another reason the elder was called an unlucky tree was because of its associations with witchcraft and as a bringer of doom. Many countrymen still regard the cutting of elder in a hedgerow as ill luck, and burning elder wood in the hearth is said to 'Bring the devil into the house'. It as considered particularly foolhardy to make an infant cradle from elder wood. My father used to pick pieces of elder to stick inside the front of the harness of his working horse team to keep flies away from the horses' eyes.

However, some good came out of this wood, as the elder bush is thought to be a protection against lightning - perhaps because it had a touch of magic.

'Under the oak, there comes a stroke
Under the ash there comes a flash
Under the elder there comes no harm.'

Elder was also believed to provide a cure for warts; if warts were touched with a pin and this was then inserted into a length of elder bough, which was then buried and left to rot.

I like the elder for its wine and cordial, both from the flowers in June and from its berries in the autumn.

'There was a crooked man who walked a crooked mile
He found a crooked sixpence upon a crooked stile.
He bought a crooked cat, who caught a crooked mouse,
And they all lived together in a little crooked house.'

There is a story behind that rhyme, which goes back to the reign of George III. Conrad Robinson, who hunts for treasure with a metal detector, found a lot of crooked sixpences in one area. At first it was assumed that these sixpences had been hit by ploughshares or damaged by a heath fire. However, when twenty or more specimens were found, they were all bent in the same manner. The solution was found in an old book where it was discovered that the crooked sixpence was a token of betrothal. This was commonly used by shepherds and drovers when they met the girl of their dreams at the great sheep and cattle fairs once held throughout the land. It would seem that one particular great fair was more famous for its broken engagements than it was for its cattle and sheep. Any girl who wished to indicate refusal of a potential bridegroom did so by throwing away the bent coin - hence the number of coins found. Metal detectors have helped to find these crooked sixpences, and a large number were also found at a site near the Yorkshire borders at Appleby - renowned for its annual horse fair.

The late Dr E. Rudge told a meeting of the Essex Field Club 25 years ago of his remarkable discovery of a series of boulders, some quite small, but all of the same kind of stone and placed within sighting distance of each other. The stone was called 'Conglomerate' or 'Pudding' stone and consists of a large number of flints or pebbles, set in sandstone, like raisins in a plum pudding. It is found in small patches underground in many parts of southern England, and is exposed in the beds of streams where the overlying clays and gravels have been eroded away. About 5,000 years ago, people placed these stones along well-used tracks to mark the way for others. We can only marvel at the ingenuity of early man who, with no roads or written language, hit upon this infallible method of keeping himself on the right track.

Nothing remains of the original tracks, except the stones that marked their courses. 125 of such tracks have been found in all sorts of places and spaced in a variable manner. Often one is found to mark the crossing of a ford over a stream, and others were set at the top of hills, where they would be visible for long distances. A typical section of such a track used to run through East Anglia and was easily traceable from Essex through East Anglia and entering Suffolk at Nayland. The first pudding stone was found at Whitestreet Green, near Boxford, and is said to be a magnificent boulder, well known in the district. From this stone the direction lies over Hadleigh Heath to Kersey, where there were two track stones. No fewer than 15 track stones have been found in or near churches and another is at Thurston, where the stone stands in the churchyard, a few feet from the church wall. Traces of the track with pudding stones, have been found at Bildeston, Hitcham, Wetherden, Hessett and Livermere.

Parts of the track have disappeared except where they are now incorporated into roads used by modern traffic. However, given that the track must have been used only by foot travellers and riders, well before the days of wheeled traffic, it is remarkable that so many of the smaller stones still exist so that we are able to follow its route today.

Many pudding stones have been incorporated into church walls during rebuilding and repair work. An example of this is at Clopton church where a pudding stone - which I am told had been used as a door-stop by an old man in the village for many years - has now been built into the church wall. When visiting Laxfield All Saints church I noticed a large stone at the right hand side of the door and thought to myself 'Ah, is this yet another pudding stone?'

Today we all use tissues, but years ago we bought, or were given, boxes of handkerchiefs, one for each day of the week. When staying with my aunt, she would say, 'Aren't you going to put your Sunday handkerchief in your top pocket?' I remember how I kept my handkerchiefs in a nice box, each one neatly folded and showing the day of the week. The white one with a church in the corner was for Sunday, and the one with a picture of a washtub in the corner was right for Monday - which was always washday. The flat-iron in the corner of the Tuesday handkerchief was of the kind every housewife used. This would be placed on the bar in front of the red-hot fire. After a while, it was taken up and tested for heat by spitting on it. If the little sizzling ball danced on the surface before bouncing on to the floor, then the iron was hot enough to start on the linen.

The besom on the Wednesday handkerchief was a little out of date even when I was young. Made of twigs tied to a pole, this type of broom was only used for sweeping the floor of the wash-house and keeping the back yard tidy. Thursday was the recognised day for baking and the handkerchief was decorated with an iced cake. I could not imagine any housewife, certainly not in our village, icing a cake except at Christmas. Even birthdays were not celebrated with such extravagance, and in many families they passed unobserved.

The picture on the Friday handkerchief showed a shopping basket, but to me, Friday was always baking day while Saturday was used for shopping and cleaning up the house ready for Sunday. Saturday's picture depicted a skipping rope, as if it was a day entirely for play. This was not often the case, as babies and toddlers were left in the charge of we older children while mother set off on the long walk into town, where it was market day. Then the tiring trek home, with the baskets becoming heavier with each mile. I think the Saturday handkerchief should really have shown a tin bath, for this is what I remember most about Saturdays. Everyone, from the youngest to the oldest, would have a bath on Saturday, always using the same water, which was heated up from time to time from the copper. The oldest child had more water in the bath, but it was certainly less clean than at the start. By the end of this process, everyone would be scrubbed clean in readiness for the Sabbath, which was a family day when no work would be done. If any small job had to be done on a Sunday, it was done in secret. Perhaps some garment had to be washed because of an emergency, it was never hung outside to dry. As one old lady said to me, 'That would be asking for Old Nick to come and get me'.

June is the month for swarms, the time when bees feel the urge to found new colonies. These are swift and fruitful workers but inclined to be possessed by a fever for swarming, a law to themselves as if compelled by some strange power and restlessness. Gathering in groups on the alighting board, they creep up to the opening of the hive then suddenly, without warning, the swarm rushes out with a deeper sounding roar that can be heard from a distance. They swirl about high in the air, descending like stinging hail on any onlooker who dares to approach too closely. The swarming mass will eventually form a great living ball and hang suspended from the branch of a tree or a ledge. Usually a local bee-keeper will come and collect the swarm, first puffing smoke at it to make the bees drowsy and then tapping the branch so that it drops into a bee 'skep' or box. I have heard that rattling two spoons together will bring the bees down, but I am not a beekeeper, and would not try this.

The few bees left behind will, in due course, return to the hive where they fill it with a contented hum as if to confirm their satisfaction. As dusk falls, all that remains of the swarm are a few exhausted stragglers.

Beekeepers tell me that the parasitic mite 'varroosis', which has been infesting colonies of bees, is getting less harmful now. A colony may show no signs of harm until late summer, and may well produce good honey yields, then a colony can collapse very quickly - within two to four weeks. 1995 was the worst year for this, and colonies all over the country were destroyed. Thank goodness this now seems to be under control - what would we do if we could not buy good

English honey?

Bee-keeping must be one of the oldest hobbies, and beeswax has been used to make candles since the earliest times. Over the years, beeswax has had many other uses, from sealing wax for documents to polish for wooden furniture and cosmetics.

For more information about bee-keeping, contact the Suffolk Bee-Keepers Association. The Hon. Secretary is Jeremy Quinlan, The Old Rectory, Dallinghoo, nr Woodbridge, IP13 0LA.

To make an effective dowsing rod, it was traditional to cut it from the hazel tree on 23 June, the eve of St John's day. In the Austrian Tyrol the rods had to be cut on Good Friday. Hazel divining rods have been employed throughout Britain, not only to search for water, but also to search for hidden treasure. After the seventeenth century such practices became too strongly linked with witchcraft and died out.

Anyone can go divining, but there is an art in the cutting of the diviner's twig. There is more to this than just slashing the twig from the hedge with a knife or hedging hook. I used to know an old gentleman who was a diviner and he told me that copper wire can also be used, but never elder, which was taboo. He used a hazel twig shaped like a slender catapult, others use two twigs held parallel to the ground. The diviner walks slowly over the ground, holding the rod or twig firmly until it starts to dip and point downwards. If he is using two rods or twigs, these are held loosely in the hands and where the two cross over is the place to dig for water.

Many churches will now be getting ready for their annual fetes. This is an old custom, which has been going on for centuries. Many of the old-time fairs had the authority of a Royal Charter or Statute, and some extended over a period of several days, or even weeks. Although we now take it for granted that such events should be held during the summer months, the ancient fairs were always held on religious festivals or Saints' Days. What we now call a holiday was originally known as a 'holy day'.

It's always difficult to find new attractions, but this is what village life is all about. A lady who recently moved to a nearby village told me that since she had been living there she noticed that three quarters of the inhabitants 'were busy making money'. Of course, the money is not for themselves, but for the many good causes and charities in the village; the church, village hall, silver band, school funds or the local hospice. The churches always need money, so it's the first fund-raising event in our village. Fetes have to be planned months ahead; finding volunteers to man the stalls and collecting items for sale. With annual practice, village folk are geniuses at knowing which stalls will bring in the most money. There used to be a lady who collected 'bits and pieces' for our fetes, and as soon as one event was over, she would start collecting again. She raised hundreds of pounds for her church - God bless her - sadly, she has now passed on. Most people will tell you that in the villages it is not always the money which is the important thing, but the getting together of all the villagers, some of whom one may not have seen from one yearly event to another.

Raffles are always popular and another good money-spinner would have been bowling for a pig, but nowadays it is likely to be bowling for £5 or a good joint of meat. Years ago, some kind farmer would give a 'runt' or 'pipman' (small pig) and this would have been worth winning. A makeshift sty would have been made at the bottom of the garden and the pig fed on scraps from the household. By the time it went to be slaughtered, it would have been worth a good bit of money. I can remember when lights were fixed up so that when the men turned out of the pub they could come and bowl, and this would have gone on until midnight, or even longer, if two people had the same score.

The cake stall is usually the first one to sell out, and what can be better than to take home a tasty fruit cake or sponge? A stall can be made to look very attractive with homemade preserves - jams, jellies, marmalade, lemon curd, chutneys, pickles and flavoured vinegars. To give the preserves a little something extra, cut scraps of pretty cloth with pinking shears, a size bigger than the container lid and cover the jar, fixing with an elastic band.

Plant stalls can be very colourful and it is good to get children to help in potting up plants for sale as this will help to interest them in growing all things green. The children can also make buttonholes and small pieces of jewellery to sell to people as they arrive at the fete.

Tombola is always a winner, and there are the country craft stalls, crazy golf, tug-of-war, pony rides and fishing for plastic ducks, while visitors always love the white elephant stall.

I have only recently discovered the art of making pot pourri, and what a joy it has proved to be. I gather roses in full bloom, Mrs Simpkin pinks, clove carnations and stocks then pull the petals apart and spread them out thinly on trays. To these I add lemon verbena, thyme, rosemary, geranium leaves and lavender flowers - in fact anything that I can lay my hands on that has a strong, sweet smell. In other years I have made the mistake of thinking that all these ingredients, when dried, would make a pot pourri. How wrong I was, for the scent lasted no time at all. Then an elderly friend, very skilled in these matters, advised me and I took more time and trouble. I was well rewarded although making pot pourri is a slow business and is not something that can just be dashed off in a few days.

First, I placed a piece of newspaper on my tray and scattered the petals on top, then left them in a dry, sunny room. I had trays all over the house in various stages of drying. When the petals are completely dry - this took about a fortnight - I put them in a large mixing basin and added some bay salt, a little powdered nutmeg, cinnamon, cloves and orris root, together with some lasting flower oils. These oils do cost more than the powdered variety but very little is needed and they certainly help to keep the sweet scent much longer. For my mixture I added a teaspoonful of oils of lavender and sweet geranium, a few drops of bergamot - don't overdo this one as it is very strong - and a little oil of sweet orange and rose water. Lastly, I added thinly peeled lemon rind and an ounce of allspice.

All the petals are put into a large container with a tightly fitting lid, which is shaken every three to four days - I used a large glass sweet jar. Then the whole process was started again with another collection of petals on my trays. The pot pourri packs down very well and when the new lot was ready, I topped up the jar by adding a few more drops of oil and once again screwed the lid back tightly as before. Its important never to use damp petals as these will turn all the others mouldy.

I left my pot pourri in the sealed jars until the end of September then put some into little sachets and placed them in the drawers among my clothes. The bulk I emptied into a large old bowl, which I put in my sitting room, where it gave off a sweet subtle fragrance all through the winter. I often gave it a stir with my fingers as I passed and this seemed to encourage the scent.

RECIPES

Candied Flowers

Another joy was to make candied flowers from wild flowers - used as decorations on birthday and christening cakes. Take 3 teaspoons of gum arabic in crystal form (this is important), then put this into a bottle and cover with 3 tablespoonsful of orange water. Leave for three days to dissolve, shaking it often. Use a small paintbrush to cover the petals of the flowers, the calyx and all the parts accurately. Then dredge lightly with caster sugar. Gently shake off the loose sugar and dry on paper in a hot cupboard, then store in a box.

Gooseberries:- Muscat Syrup

Soon we shall be seeing the first green gooseberries and with the elderflowers coming out in the hedgerows, try making this nice syrup, which is delicious served with ice cream.

> 2lb green gooseberries
> 1¹/₂lb sugar
> ³/₄ pints water
> Good bunch fresh elderflowers

Dissolve the sugar gradually in the water, add the gooseberries and simmer gently without allowing the fruit to burst. When the fruit shows by its shrinkage that the juice has escaped into the syrup, bring the mixture to the boil quickly, and plunge in the elderflowers, washed but left on the stalk.
Leave the flowers in the pan for a minute or two, tasting to be sure that enough flavour has been imparted to the syrup. Strain and put into bottles
The syrup does not keep well, and it is best to make it for special occasions.

Gooseberry jelly may be flavoured in the same way with perfumed leaves of eau-de-cologne mint or lemon thyme, but first the leaves must be lightly bruised with a small quantity of sugar and a few spoonsful of water added. They are then set in a cool oven for an hour or more. The whole thing may then be added to the jelly mixture, which is then strained and boiled. In this way, the flavour of the leaves is imparted to the jelly.

Gooseberry Cake

> 8oz Self-raising flour
> 1 level tsp baking powder
> Grated rind of 1 lemon
> 4oz muscovado sugar
> 4oz block margarine, melted
> 1 egg, beaten
> 4 tbsp milk
> 12oz gooseberries, topped and tailed

Heat the oven to 180°C, Gas Mark 4. Lightly grease an 8in, loose-bottomed round cake tin. Measure all the ingredients except the gooseberries into a bowl and mix well until thoroughly blended. Spoon half the mixture into the tin and level out. Spread out the gooseberries over the mixture and roughly spoon the remaining mixture on top.

Sprinkle with the demerara sugar and bake in the oven for one hour and twenty minutes until golden brown and shrinking away from the sides of the tin. Allow to cool for a few minutes then remove from the tin. Serve warm with cream or real custard

Lamb Chops with Rosemary

 1 tbsp fresh, chopped rosemary
 $1/2$ tbsp fresh sage or marjoram
 6 lamb chops
 2 crushed cloves of garlic
 2 tbsp olive oil
 1 tbsp lemon juice
 Salt and pepper to taste

Mix the herbs and place in a bowl, along with the lamb chops, add the garlic and oil and allow to marinate overnight.

Grill or bake in the oven until tender.

Summer Fruits

At last the first of the wonderful English summer fruits are ripening in the garden and starting to come into the market. No made-up dish can surpass a bowl of raspberries or strawberries served with fresh cream. However, it is not always possible to serve this feast, and some recipes for using the first sparse pickings are useful.

Summer Pudding

I think this is one of the best puddings and as children, how we loved mother to make this for us. She would tell us to pick some blackberries when we came home from school and then she would make our favourite pudding using stale bread. We thought it was wonderful to see the bread change colour to deep reds or purple from all the juices of the mixed fruits. I think we enjoyed the fruits more when we could only eat them in season; nowadays the freezer gives us the opportunity to have all sorts of soft fruits all year round.

Butter a smooth, deep basin and cut a round of bread to fit the bottom, then cut slices sloping so that they fit the sides of the bowl and press into place.
Boil about 1¹/₂lb mixed fruit, raspberries, currants or strawberries in sugar to taste. When boiled, lift this into the basin, packing it in carefully. Fill up with the hot juice and put left over cuttings of bread on top.
Fit a saucer or plate on top of the basin so that it presses down on the fruit and bread. Put a weight on it and leave it until the next day.
Turn it out on a glass dish, decorate with whole fruit and serve with cream.

Rose Petal Wine

The roses are out in full colour and the scents are heavenly. For wine makers this is the time to make rose petal wine. Most petals finish up in the compost heap so take advantage of their glorious scent - the more strongly scented the better.

A small bucket full of petals
Juice of 2 lemons
2³/₄lb sugar
1 gallon water
1 level tsp wine yeast and nutrient
¹/₂ pint grape concentrate or ³/₄lb raisins

Bring the water to the boil, then add the sugar and rose petals, add the lemon juice and raisins or grape concentrate and stir well. Cool to 21°C, add the yeast and nutrient
Cover the pan closely and leave to ferment for 5 days, stirring daily. Strain into a jar until finished fermenting
This wine can be ready in six months, but I like to keep all flower wines for a year before drinking.

JULY

The Dog Days are 3 July to 11 August - why dog days you may ask? The Romans wrongly supposed that Sirius, the Dog Star, the brightest in the sky, which rose and set approximately with the sun at this season, reinforced the heat of the sun, and so caused the greatest summer heat in this period. Of course, all the stars put together do not give us a fraction of a millionth of the heat we receive from the sun, and the sun sets half an hour earlier at the end of the month than at the beginning.

Around Suffolk there are a few roads where oak and ash trees grow along the verges, at one time they were hedges and now have grown up to a height of thirty feet. The branches have joined overhead and the interwoven leaves enclose a mystic glade below, cool and dim, on even the hottest, brightest summer's day. It's like driving in another world, so peaceful. After a while the lane breaks away from the mystic past into the sunshine of open country and the acres and acres of tender, green crops. Each year I look for the red poppies. Some years the corn is full of the red heads blowing in the wind. I often stop my car to gaze at the scene. If you look into the heart of this simple flower, you will notice a dainty, embossed seed-box and standing all around this a little forest of pollen-laden stamens. Each time I see this country picture I think of the service given by men and women in the war years.

The corn and barley reaches maturity and the inhabitants busy themselves in the miniature forest of stems unaware of the catastrophe of the harvest to come. Stoats stalk the rows like tigers in an Indian bamboo jungle, catching unwary voles who nibble blunt-nosed into the springing wheat. At night barn owls hover like enormous white moths over the waving array of stalks, waiting to pounce on any unwary animal that ventures into the open.

July is the month when we have the succulent harvest of soft fruit, and how the birds envy us; if they can possibly find their way under the strawberry nets, they will do so. You will see the orange scissors of the blackbird's bill where he has found a hole in the countrywoman's lace curtains that were laid over the

141

currant bushes. There are the last strawberries, the first raspberries and green gooseberries in abundance. At last the garden is full of crops, even the bedding plants are beginning to flourish. Soon it will be the village flower shows in countless marquees and village halls.

Tea in the garden is one of the oldest of English pastimes (provided the wasps and ants have been properly attended to). A childhood memory remains very clear: as we walked home from school an old lady from the Farmhouse was sitting in the shade of a great cedar tree with her children and grandchildren around her and her hands folded over a white parasol. Just behind her chair was a huge bush of bright red roses. As we peeped through the hole in the hedge, we saw the butler bring the silver kettle and its stand followed by the parlour maid carrying a silver tray with pretty cups, saucers and plates. There was a cake stand and a plate of sandwiches. No jets screamed across the sky, instead there was the sound of a pony-drawn lawnmower at work. The old lady has gone, so have the butler and parlour maid, but I often think of that picture as I drive past in my car. How we children would have loved a taste of those cakes and sandwiches!

When out walking near local rivers or streams, you will see the great willow herb, which likes damp areas and open woodland where it can see the sun. Like its near relative, the rosebay willow herb, it is a tall plant, but the flowers are distinctly different; those on the great willow herb are clustered towards the top of the stem, whereas those on the rosebay willow herb form a tall conical spike. The great willow herb is also known as 'codlin and cream', 'cherry pie' and 'apple pie'. There have been various explanations for the name 'codlin' - some suggest it refers to the codlin apple, because the flowers of the willow herb give off a smell similar to that of apples. However, it is not easy to detect, and I think countrymen liked using the word 'codlin', it comes up a lot in old books on country matters.

A wild plant that needs to be watched, especially if you have horses, is the ragwort (Senecio Jacobaea). Ragwort is a perennial with bright yellow flower heads of the compositae family. It is often seen covered in cankers and brown striped caterpillars, and is poisonous, especially to horses who particularly like to eat the plants when they are young and sweet. As the plants mature they become bitter and are only palatable when wilted. They need to be pulled up regularly from areas of grazing and taken away. The poison in horses can build up over several years and can start with what appears to be skin problems in their feet. Eventually, the liver is damaged and death results. The plant can also get into hay and is deadly when eaten. Cows have more than one stomach and so are not so badly affected as the horse.

While on the subject of poisonous plants, many plants produce berries and seeds that look good to eat, particularly the deadly nightshade plant with its attractive purple berries. Watch out for laburnum seed pods too. Laburnum is the most poisonous tree grown in Britain; all parts of the wood are toxic, but the leaves lose some of their poison as the fruits ripen and the seeds mature. The poison is then concentrated in the pods and the seed - so don't plant the tree if you have small children.

Years ago we used to repair, and re-use as much as possible. Sheets generally wear down the centre and we used to slit them from top to bottom, cut out the worn strip, seam the two selvages together and hem the cut edges on the outsides of the sheet. This was known as 'Sides to middle'. Worn double blankets were cut down for single beds or cots. Older children's clothes were cut down and mended to suit younger brothers or sisters as they grew out of them. Stockings and socks were darned and mended and white towels cut down to make babies' nappies. White muslin nappies were made from yards of this soft material bought from the local store. Today we have disposable nappies and girls don't seem to go in for sewing so much. I can remember how we made our own handkerchiefs, embroidering our initials in the corner. My mother used old woollen stockings for floor polishing by cutting off the feet and drawing one leg over the other and folding it over and tacked up the sides. Sometimes we tried to make our clothes look different by dyeing them, and most linen stores sold dyes.

What did we do in the old days without a fridge? Pantries were always whitewashed every spring 'before it got too hot'. Heat is absorbed much more easily into a dark surface and whitewash helped to keep the houses cool in summer inside and out. Some of the old farm workers would take bottles of beer and bury them under a big tree at the back of the garden. It was a good place to keep milk too. We never had milk in bottles, but my father dug a hole and put a box with a lid on it in the ground, so mother could stand a jug of milk down in the box. Some old farm cottages had a larder with shelves covered with old roofing slates - very cool and easy to wipe down.

Most houses had a food safe on the northern outside wall of the house. I can remember my mother used to spread a length of butter muslin over the safe in very hot weather, with the ends of the muslin dangling into a bucket of water. The water crept up the muslin by capillary action and kept the safe permanently damp; as long as there was a current of air, the safe would remain beautifully cool.

Vegetables were not a problem for most country dwellers as they came in fresh from the garden as we wanted them, but if necessary we kept green vegetables fresh and crisp by wrapping them in newspaper and putting them in a container with a close-fitting lid. We did not have to worry about keeping meat cool as we never had much, but if there was any left, then muslin wrung out in vinegar was put round the meat to keep it cool.

15 July is St Swithin's Day; the most well-known of the saints' days for weather lore, and still very dearly and stubbornly believed in. St Swithin, who was an Anglo-Saxon bishop of Winchester, originated the rain legend by wishing to be buried in the churchyard where the rain from the church eaves might fall upon his grave. When he was removed to Winchester Cathedral on 15 July, 971, it poured with rain for 40 days - 15 July to 23 August - so the legend has it. On 15 July, 1870, a Huntingdonshire cottager pointing to his apples said, 'I shall get a few o' them codlins for a dumplin' for my Sabbath dinner. I never taste an apple 'till the Sabbath after St Swithin'. He also quoted the old saying, 'Till St Swithins Day be past, the apples be not fit to taste'.

There are a lot of sayings about apple trees around St Swithin's time, hence the phrase, 'Christening the apples'. We don't hear the term 'codlin apple' so much today. When I was young, we had an apple tree in the garden that my father called the 'codlin tree', on which small apples grew. Since fruit trees need so much water to help the fruit to swell, forty days of rain is a good thing for them, and it is lovely to see a fine crop of apples swelling on the trees.

This is the time of year when we reap what we have sown in our gardens. What can be nicer than walking up the garden and thinking, shall I have peas, broad beans, cabbage, carrots or cauliflower? It all comes at once, and once the cauliflowers are ready, I like to make mustard pickle - Piccalilli (see July Recipes). You can't make piccalilli without mustard powder, and I wonder how many people know that mustard powder started as a little grain of seed. Colmans of Norwich must be known all over the world; they have been growing, milling and blending mustard for over 180 years.

This hot pungent yellow powder has been used either as a condiment or in medicines as an emetic and in poultices since the earliest times. The king of Persia was reputed to have given Alexander the Great a bag of sesame seed as a boastful indication of the strength of his troops. Undaunted, Alexander responded with a sack of mustard seed to symbolise not only the vastness of his army, but also the fiery energy of his soldiers. In the beginning, mustard seeds were most likely ground at dining table and then sprinkled over the food. Then in 1720, Mrs Clements of Durham hit on the simple idea of grinding and pounding the seed, then sifting it in the same way that flour is produced from wheat. Pleased with the result of her experiment, she took her powder to sell in London. Her brave enterprise met with enthusiasm, even finding a place on the table of George I who preferred mustard powder to any other condiment. Mrs Clement guarded her secret and it died with her, but the method of obtaining a finer mustard powder soon led to the beginning of a new industry. In 1742 Messrs Keen opened a factory at Garlick Hill in London for the manufacture of mustard powder and were in business for over a century; 'As keen as mustard' was their slogan.

In 1814, Jeremiah Colman moved to the water mill at Stoke Holy Cross near Norwich and started to mill mustard. From this period, most of the other mustard interests in Great Britain came under his supervision, including Keens, which he took over in 1903. The company moved to Norwich in 1854, where they have remained since.

The plant breeders at Colmans have devoted many years of experimental work and introduced a succession of improved strains of mustard for cultivation.

The yellow flowering mustard can be seen in fields in June. Once the kernel is separated from the husk, it is pulverised to a fine powder and made into white or brown mustard, without which our Sunday roast beef would not be complete.

If you take children out on heathland, watch out for adders. They are creatures of dry places and like a heath and heather environment. Despite its reputation, the adder is not aggressive and, if disturbed, will slide away to cover - but if trodden on, it will bite in self defence. The bites are serious and should be seen by a doctor as soon as possible.

For some obscure reason, ferns have always been associated with snakes and it was widely thought that the spore of the fern helped the snakes to see.

Sometimes you will see grass snakes in churchyards and gardens, but they won't harm you. As children we would go looking for them, put them in a box and take them to school. The teacher was not very pleased and soon told us to let them go, but we liked to show our schoolmates how clever we were in catching them as they do move very quickly.

Recently I was out walking with my grandchildren and I showed them a 'robin's pincushion'. Many country people will know that this occurs on a wild rose bush and has a variety of names, including 'bedegaur gall'. It appears as a strange, irregularly shaped growth and is one of a variety of pests that can be found on many different plants, caused by the gall wasp. Towards the end of spring, the female wasp lays her eggs in the bud of the wild rose. The gall wasps are not responsible for the growth, but their presence causes the rose to react so that a deformed bud is produced. The gall is green at first but has a series of colour changes. Inside the gall there are a number of chambers, each home to a small white grub, and these feed on the inside of the gall.

Among the minor discomforts of hot weather are sunburn and insect bites. I suppose we all have our favourite way of protecting our skin from the sun, but I still use the same remedies my mother used - malt vinegar or cold tea. One or other of these should be rubbed onto the skin and allowed to dry before exposure to the sun. For wasp stings, the old remedy of rubbing the sting with a moistened lump of washing soda is probably the easiest and quickest way to give relief, although I wonder how many people now keep a packet of soda in their store cupboard. Elder leaves are used for relieving mosquito bites and a pot of elder flower ointment is a remedy for many stings and bites.

To relieve the pain of sunburn, apply egg white or a paste made out of milk and bicarbonate of soda. The fastest way to take the sting and redness out of sunburnt skin is to apply either a liberal coating of natural yoghurt, or to smooth the juice of half a tomato on the skin - the acid content of either will calm the skin within six to eight hours. When we were children, we would look in the nearest hedgerow for a dock leaf and this would help if we fell into stinging nettles or got a wasp bite. Last but not least, there always used to be a small jar on the kitchen window sill with a little blue bag in it, which mother used for a final rinse to bring her white washing up nice and white. This little blue bag was often dampened and rubbed on our bites and stings.

My brother still makes fly and wasp traps every year by putting a little jam into an old jam jar and then half filling the jar with water and giving it a good stir. He then fixes on a lid with holes in it, ties string around the neck of the jar and hangs it up near the back door or in one of the fruit trees. The wasps and flies soon scent the sweet jam and climb into the jar and drown in the water. We do this every year and it is surprising how many flies and wasps we catch; it is the best fly-catcher I know.

Then we would have the Sunday school outing to look forward to - the treat of the year and always to Felixstowe. We used to go fruit picking and pea picking to earn extra spending money to pay for our rides in the Amusement Park. We all had our money in little cloth bags, usually each child had about the same amount.

Often, two or three buses would leave the village with mums and dads, grandmothers and grandfathers, aunts and uncles; it was a real family outing. To us there was nothing like the taste of ice-cream by the seaside. We had packed lunches and the sand usually got into the sandwiches, but we never worried about that, and often finished our lunch well before lunchtime, as once by the sea, we always felt hungry. We made sandcastles, running forwards and backwards up the beach to fill the 'moats' around our castles. We had games with bat and ball, and loved to collect seashells and pieces of seaweed to take home. Often the seaweed was hung near the back door to forecast the weather - if it remained dry, the weather would be fine, but if it turned damp, rain was on the way. Today if you see children paddling, they just wear a small pair of pants, but years ago costumes were long, knicker-like garments made of stockinette or wool. I can remember how difficult it was to peel off this wet costume when coming out of the sea. Grown-ups did not go into the sea - if any men were on the beach, they may have taken off their boots and socks, rolled up their flannel trouser legs and just paddled. They still wore their waistcoats or brightly patterned 'Fair Isle' pullovers and always wore a cap. Mothers wore long dresses, overcoats and hats, it was only in later years that less and less clothing was worn.

In the afternoon we would sometimes go to Woolworths but did not have much to spend. The Amusement Park was another world to us with all its noise and entertainment. Then we went back to meet up at the restaurant for our special tea - sandwiches and fairy cakes and often the first time some of the children had seen cream cakes. In later years we had fish and chips which was a real treat. Then it was back to the coach to return home, some children looking very tired and with dirty little faces, but they all had a good time. How we enjoyed the day, and it was talked about for days afterwards. Our next glimpse of the sea with all the excitement of the Sunday school outing would have to wait until the next year.

My brother-in-law is in his seventies and he told me that when he was a child there were no seaside outings for him until later in life. There was a Sunday school sports day with races such as the egg and spoon and sack races, also ball games were played on a local meadow. After the games, they were all invited to the Squire's house for sandwiches, cake and lemonade. Later, when the first bus (charabanc) came into the village, it was a great treat to ride in it, especially when going to the seaside for an outing.

This month a good many sweet-scented flowers pass to the seed stage, noticeably those of elder and of meadow sweet. However this lack of scent is more than made up for by the lime trees which are now in full flower. The bees love the lime blooms and when one hears a hectic buzzing coming from the hive, it is fairly certain that lime trees are not far away.

Towards the end of the month the brilliant red berries of the woody or deadly nightshade appear and as they are extremely poisonous, children should be warned not to touch them. Another seed pod that is dangerous is the laburnum, while the black seed of the bryony, often seen growing wild in the hedgerows is also attractive to children as are the red berries of the yew tree. Although they are so attractive, they are all poisonous, and I mention this because with school holidays starting, children will be on holiday and going on walks and picnics. They can be very inquisitive and often imagine that all berries and seeds are for eating.

There is a story that an old Suffolk farm labourer was asked why he was so lethargic on morning, he solemnly explained that he had 'just heard the death-watch beetle ticking in his room, and was therefore expecting a death in his family any minute'.

There are many beliefs about the weather, and I recall chatting to an old gardener on a peaceful summer afternoon, when a green woodpecker began shattering the peace with his 'horsey laugh'. The old gardener began grumbling and mumbling under his breath, so I asked him what was the matter. He told me that it would surely rain the next day, because 'that there wood-sprite was laughing again'. He went on to explain that in Suffolk, the woodpecker was understood to say, 'Wet, wet, wet, wet', when it cried - thus predicting rain. I may add that the next day was one of the finest that we had that summer!

It is said that rain is not far off when a horse shakes in its harness while at work. Others say that this means the birth of a child in the village.

Approaching rain is also heralded when a skylark is seen to drop like a stone from the sky, only checking its headlong rush within a few feet of the earth. Country people also used to say 'when the new moon is lying on its back, a dry month is predicted', because the moon is said to hold the water better than when it is a 'dripping moon'- when it is standing on end. In this position, the water is said to run out, and so there would be a wet month. Thunder is predicted when midges are seen swarming on a hot summer's day.

It is interesting to note that most beliefs predict rain, and hardly ever fine weather. Similarly, it is usually a death or some other dire happening that is predicted in other beliefs. For instance, Suffolk people say that should a watch stop and the owner fail to make it go again through their own particular efforts, there is sure to be a death in the family. When my husband died all my clocks stopped and it was a long time before I could get them going again. A death is also predicted when a picture falls from its place on the wall, and there is a gruesome superstition that if a person dies in the village and 'lays' over the Sunday, we always say that this will be followed by at least two more.

'The weather will soon change' said my old country friend 'when they start the haysel' (the hay carting - sael means time or season) 'for it allus rains'. Before field cultivation of hay, village commoners were allotted a strip or strips of land and they would have been responsible for the cutting and carting of the hay from their own strip before 1 August (Lammas Day), after which stock were allowed to graze on the meadows.

In years with little rain, the tall grass, as we used to call it, is not so tall, and the hay season is short. Hay is very important; without it no stock keeper could carry on. A generation ago scythes, rakes and picks (pitchforks) were the only tools used to make hay. During the last thirty years or so, more and more machines have invaded the hayfields. Years ago it used to take about two months or more to do hay-making, now it is done in weeks with fine weather. You can always tell a 'good chap' with a scythe - not so much by what the finished job looks like, but by how it sounds. A sharp scythe sizzles through the grass, it hisses and whispers, because the blade is so keen, and the stems do not slow down its swinging movements. A man doesn't fit his scythe, he adjusts it to fit him. The toe and heel of a scythe can be adjusted until the blade swings level, parallel to the ground, to suit the mower's natural swing. It seems as though the very handle of the scythe has grown onto the ends of the mower's arm! My late husband cut up an old piece of leather or a rubber boot to make a sling which he then fixed to his belt and strapped around his waist to carry the 'rub' (whetstone). The rub whistled along the blade, sending out a ringing note into the air, a wetted thumb tested the sharpness, until a cut-throat razor seemed as blunt as a penknife by comparison. It took a good man to use one of these ungainly country tools, so often seen hanging from the apple tree at the bottom of the cottage garden when not in use.

I can remember going into the hayfields where my father and other farm workers would be piling the hay into large heaps, or turning it, as it had to be nice and dry before it was carted to the stack-yard to be made into a haystack. Women and children helped to get the hay in, using the traditional wooden hay rakes, which have been used for centuries. The hay rake was made entirely of wood with about 30 tines or teeth, fixed into the head so that the hay could be pulled more easily into a continuous swathe. The handle was made of ash, which was split down from one end about 18 inches, the two halves then being spread apart and inserted into drilled holes situated on the head. Another way of fixing the handle was simply to insert it in a central hole in the head then securing it with wire stays to the two ends. The teeth of the rake were made of oak and were pushed into holes which were drilled in the head at 2 inch intervals with alternate teeth being glued into place.

It was important to shake and turn the hay before it was made up into large piles or 'cocks'. Years ago, many different types of hay stack could be seen around the countryside, each stack usually containing one day's carting, which was then left for a time to settle before it was eventually thatched. If the hay was damp when taken to the stack, it would bind together so tightly that any heat formed could not escape quickly. The grasses or clover 'sweat' and bacteria becomes active, and this means heat is given off. Occasionally the hay would heat up so much that the stack burst into flames. Nowadays we only see bales of hay in the fields, and most grass is cut and stored green for silage.

In cherry orchards now, the fruit is ripening. Kent is famous for its cherries, good for both cooking and for dessert. Cherry orchards flourish in many other counties especially Hertfordshire and Lincolnshire as well as in East Anglia. The history of the cherry goes back further than most other fruits. One of the earliest records of its cultivation is in the gardens and orchards of the monasteries of Norwich, as well as the 'Pomerium' there was a 'cherruzerd; or orto-cerser, the cherry garden. At Ely, besides the famous vineyard planted in the garden of the bishop, the records of sales show that cherry trees were also grown in the vineyard area. As the years went by and the cherry became more popular, the smaller tree was introduced and made cropping and picking easier, producing fruit of better, disease-resistant quality. Sadly, the cherry orchards of England today no longer occupy the place they did even 50 years ago. Imports of cherries from Europe have invaded the markets of Britain as they did in the fifteenth and sixteenth centuries, before the Flanders fruit was replaced with fruit from the orchards of Kent, encouraged by the lead given by Henry VIII.

The most popular sour cherry is the Morello, a good cooker, but grown chiefly in large orchards for the making of cherry brandy. These are risky crops as even a thunderstorm or heavy rain can be a catastrophe, splitting the cherries just before they are ripe and the grower could lose his whole crop in one day. As a rule, as soon as the cherries begin to ripen, bird scarers are necessary, and the crack of scarers - known as 'cherry-bangers' in Kent - is often heard from dawn to dusk. Picking the fruit is not as easy as one might think as all the cherries have to be cut from the tree with secateurs - if they are pulled off the tree, the stalks would be separated from the fruit, which then becomes spotted and squashy. A recipe for cherry brandy is included in the recipe section at the end of the chapter.

I have driven between Newmarket and Bury St Edmunds many times, yet I have never done so without sparing a sympathetic thought for the nameless shepherd boy whose wayside grave one passes at the crossroads about three miles from Newmarket. There are always flowers upon the neatly trimmed mound - who puts them there, and who cares so lovingly for the grave? I have heard some say that it is the roadmen while others think that it is passing gypsies. The shepherd boy was employed by a local farmer and one evening, on counting the flock, he found one sheep missing. Fearing that he would be accused of stealing the sheep, the penalty for which at that time was hanging, the lad took his own life. As was the custom with suicides then, he was buried unceremoniously at the nearest cross roads. There is a tale that many racegoers driving towards Newmarket will take special note of such flowers as happen to be on the boy's grave for legend has it that luck will be with the owner whose racing colours correspond to those of the grave's flowers.

July is the time to start preparing for the craft and produce shows that are held in the autumn. Preserves, fruit and vegetables and craft items such as aprons, stuffed toys, character toys and rag dolls all need to be planned well in advance.

Decorated cakes are often an item of such shows, and I love to see the variety of designs that are entered. Over the years, cake icings and sugar craft have come a long way and I marvel at what friends have done with a small piece of fondant icing, creating the most beautiful display of miniature flowers and decorations. There are now classes in sugar craft and it is possible to make birthday cakes iced with a child's favourite cartoon character or even a replica of the famous blue willow pattern.

Over the years, I have judged flowers and produce at many shows and the following is my advice to anyone who wishes to win prizes. Preserves should have cellulose covers - vinegar resistant in the case of pickles. Tie-down covers are not recommended for show work and labels must contain all necessary information, including the date of making. With jam, the jars should be full, the colour bright and the flavour true with a jelly consistency - no hard skin or too many stones. The jam should be neatly finished and the label should not be too big or fancy. The same rules apply to jellies, brilliant clarity and when small pieces are cut with a knife, they should hold their shape but still quiver. Marmalade is basically the same as jam but based on citrus fruits and with a specific label. The peel must be soft and evenly cut and the distribution of peel and pulp should be even. For pickles, fill the jars to within a half-inch of the top covered by a half-inch of liquid. Clear pickles and piccalilli should be crisp, and sweet pickle tender but not broken down, the pieces neat, bite-sized, attractive and bright. Chutney jars must also be well-filled and the mixture bright and smooth, firm and mature. Remember that chutney should be made three months before showing so that it is fully matured.

A large number of butterflies are on the wing - one of the most prominent being the white admiral the colouring on the upper surfaces of their wings being most noticeable. Rivers and streams start to run low and the fish can suffer from the heat. We sometimes forget that, like us, animals can also suffer from the heat. Fish in ornamental gardens can suffer from a lack of oxygen, and you will often see fish lying on their sides or trying to get as near to the waterfall in their ponds as they can. When this happens it is a good thing to spray the pool with the hose, as this will help to put oxygen back into the water.

Birds need water, and we have a container near our garden, which my brother fills every day for the birds. You would be surprised at the different sorts of animals and birds that come to drink at our 'water hole'. Some of them become quite tame when they realise that there is water about.

We are often asked what sort of manure we use in the garden, and one old gentleman told me the following story. There was a farmer in his village who, during the First World War, was short of men to help clean out the hen houses and pig sties. While walking round the farm, a visitor expressed surprise to see the muck so high and asked the farmer what he was going to do about it. He replied, 'Oh, don't worry bor, I'll lift the perches!'

RECIPES

Barbeques

With the warm evenings it is very fashionable to have food cooked out in the open air. Steak tastes so much better cooked over a wood and charcoal fire, and we might well borrow ideas from the USA where it has long been recognised that a return to the primitive conditions of cookery gives a special flavour to the food. The barbeque was originally the communal meal of the Boucaniers or wild cattle hunters of the West Indies, in which a beast was roasted whole over a driftwood fire. Today, chicken supplements steak, and grilled chicken in America means a 'spatch' cooked bird, that is to say split down the back, opened out and beaten as flat as possible.

If you are restricted to low salt and low fat, try this sauce on chicken (without the skin) or on fish or any meat from which you have first trimmed the fat.

12oz can 'no salt added' tomato paste
1 tbs dry mustard
$^1/_2$ cup dry white wine
1 tbs red wine vinegar
1 tbs Worcestershire sauce
Dash of Tabasco to taste
$^1/_4$ cup brown sugar
1 tbs chopped onions
Juice of 1 lemon
$1^1/_2$ cups of water

Blend all the ingredients well and simmer for 15 minutes. Be careful as this sauce bubbles quite hard and can splash over onto your clothes. It keeps for up to ten days in the fridge.

Broad Beans
The broad bean is one of the oldest cultivated vegetables, and has been eaten in Britain for centuries. They were the food of the common people,

and Chaucer referred to things as 'not being worth a bean'. Bacon was another staple food of the time, and not surprisingly, the foods came to be eaten together and this association lasted for hundreds of years. Try cooking them with a sprig of savory, this is like adding mint to peas, and enhances the flavour of the beans. The very young beans can be eaten pods and all, and beans in parsley sauce served with ham is one of my favourite dishes. This was also a Victorian speciality. Salads would not be the same without lettuce, and these were first mentioned in a fifteenth century book on gardening. At that time, they were more likely to be cooked with other pot herbs or green vegetables than eaten raw. Fresh peas will also be available for salads, or to be cooked and eaten hot. The peas we know today are of a much finer quality than those which fed our ancestors. It is rare these days to find good fresh peas, since so many are sent to the frozen food producers. However, young peas, straight from the pod are really worth looking for - or growing in your garden. Do try the Asparagus pea and the Sugar-snap, where the pods are eaten as well as the peas, but you must eat them when they are young and don't overcook. Pea pod wine is also very good! Don't forget to add a sprig of mint when cooking peas, also to new potatoes.

Mint can also be used in a pastry dish, so try this one for a change. Line a plate with shortcrust pastry and cover it with mixed sultanas, well-chopped mint and a few slices of cooking apple (time to use them out of the freezer). Sprinkle liberally with sugar and moisten with a few drops of lemon juice or water. Add a dab or two of butter and cover with pastry, making cuts in the top to allow the steam to escape. Cook until the pastry is brown and crisp.

It is worth noting that the addition of a little chopped mint will improve salads, scrambled eggs and toasted cheese and a bunch of fresh mint hung in the kitchen helps to keep flies away.

Rabbit

There are several ways to cook rabbit, but first they must be skinned then cut away the portion between the hind legs and trim off the flaps of the chest cavity. Put the meat in to soak in salted water with a little vinegar added to blanch the meat. The basic way to cook rabbit is to brown or seal the meat by frying in fat for about ten minutes. This should not be too hot, and frequent turning is essential. The joints can also be dipped into a mixture of flour, thyme, tarragon and pepper before browning, and if you have time, leave the rabbit in a marinade overnight before browning.

Marinade

$^1/_2$ glass wine
6 bay leaves
Some onion rings
2 sprigs of thyme
2 sprigs of parsley

The joints should be turned in the marinade at intervals so that the flavours will penetrate the meat. The marinade can later be heated and reduced to form a sauce for the rabbit.

Rabbit Pie

My father used to love this for breakfast on Christmas Day. There are many ways of making the pie, but it is best to cook the joints first and then place them in a pie dish, adding slices of fat bacon or fat and lean pork. You can also add chopped onions, mushrooms, leeks or any other vegetables you wish, although my mother never used vegetables. Season well, cover the dish with pastry, making a hole in the centre for the steam to escape, and bake in the oven. The juice from the cooked rabbit was poured through the hole in the crust, and when cold, the pie was cut and there would be a lot of tasty jelly as well as the meat.

The above mixture can also be used for a rabbit pudding by putting the ingredients into a basin lined with suet crust and steam this for a few hours - for this dish you would not have to cook the rabbit first.

Cherry Brandy

1lb top quality morello cherries
$^1/_2$lb caster sugar
1 bottle vodka or brandy (lower strength)

Stalk and wash the fruit and drain to dry. Prick each cherry several times with a large needle and place in a Kilner jar or similar. Sprinkle the sugar over the fruit in layers. Cover with several layers of polythene, secure with a rubber band and leave for a few days until the juice runs and the sugar is dissolved. Pour the vodka or brandy over the fruit, re-cover and shake the jar to ensure dissolution of the sugar.

Store for six months, then strain off the liqueur and pour into bottles; it is now ready for use.

Preserving

There were no freezers in my mother's day, so there was much drying and salting down of vegetables and fruit. She used lump salt, which was bought in brick form, and broken up with a rolling pin. Runner beans were put in stone jars - a layer of cut-up runner beans, then a layer of salt - and when we came to use the beans, we would soak them overnight in cold water before cooking them to draw out the salt. It's a pity firms have stopped making lump salt, as the salt of today does not preserve so well. It is possible to substitute sea salt, but this is expensive.

I am often asked if I would like some kilner jars for bottling fruit, and sadly I have to say 'no'. Like most people, I now own a freezer, and use it to store and freeze all my vegetables and fruit. My mother used to bottle large quantities of fruit, using a large saucepan, with a cardboard lining inserted between and around the jars, and this she would stand on top of the oil stove. Sometimes we would hear a crack, and my mother would be cross as this would mean that one of the jars had cracked all round the bottom. It would be such a clean cut that the entire bottom of the jar would come out, meaning the loss of the jar's contents. So we had to make sure we did not screw the tops on too tightly until after the cooking period. Some people used to bottle fruit in an oven on a low heat, but whichever method is used, there is an art in the preserving of fruit which is very apparent at all local flower shows.

July is the pickling season, and pickles are a traditional English dish, as old as Shakespeare ('A plague o' these pickle herrings') and seem to have been continuously popular ever since. Chutney came from India via the army sometime in the nineteenth century. There it was traditionally eaten with curry and was soon adopted in Britain.

The equipment for making all types of vinegar-based pickles is simple, but it is essential that the correct items are used or acid may affect both the equipment and the finished product. Copper, brass or iron utensils must not be used - I always use a large stainless steel or aluminium preserving pan or big saucepan.

Fruit and herb vinegars would be on the shelves of all well-stocked Victorian larders. They give a most unexpected lift when used as the basis for salad dressings and are also useful for drinks. Try these vinegar recipes.

Flavoured Vinegars

Fruit and herb vinegars were always in Victorian larders. They give a most unexpected lift when used in salad dressings and are also useful for drinks.

Horseradish Vinegar

Put a large, sliced shallot into a pint of mild vinegar and warm through. Fill a jar with shredded horseradish and pour over the vinegar to cover. Cover tightly and let it stand on the stove infusing, keeping it hot for a week (an Aga-type cooker is best for this). Strain and boil the mixture. Bottle and seal down whilst hot.

This vinegar is strong, and you will only need a spot or two when using.

Herbal Vinegar

Chop the herbs of your choice into small pieces and add as much to white wine vinegar as the jar will hold. Leave the herbs to infuse for two to three weeks, shaking the jar every time you pass it. Taste the vinegar after this time, strain the liquid from the herbs and pour into a bottle adding a sprig of one of the herbs. Seal, and you will find this very good if making up a tomato salad and so on.

Lavender Vinegar

This is very good for the treatment of migraine.
Rub the lavender flowers off the spikes, crush them and fill the bottle. Top up with white wine vinegar. Leave for two to three weeks then strain the vinegar into a bottle. You may have to repeat the process as a lot of liquid can be lost in the straining. Lavender vinegar can be very strong and may be used by putting a few drops on a handkerchief.

Raspberry Vinegar

Take 2lb raspberries and 2 pints red wine vinegar. Place the fruit in a bowl, crush slightly and pour the vinegar over the fruit. Leave for a week, stirring every day. Strain the fruit through a jelly bag and measure the liquid. Allow 1lb sugar to every pint of juice and place together in a preserving pan. Stir to dissolve the sugar, boil for 10 minutes and bottle when cold. This is very handy in winter, diluted in hot water.
Blackberries and elderberries may be used in the same way.

Pickled Walnuts

This is an old recipe given to me by a visitor to my garden some years ago. When pickling walnuts, always wear rubber gloves as the stain from the walnuts is very difficult to remove and virtually has to wear off the skin!

> Walnuts - green but well-grown with the skins still soft.
> Quantity of salt water
> Quantity of spiced vinegar

To make sure that no shell has begun to form, take a knitting needle or something equally sharp, and prick each one thoroughly. After the pricking, soak the green nuts in a solution of brine made up with one pound of salt to three pints of water. This needs to be changed every three days.
After twelve days, strain off the brine, and put the nuts in the sun to dry until they have turned black. When the nuts have turned black, simply pack them into jars and pour spiced vinegar over them.

At the time of pickling the walnuts, reserve the youngest and most tender to make walnut ketchup. These nuts should be chopped finely with shallots and the mixture boiled in spiced vinegar for two hours, then strained and bottled.

Pickled Onions

As all good gardeners know, shallots should be planted on the shortest day, lifted on the longest day. Therefore should have been harvested by July.

>   6lb shallots
>   1lb salt
>   1gallon water

Peel the onions. Make up a brine solution with the salt and water and put in the onions. Leave the onions in the brine for 24 hours. Drain the onions, pack into jars and cover with spiced vinegar. A teaspoon of sugar may be added to each jar, but this is a matter of taste

You may notice small yellow spots appearing on the onions after being stored for a while, this is quite harmless and will not affect the eating quality

Parsley

I would not like to be without parsley as it is such a useful and versatile herb. I use it for flavouring stews and casseroles, and always keep a stock of it in the freezer for use in the winter months. If you only need small amount, you can chop up the parsley and freeze it in ice cube trays. Otherwise, just wash small bunches, shake, put into small bags and pop them into the freezer. When you take it out it will crumble up and does not need to be chopped, and the flavour is just as good. Parsley is also useful for garnishes.

There is a saying, 'Parsley seed goes nine times to the devil' - parsley is tricky to grow, so it was believed to be planted nine times before it sprouted - it goes to the devil nine times, and very often forgets to come back again! Another old saying is 'Parsley goes to hell and back before it sprouts'. It was also thought very unlucky to give parsley plants away, and transplanting parsley could mean a death in the family. I don't believe this for one moment, as every year

I sow parsley in a tray in my greenhouse, prick it out and then transplant it!

Edible Wild Plants
Lime
Commonly found in our parks and by the roadsides, lime flowers in July and has a drooping cluster of heavily scented yellow blooms. Some people like to eat the leaves in sandwiches with just a dash of lemon juice or Worcestershire sauce. The flowers also make a nice home made wine and, in France, people make a tea with the dried flowers known as 'Tilleul'.

Hop (Humulus Lupulus)
Hops can frequently be found growing in hedges and damp thickets from July to August. The cone-like green flowers have been used for flavouring beer since the ninth century, but the young shoots can also be used chopped up and simmered in butter as a sauce or cooked like asparagus.

August

S.E. Burrows
2007

AUGUST

August was named after the Roman emperor Augustus. He thought it was his lucky month. Years ago, 1 August was known as 'Lammas' and was an important day - the day when the first loaves of bread, made from the new grain, were consecrated. Lammas is one of the quarter days in Scotland, but no longer recognised as such in England.

Some of the smaller birds are starting to sing again. Starlings whistle on rooftops and in the garden trees the 'saw-sharpening' song of the great tit, and the musical whisper of the blue tit are heard. House sparrows hover over flowers where insects are abundant and wood pigeons have started on the rowan trees, fluttering as they lean over to eat the orange berries. The dandelion tribe, common sow thistle and the larger, pricklier corn sow thistle stand conspicuously at the edges of fields everywhere, and thistledown begins to float in the air. Walking the country roads and lanes, we can hear the snap and crackle as the fields of August corn ripen in the sun and the sap dries out of the stalks.

Although August is the month of golden corn and ripe fruit, it also alas, brings summer to a close and we shall soon be saying 'the nights are pulling in'. Orchard and hedgerow fruit begin to ripen and this is one of the busiest months of the year for harvesting from our gardens, preparing vegetables for freezing and making jams, pickles and preserves. Whilst we harvest our crops, nature too shows an abundant crop of seeds and fruits and as daily they increase, the flowers diminish.

This month is the thrilling climax to the farmer's year and unless you have lived on a farm or worked in the fields, you will never fully understand the excitement and satisfaction of harvest time. The wheat, which the farmer drilled last autumn and watched break through the brown earth in little green spears before the winter, is now red-gold straw, bowed down with heavy ears of corn. As one looks over the gate at fields of wheat, oats and barley waiting to be cut, one remembers that nothing stops the march of the seasons. From seed-time to harvest, man must work to nature's plan, and August and September are the months of fulfilment. Nowadays the corn is taken from the combine to be stored in large barns or hoppers, so if the weather does turn to thunder storms, all is safely in the dry.

In the year 1912 a flood in August devastated the crops. I have seen photographs of stooks of corn standing in a field of water, and on the back of the photograph was a long account of the disaster which befell Norwich and the surrounding villages. Within the space of 29 hours between Monday and Tuesday, the rainfall exceeded seven inches, an amount equal to that of three average months.

The floods reached their height at 2am on the Wednesday morning, by which time the state of affairs in Norwich was critical. Railway and telegraphic communication was cut off and about a square mile of the city was covered with water, which in some places reached to the bedroom windows. Houses collapsed and thousands of people were homeless and destitute, while the work of rescuing them was made still more difficult by the failure of the electric light owing to the flooding of the power station. To add to the calamity, the engines at the pumping stations were stopped and notices were issued that there was only three days' supply of drinking water available. Fortunately the rain stopped on the Wednesday and railway communication was restored. Ten thousand shops and factories had been idle, bridges had been swept away and tens of thousands of acres of crops were devastated. It has been stated that the Norwich rainfall of 26 August, 1912 would have a unique place in the history of English floods.

Many hotels in London will now be getting ready for the grouse season, which starts on the twelfth. Grouse is game and any good cook will tell you that game birds need to be hung for five to six days before eating, so I was wondering how restaurants manage to serve this bird on the evening of 12 August. I am sure they do not employ people to creep around the Scottish moors a week or so before the twelfth, with silencers fitted to their guns, to bag a few grouse so that enough can be brought down by air to fill the first few days' menus. However, I have been told that the grouse eaten on the twelfth has not been hung.

Hanging is important for game birds to enable the fibres of the flesh to break down, this makes the meat more tender and improves the flavour. There are no hard and fast rules on how long to hang birds or ground game as much depends on the weather and the individual taste of the consumer. An August grouse may need hanging for only three days, whereas a cock pheasant, shot in cold January, will hang for two or three weeks and still be in perfect condition. I have plucked and dressed pheasants with maggots at the tail-end and the meat almost green - but that is how my friends wish to eat them.

In this holiday month, our village inns and country pubs are invaded by holiday - makers. The regulars welcome the newcomers with their bright chatter and faster habit of drinking. The visitors come for a breath of fresh country air and are quite oblivious to the fact that they bring with them a brightness and freshness from another world. The old locals used to say, 'They'll soon be here. I reckon they will make a pleasant break in our daily routine, and there will be a free pint or two to be had in return for a bit of well put on local colour and entertainment'.

In spite of all the traffic, hikers still manage to hold their own and walk on bravely, undeterred by the traffic thundering past them. Walking is an art if full enjoyment and benefit is to be obtained. Many people walk along leaning forward from the waist, in an eager do-or-die fashion but I am told that to give the lungs an opportunity to do their stuff properly, it is essential to walk upright, swinging the arms in rhythm with the stride and being as relaxed as possible. I can see how a badly packed or ill-adjusted rucksack will tend to make the body bend forward and why it is important to get the load well up on the shoulders so that it does not sag like a dead weight half-way down the back.

I once met two Belgian visitors who were carrying huge rucksacks. They insisted that they did not get tired as they are regular walkers, but told me that it is important not to bathe the feet in hot water when on a walking holiday as this tends to soften the skin and cause blisters. You can't do better than to wash your feet in the cold water of a running stream. I wished them an enjoyable holiday, but to myself I hoped that if they put up their tent in a farmer's field, they would leave the place as they found it, by closing gates behind them, keeping to footpaths and not taking short-cuts through standing crops - and, of course, not leaving litter behind.

Although there is still considerable social etiquette in existence in country pubs, the pubs themselves are changing fast. Today they can't get by just by serving beer, they must be restaurants as well. Gone are the days when you saw old men, full of character and rural assurance, sitting in their special chairs. Men wearing striped farm-workers' shirts, and colourful braces, and a large leather belt round their bellies, were almost as appreciative of good liquor as the barrels themselves. My husband used to say that the belts eased backache, and farm workers always wore this wide belt whatever the weather, plus an old red handkerchief around their necks. You could tell a countryman from a holiday-maker just by looking at his dress.

I often wonder how the ladies managed to keep their long dresses clean when they went to work in the fields in Victorian times. It was often said that the men's trousers could stand up by the bedside, so that they could just step into them in the mornings, and I could believe this to be true. My father wore his thick cords winter and summer, and I can't remember him changing them very often.

The last of the summer lies upon the land, sometimes sultry, often thundery. August shimmers on to harvest. The farming community pray to gods old and new for a period of continuous dry weather to ripen the grain. Waving fields of corn are streaked blond and green, here and there dotted with poppies like spots of blood.

We always looked forward to the harvest and as it drew nearer, straw hats of unpredictable shapes and ages were taken down from their pegs, not to be hung up again, come rain or shine until 'all is safely gathered in'. The subject of the weather became very important and neither wireless nor newspapers were allowed to mention it until it no longer mattered. Old men who could foretell the weather by various natural signs or by 'feeling it in their bones' suddenly came into their own again and their predictions were carefully observed. Ears of corn were rubbed between the palms of the hands to see how readily the husks fell away. The corn kernel was crushed between the teeth and should taste like cheese.

As children, how we used to love going into the harvest fields. There was not so much heavy machinery in the fields and mother used to send us off in the mornings and tell us to amuse ourselves for the day. I have wonderful memories of creaking waggons, the horses straining under the weight of the load of corn, the grizzled old men in corduroy trousers, tied at the legs with binder twine and red dotted 'wroppers' around their necks to catch the sweat that trickled down their faces. Some of the men had straw hats to keep the sun off their necks. We loved to take the 'fourses' that mother had packed up to take into the fields or stack yard. There were harvest shortcakes and milk cans full of hot tea. We loved to ride in the last waggon full of sheaves to the stack yard, mingling joy and terror as we ducked to avoid overhanging boughs which threatened to sweep us from our lofty perches and singing at the tops of our voices.

August

I can remember going to the farm with my father and watching him, together with another farmworker, pushing the ancient Massey Harris binder out of the shed, brushing off the hen's droppings, checking the canvasses and threading the twine. Once started, it worked - I don't know how. The faithful old machine kept going pretty well but occasionally it threw a temperamental fit and left sheaf after sheaf untied, usually the thistley ones. As we got older, we helped with the stooking, or shocking as we called it, and we soon learned that there was an art in this. Each sheaf had to be banged down firmly, with the knot facing the right way, otherwise the whole thing would collapse before we were out of the field. There would be six or eight sheaves to a stook, sometimes helpers would build enormous stooks of ten or twelve sheaves and these took ages to dry out.

A foreman was elected by the rest of the workers and called 'Lord of the Harvest'. Appointment depended upon no special favouritism, and no greater honour could come to the man chosen. Once appointed, there was no appeal against the Lord's rulings, any unseemly conduct, bad language or over-drinking of ale or cider would come under judgement and often, if found guilty, the culprit was ordered off the field and forbidden to return. It was the lord of the harvest who decided when it was time for a 'breather' and a much-earned drink. He would set the hour of starting the break for meals and the moment when the exhausting day should end. His final duty was to preside over the Harvest Supper. We often talk about the beer being drunk by the youngsters at football matches, but think how much the reapers used to drink when mowing corn all day. The men had enormous thirsts in the dusty fields and would think nothing of downing 15 or 16 pints of ale in a day and then they would not be drunk, only happy maybe!

As teenagers, we always looked for the fields where the tractor and binder were nearly at the middle of the field. As they cut round and round, we knew that the rabbits would creep towards the centre of the field. We all had our prized club-sticks, usually made of hazel wood cut from the hedge, and each time we managed to kill a rabbit, we would make a snotch (a mark) in the stick - our mothers used to be pleased when we took home an extra meal. We soon learned to kill the rabbits with a quick knock on the head, then we cut them underneath to disembowel, or 'hulk' them as we said. We then cut a slit in one of the back legs to thread the other leg through and put the rabbits on a stick to take them home over our shoulders. Sometimes the farmer would make us take all the rabbits to the gateway of the field, where they would be shared out so that we all had one each. Sadly, myxamatosis has put people off eating rabbits, but I have included some recipes for cooking rabbit in this month's recipe section.

I have heard that there was an old custom in many parishes of putting a green oak bough up at the end of the barn when the last load of corn came back. The bough remained there until displaced by another bough, and was supposed to bring good luck and crops for the following harvest.

At threshing time, there would be plenty of help as the threshing engine pulled into the stackyard. All day the machine would be whirring and throbbing and chaff would fly about in the air. My father used to bring home some of the barley chaff to put on the garden to kill the slugs. After three days or so the threshing was finished and the harvest was coming to an end. The old men would say how the stacks of beans, barley, oats and wheat were to be made, to stand until it was time for threshing. Later, sacks would be sorted out to hold all the corn to stand in the barn where rats would soon gnaw at them. Then a wisp of straw would be pushed into the holes to keep the corn from spilling out, but it was a constant job, trying to stop the rats eating the sacks - the rat catcher was a busy man years ago.

In the old days, women and children were allowed to go into the fields to collect any ears of corn missed by the farm workers, but there were strict rules to be observed. No woman was allowed to glean in a field that was not in her parish, and the gleaning could not start until the farmers had carted all the shocks of corn from the field and had collected up the rakings as well. Often one shock of corn was left in the field to stop the gleaners until farmer was satisfied that the field was cleared - this was known as 'the policeman'. The field would be raked with a hay rake pulled by a horse and after the last of the straw was collected the 'policeman' was taken away. Then the women and children lined up in the field early in the morning, waiting for the church bell to ring, then with a cry of 'All on, all on', they would rush to pick up the ears of corn. This was very hard work and continued until six o'clock in the afternoon, when the church bell rang again and all work had to stop - then the cry was 'All off, all off'. The ears of corn were taken to the cottage and threshed with a flail and the corn was then taken to the windmill to be ground into flour for bread making, helping to provide bread for the winter. When I was young, although we no longer gleaned for grain to make flour, we gathered the corn to provide food for the chickens.

August

Fields are often named after trees and there is often a mystery surrounding the names. There are sometimes small wedges of grassland between a wood and the boundary of a field, in which a horse may be left to graze for a day or so, and this will be called 'Forty Acre' - of course this is a country joke. Then there are the 'Oak Fields', 'Nut Acres' and 'Alder Field' and when you walk into them, there are no sign of oaks, nuts or alders. Obviously these trees surrounded the fields at one time, and the custom of naming fields goes back into the mists of time. I expect 'Golden Meadow' was given its name because at one time it was ablaze with golden buttercups. Some fields have odd names like 'Hungry Hill' because of the poor soil that did not produce very good crops. We have some interesting field names in my village; 'Sandpit', 'Blackbird', 'Scarlet Hill' and 'Maypole'.

After the gathering of the corn comes the gathering of the cottage fruit and vegetables - the farmer's harvest has finished and now the farm labourer gathers his own harvest in. The onions have been pulled and lie in rows across the garden with their silky roots turned to the sun and the leaves slowly whitening like winter grass. As children, we used to help father tie the onions up in bunches, then hang them around the shed and the old 'Bumby' (the outside toilet) on large nails. There they would hang all winter and we would use them as needed. Various roots too were taken up and left strewn about the land during the day to dry, then they would be stored later in neat clamps down at the far end of the garden. The clamps were like a little village of igloos, each with its mud walls patted firm, smooth and shapely with a straw chimney at the top.

Plums, bullaces and early damsons would have been gathered and handed over to mother, who would bottle and store them away for the winter. Then it was time to slice the runner beans to put them down in salt. How I wish we could still get those large blocks of cooking salt - the salt of today is no good for preserving vegetables. Many a time I helped my mother by putting the lumps of salt into a pillowcase and then smashing them with a rolling pin. The salt was then put onto the beans layer by layer. Pickling onions and red cabbage were next; I can see the red cabbages hanging in pairs on the washing line posts to dry ready to be pickled.

In the school summer holidays there were never enough hours in the day for playing around. With all the gloriously hot days, there was plenty to occupy us, even if it was simply lying in the long grass making daisy chains. If the weather happened to turn chilly, we would make a den or old cover with bits of wood and tin. Summer brought the boats out to sail on ponds and we loved to wade into the streams looking for tiddlers. Using jam jars on a length of string, we would see what we could fish out of the water. When we could not find much to interest us at the water's edge, we went off to play rounders or hopscotch on the tarmac roads. With a lump of chalk brought from the fields, we marked our squares out and played for many hours. If we heard the unusual sound of a car or lorry coming, we just got into the side until it had passed. Often we went out as early as half past eight in the mornings and would be out all day roaming far and wide.

I used to love to collect wild flowers and my bedroom windowsill would be filled with them. Sometimes we made swings out of old car tyres which we suspended from the branches of trees. With so much to do, we lost track of time and on many a summer's evening, mother would come looking for us because it was getting late. Often we lost hair ribbons, plimsolls and cardigans; we received cuts and bruises and tore our clothes, but we gained so much more - healthy bodies, joyful memories and a happy sense of freedom.

Human beings are not the only creatures who derive pleasure and satisfaction from obtaining the maximum amount of sunshine on their bodies whenever the opportunity presents itself, especially in our varied English climate. I know that some carry the sunbathing cult rather too far but, on very hot days I have often noticed house martins massed together on the roof of my house. The roof faces the full morning sun and the birds recline flat out, with their wings and tails outstretched, apparently taking full advantage of the hot rays. Among the other common species that I have observed sunbathing are blackbirds and starlings. Some have characteristic postures, leaning sideways with feathers erect and the near wing and near half of the tail spread. The bill is often open while the eye nearest to the sun is closed or partially so. Pigeons squat on the ground with the tail and the wing nearest the sun extended and partially spread.

When I was a young girl, I loved to watch as the cows ran round the meadows, careering at top speed back and forth from one end of the field to the other. With their tails in the air and heads down, they galloped as fast as they could for no apparent reason. I now know that this was not a game they were playing but it was caused by an insect - the warble fly - which can be found on our grasslands from May to August. The female fly makes an ugly buzzing noise as she flies around the cattle before landing and laying her eggs on the cow's soft hair. A few days after the eggs are laid, they hatch into larvae which work their way towards the base of the hair and then bore their way under the skin. Little wonder the poor old cows get upset! I remember my father telling me that the cows would seem to be frightened by the fly and that often it would upset the milk yield, and even cause quiet old bullocks to run off their fat. Today farmers have a spray to treat the animals and kill off this rotten little fly.

One of the most beautiful sights in August is the flight of the large dragonfly, which is so like that of a helicopter, flying directly up and down, backwards and forwards. Their jewelled coat can be seen even in the centre of cities, flying over land and water. At one time, naturalists would collect them, but they soon found that the beauty of the larger hawking dragonflies is less than skin deep and once the dragonfly is killed, the colours fade in under an hour.

The colourful dragonfly is among the fastest-flying and oldest insects in the world, and their speed is estimated at between 35 and 60 miles per hour.

This is the time of year when we have problems with wasps. These live in large communities that stem from a single queen. The nest hangs in any convenient space, often underground in old mouse holes, and is enlarged as the swarm grows. It consists of a cluster of vertical cells hung about a stalk, similar to a chandelier, and is covered by a 'paper' envelope made in the same way as the cells, from wood pulp gathered from fence posts or trees and mixed with saliva. This envelope is made larger by tearing up, pulping and re-issuing its paper. The grubs of the common wasp are carniverous, and feed on caterpillars and insects, which the adults paralyse with their stings before taking them to the larder in the depths of the colony. Although wasps do not store or even collect honey, they have the same taste for sugar delicacies as their relatives the bees. By August, with a large colony to suport, wasps are looking for bigger and better picnics, such as ripe fruit. As the season goes on, the wasps get rather dopey and this is often when one is stung - try a dab of solution of ammonia, another old method is to rub in parsley. When the first frost comes, it will kill the entire swarm, leaving the young queens, hanging by their jaws, to start a new family for the following May.

The wasp's larger, handsome and much-feared relative, the hornet, also builds paper nests, often in a hollow tree or a barn and occasionally in the roof space of country houses. A hornet sting can be exceedingly painful but, like the wasp, it will rarely attack unless provoked. As hornets fly strong and high, they do not usually get mixed up with people. So remember, do not fling your arms about if you see them, just walk calmly by with as little noise as possible. If you don't upset them, they won't harm you.

There are many superstitions and customs connected with church bells; their ringing was widely believed to drive away the demons of storm and disaster. This probably came about through the idea that spirits dislike loud noises, and our superstitious ancestors believed that the bells chased away evil spirits when a person died. - pagans made a lot of noise at funeral rituals to give the dead person a safe passage to the hereafter. The sound of church bells is also said to chase away thunder and lightning.

Campanology - bell ringing - is a very old art; it is believed that the sound obtained by striking metal was first discovered in the Bronze Age, when the earliest bells were saucer-shaped, and the notes were produced by striking the bell with a hammer. Our modern bells are modelled on these early bells; today they are made of a mixture of copper and tin, and the clapper to strike the bell was a later improvement.

Church bells are rung for various reasons; to inform the congregation that a service is due to start, and during the last War, they remained silent for the duration of the War only to be rung as a warning if the country were invaded. On the brighter side, bells are rung joyously to announce a wedding service.

It was once thought that the grease taken from a church bell had miraculous powers when applied as an ointment and was used to cure ringworm, shingles and various other skin diseases. Unaccountable ringing of a ship's bell was said to be coincidental with the loss of another ship at sea. Ships' bells have many strange legends connected with them and are regarded by many sailors as the embodiment of the ship's soul.

East Anglia, and Suffolk in particular, is noted for its churches and their bells, and I love to hear the bells ringing. As some of our church bells go back to the thirteenth century, the time comes when they have to come down and be re-hung. This happened in 1990 at St Mary's Church at Monewden, where the six bells were taken down and sent to Whitechapel in London for restoration. On 17 September, 1990 the village celebrated the first ringing of the new peal - on this day, the bells were rung from 9.45am until 6.30pm and there were lunches served and sports such as tennis and quoits were played. This scene was recreated to celebrate the hanging of the new bells under the bell-master Brian Martin.

There is nothing nicer than a new crust of bread spread with home made jam or that favourite pickle. In years gone by, there were many women and children from my village who would go blackcurrant picking. This was a slow and laborious job, reaching in and around the branches for every last currant. The season only lasted two or three weeks, and I remember my poor mother coming home with a sick headache after sitting in the sweltering sun all day. She would wrap a rag soaked in vinegar round her head to relieve her suffering.
Today, with the invention of a wonderful currant-picking machine, these days are gone. The machine is fascinating to watch as it straddles the rows of bushes, shaking off the fruit. The fruit then goes up an elevator - rather like a combine harvester - and comes out at the back of the machine where two men check the trays as the fruit flows into them. One would expect the fruit to be squashed after travelling through the machine, but it remains quite whole. The majority of the currants are taken to Beecham's factory in Gloucestershire where they are made into that famous blackcurrant drink, and a few are sold, ready picked, to the public. Looking at the bushes after the machine had gone, there was no apparent damage and I have been told that, with a minimum of pruning, this is the way of picking blackcurrants in the future. I can only marvel at man's ingenuity.

The blackthorn (sloe) grows abundantly in woods and hedgerows. The flowers are small and white and appear before the leaves, often in cold spring weather - the 'blackthorn winter'. The fruit is small, round and purple in colour and it is the ancestor of all cultivated plums. The sloe was crossed with the cherry plum and eventually produced sweet plums such as the Victoria, yet the sloe is the tartest of them all and with one bite, the whole of your mouth 'creeps'. I think they are our best wild fruit and will go miles in search of them, as sloe wine is hard to beat. Sloe and Apple Jelly is wonderful and as for Sloe Gin, it is one of those special joys which makes living in the country worthwhile.

We have had some good fruiting seasons lately, and plums are one of my favourite fruits. Early Rivers are one of the first to appear in the shops, followed by the Czar and the Victoria plums. These varieties all make good jam but the one I like best for making preserves is the Yellow Pershore. Sadly, we don't see many of the true Greengages around today, so Yellow Pershores are the next best thing.

The same can be said of the Bullace, a form of wild plum and the true Damsons are another variety we see less frequently nowadays. What a treat it was to rush home from school when mother was making plum jam. She used to leave us a plate of plum stones to lick and, with a crust of new bread, the first plum jam always tasted the best.

With all the do's and don'ts of what we should eat today, just think back to the time when as children -whether in town or country - we were brought up on good wholesome bread and jam. We are so lucky in the country to be able to pick wild fruits as well as to know where to find the best buys during the season.

August sees the beginning of another rich harvest, the edible fungi, which used to be abundant in Britain but sadly we don't see so many these days. Before the last World War, few people could be induced to eat any other fungi than the Common Field Mushroom, but then the Polish soldiers and later the Italian and German prisoners of war working on the land, spread a far wider knowledge of the many wild edible fungi.

Of course, fungi should be studied before they are safe to be brought into the kitchen. If you are not sure, stick to the common field mushroom and its larger cousin, the Horse mushroom, both of which have pink gills, deepening to purple-brown with age. Puff balls are also tasty, but they must be eaten young. It makes my mouth water to think of those large mushrooms that my father used to bring home from the farm meadows - mother would soon get the frying pan out!

In good years, it is worth preserving some hazelnuts (filberts). There is a very old superstition that a double nut will bring you luck. However, there are conditions attached; to have good luck, you must gather the coupled nuts yourself and they must be ripe enough to hear the kernels rattle inside the shells. I have often seen couples of unripe hazels but invariably one side drops off before ripening takes place. The nuts should only be gathered when they have turned brown or fallen out of their cups. Dry them on trays or on a floor and when the shells are dry, pack them in containers - boxes or tins. For keeping, the best method is to layer them with dry sand. Put half an inch of sand in the base of a container, cover with a layer of nuts, sprinkle over enough sand to cover and then sprinkle with cooking salt. Repeat until the container is full, finishing with a half inch layer of sand. Store in a cool, dry place.

English nuts contain more moisture than those grown in warmer countries and some shrinkage of the kernels will occur if kept too long. In the case of walnuts, remove the green husk or outer casing. As a rule, only those from which the green husk splits and comes away easily are likely to be nuts worth keeping - the nut should be dry, If the nuts have blown down prematurely, the husk is difficult to remove and the kernels are likely to be immature. Walnuts can be stored in the same way as hazelnuts, but you have to keep a watch out that the squirrels don't get there first!

The Government is trying to get us to leave our cars at home - I do believe some of our MPs do not understand how we live in the country. I don't know what I would do if I did not have my car. Some village people live four miles from a doctor and their local post office, and rely on those who own a car to do their shopping and collect their penions for them. In our village we have a bus service - one a day - but owning a car is one way we can still lead an independent life.

When I married in the early 1950's, we did not need cars so much, as there were always tradesmen calling at the door. I could not afford to buy goods from all of them, as there were so many. Bakers called three times a week, butchers came twice and the grocery man used to come at the beginning of the week to collect my order which he then delivered at the end of the week. The milkman called every day, newspapers were delivered in all weathers and the postman delivered the post by bicycle. Apart from these regulars, there was a fish man who came around every month or so, a man who call around on his motorcycle to see if any shoes needed repairing and another man selling brushes and cleaning materials.

As children we looked forward to all the doorstep deliveries; what an adventure for a small child to see all the tradesmen coming up the front path with the weekly items that had been ordered. Meat was wrapped in paper, and the butcher still delivered even if mother had only ordered 1lb of sausages. The baker wore a cap that looked too big for him, a brown overall that flapped around his ankles and a pencil stuck behind one ear. I was rather frightened of him, but I loved the smell that came from his basket. Gypsies brought baskets of lace, pegs and bits and pieces, and the haberdashery man sold everything from teacloths to kettles. If he didn't have what you needed, you could be sure he would bring the item next time he called. If you could not pay immediately, he would let you pay so much a week 'on tick'.

There was the 'Ginger Beer and Vinegar Man' from Arden Brothers in Whitton, who used to come round in a van with open sides with the nice old gallon stone jars lined up on the shelves. We looked forward to seeing this kind old gentleman who often gave us a sweet when he called. There was even a man who came around with a 'funny cycle', as we called it. He was the knife grinder, and used to stop outside the cottage, put his cycle on a stand then sit and pedal with the wheel spinning a grinding stone. Sparks would fly when he put the knife to the stone, and it was great fun to watch. Another regular visitor was the little man in a yellow van who brought the accumulator each week for the wireless. This had to be used sparingly so that the power from the accumulator was not used up before the man returned the following week.

As the years went by, tradesmen called less and our village shops closed as the big supermarkets and out-of-town shopping centres took over, and now we would find it hard to manage without our cars.

The roads are so busy now, and in August there is the added traffic of touring caravans, camper vans and boats, all travelling to the seaside and country. With harvest in full swing, there is extra traffic as combine harvesters move from one field to another and tractors transport loads of corn and straw to the yards. One has to be patient on our narrow country roads, many accidents are caused by impatience.

Country people used to say that it is unlucky to kill a pig in the wane of the moon, and if you do, it will waste in the boiling. Another old saying was that it is unlucky to go in by the back door to a house you are going to live in Fishermen say that if you count the fish you've taken, you won't catch any more.

Although August is the month of golden corn and ripe fruits, it also brings summer to a close. It makes me feel rather sad when we come to August Bank Holiday and know that it is the last before Christmas, and summer is nearly over. We are coming to the time of early-morning mists, trailing over the fields of cobwebs, hanging from the leaves and grasses, and of cold blue air, fresh as well water. The sheep in the fields are hidden by these mists until the sun rises and gathers strength, scattering the mists in wisps of dissolving cloud. Then the land shines clean and fresh under the quickening light, each blade of grass trembling with its drop of dew, each leaf bent under the weight of its crystal bead. But most beautiful of all these mornings are the cobwebs, thousands of them, some big and open, some small and as delicate as lace. They are in the hedges and the bushes, swinging like hammocks from twig to twig and thorn to thorn, sagging under the weight of their cradled dews. The spiders have spun them overnight to catch flies and vagrant insects, and behold they have caught the stars twinkling in the early morning sunshine instead!

Towards the end of August, many of the swifts start to leave us and the few stragglers scream their last song over the farm buildings and fields - their stay is short. The wild Rosebay by the wayside is pink and misty against the deepening green of the hawthorn, and the seeded thistle heads each have their attendant goldfinches, linnets and green finches, each stealing a grain and losing a score. This means more for the wind to bear away, as it has borne away the cuckoo call; 'In August, go he must', so goes the old jingle. How true it is, as we shall not hear the cuckoo again until next year's spring.

Many of the young cuckoos will not leave the country until some weeks after the adult birds have migrated, and there lives one of nature's miracles. The young cuckoo begins life under what would appear to be a decided handicap; he has been brought up, not by his travelled parents, but by a pair of stay-at-home foster parents. Thus his upbringing would not seem to have prepared him for the long autumnal flight to the south. Until such time as the migratory urge is upon him, the longest journey he has made is the length of a field. Then, one day, long after the older birds have gone, the fledged orphan leaves the meadows and, without leadership or guidance - with nothing but a wonderful instinct - embarks on his hazardous journey. Silently he lifts up on the quiet breeze of a late summer's night and is gone.

Little is known about St Bartholomew, although it is said that he carried the gospel into India. He is the patron saint of cheese merchants, tanners and plasterers and there is a hospital near the City of London named after him - although generally known as 'Bart's'. More than one hundred and sixty churches are dedicated to St Bartholomew.

I was given a copy of a Farm Charter, written by a group of Land Girls during the war and put up in the farmer's barn:

'God gave us the land
It had been pillaged by man's greed
The soil was starved and the buildings were neglected
We pledge ourselves to hand on to the future
Better than we have received from the past
It is our purpose to make this place perfect.
We neither expect ease, nor ask for it.
We look to each other's hardship as an opportunity
And each new job as an adventure.
Perfect work in every last detail is our aim.

August

When we have hoed a field, no weed shall be left upon it
Every tool, after a task is done, shall be put back in its proper place.
We will keep each stall and stye so clean that no disease may spread
Or spring up among our animals
The heart of the farm is the family love and loyalty to each other
And is the cement which unites us
We plan to create in our family a part of New Britain
We shall drive out of our family life everything
Wise men hate in Old Great Britain.
We shall bring to birth those things all men long for
In the new and Greater Britain that is to be.
This shall be a family where discipline replaces drift,
A Family without moods.
No demand for place, privilege or position shall deaden, dull or drive us.
We seek no profit for ourselves from the land
We hold all things in common and in trust from God.
This family has no limit, everyone who comes here
Whether for a day or a year, is part of it.
It is a family which does not depend on names or riches, class or age.
We are out to rebuild men as well as to feed them
We dedicate ourselves to sacrificial God-controlled living,
Which, when done, can create a better world.
We live not for today, and for ourselves,
But for the future and for others.'

REMEDIES

Now is the time to make the remedies we will need in the winter from the fruits of the summer days.

Blackberry Scarecold

      2 pints ripe blackberries
      1 pint white vinegar
      2lb honey

Put stripped berries into an earthenware basin with the vinegar and allow to stand for a week. Then put into a saucepan with the honey and bring to the boil. When cool, slowly strain and bottle. Dose: one tablespoonful in a little water

Cough Mixture

      $2^{1}/_{2}$lb blackberries
      1 tbs allspice berries
      1 tbs whole cloves crushed

A piece of cinnamon stick
Honey
Brandy

Place blackberries in a pan with the crushed spices and just enough water to prevent the mixture from sticking. Cover and simmer gently until soft. Then strain through a muslin cloth. For each pint of mixture, add 7fl oz honey. Return the juice and honey to a clean pan and stir over a low heat until the honey has dissolved. Bring to the boil and simmer for 10 minutes. Remove pan from the heat and add ¼ pint brandy. Bottle when cool and store in a cool place.

I have been told that the vinegar from pickled walnuts, mixed with honey will cure a night-time cough. My mother used to put three drops of eucalyptus oil on a lump of sugar to stop us coughing during the night.

Blackcurrant Rob

Put the blackcurrants, what you can spare, in an ovenproof dish and cook these in a slow oven for about 45 minutes. Cool and strain through muslin. Pour the juice into a pan and for each pint of juice add 1lb demerara sugar and stir until dissolved. Simmer this for 30 minutes then, when it is cold, strain and bottle. To use as a hot drink, put one tablespoon in a glass of hot water or, if it is needed as a soothing mixture for coughs, dilute two tablespoons of blackcurrant rob with a tablespoon of honey in a little hot water. A spot of rum added can help you to get a good night's rest in the winter.

Elderberries can also be used for this recipe.

Freezing

Over the years that I have been freezing vegetables, I have learned that the successful way is to freeze fresh and quick. Go and gather the vegetables and fruits and freeze them right away.

Runner Beans: there are different ideas about freezing runner beans, but I find that it is best to cut them into pieces (don't shred) and blanch for two minutes before packing into bags for freezing.

French beans are excellent as they only have to be topped and tailed and blanched for two minutes before freezing.

Frozen beetroot is a waste of storage space since they can be pickled and will lose their flavour if you cut the roots and stems too close to the top and bottom.

Carrots: if you have a lot of small carrots these will freeze very well, just wash, scrape, slice and blanch for three minutes.

Cauliflower: when freezing cauliflower, put a tablespoon of lemon juice in the water when blanching - this may make the freezer smell strange for a while, but the smell will disappear after a time.

Courgettes and young marrows need to be cut into half-inch slices, without peeling and blanched for three minutes before packing into boxes for freezing.

Corn on the cob will have to be frozen while it is young and tender. Remove the leaves and threads and grade the cobs for size: blanching time is four minutes for small cobs and add two minutes extra for large ones, then pack individually in foil or freezer bags.

Spinach: so often at this time of year there is a surplus of spinach and this freezes very well. Use tender leaves, remove the stems and wash well. Blanch for two minutes, cool and press out any moisture, then pack in boxes or bags. I freeze mine in cartons then store them in freezer bags.

Tomatoes should be simmered in their own juice for five minutes until soft; then sieved, cooled and packed into cartons - these are very good in winter to add flavour to soups, stews and so on.

New potatoes: when we first take up new potatoes, I pick out the small ones and freeze them so that we can enjoy new potatoes on Christmas Day - its nice to smell the mint cooking with them in the middle of winter!

As well as vegetables, most fruit can be frozen and then made up into preserves later in the year - or used in various puddings.

Runner Bean Chutney

This is a mild and sweet chutney, it has become very popular over the years and keeps well. You could try french beans in place of runner beans.

2lb trimmed, sliced runner beans
1$^1/_2$lb chopped onions
1 heaped tbsp cornflour
1 heaped tbsp mustard
12oz demerara sugar
12oz soft brown sugar
1$^1/_2$ pints white vinegar

Prepare the vegetables. Cook the sliced beans in well-salted water until tender. Cook the chopped onions in $^1/_2$ pint vinegar. Strain the beans, then add to the rest of the vinegar and cook for 10 minutes. Add the sugar and the rest of the ingredients, stir well and boil for a further 12-15 minutes until thickened. Cool slightly and then pour into prepared jars and cover.

Spicy Redcurrant Jelly

3lb redcurrants
3lb sugar
$^1/_2$ stick of cinnamon
3 cloves
1 cup white wine vinegar
1$^1/_2$ pints water

Wash and strip the redcurrants and put them into a pan with the water. Tie the spices up in a bag and add to the fruit. Cook slowly until the currants are soft and pulpy. Remove the spice bag and strain the currants and pips. Return to the pan, with the vinegar and sugar, stir over a low heat until the sugar has dissolved then boil rapidly for about ten minutes until setting point has been reached. Pour the mixture into warm clean jars and cover.

Honey Cake

        8oz clear honey
        4oz caster sugar
        2oz butter or margarine
        $1/4$ pint water
        12oz Self-raising flour
        1 large pinch salt
        1 level tsp ginger
        2 medium eggs

Put the honey, sugar, fat and water into a pan and heat slowly until the sugar dissolves and the fat melts. Cool slightly. Meanwhile, sift the dry ingredients into a mixing bowl and make a well in the centre. Beat the eggs well, mix with the liquid mixture and gradually stir in, without beating, until the ingredients are well blended. Bake in a greased and lined $8^{1}/_{2}$ x $8^{1}/_{2}$in square tin in the centre of the oven for one hour at 355°F

Fried Mushrooms

If the mushrooms are small, peel and simply wash in cold water and dry by whirling them in a cloth, but large ones need to be cut into quarters. Cook in butter with a little salt and pepper.

Large Horse mushrooms are best laid gills upwards in a frying pan and stewed slowly in a little water, with a saucepan lid covering the pan, until they are cooked through. Remove the lid, add butter, salt and pepper and finish under the grill until the juice is thoroughly reduced and the gills begin to fry.

Puff balls should be sliced into rounds about half an inch thick using a bread knife. Dip the slices into well-beaten egg and milk and then into breadcrumbs. Press the crumbs on firmly then let the slices stand for half an hour or until the coating becomes firm. Fry in hot bacon fat, turning once. Drain on kitchen paper, add pepper and salt to taste and serve piping hot - they are delicious, believe me!

RECIPES

The bounty of August seems to increase from year to year both in the fields and hedges and in our gardens. The garden produce comes in fast. Broad beans are coming to the end of their season and are one of the best vegetables to store in your freezer. French stringless beans are excellent, as they only have to be topped and tailed, and runner beans are another excellent vegetable. Beetroots are very good eaten small, but don't cut the tops and roots too close to the beetroot or or they will 'bleed'. Carrots, onions and cauliflowers are all so good for you and courgettes and marrows need to be cut young. I know gardening is hard work, but it makes it all worthwhile when you can walk up your garden path to choose from the display of vegetables before you.

Summer is picnic time - children love them in the holidays and it is good to plan in advance something that is easy to prepare and tastes good out of doors. For myself, I can think of nothing better for a wayside meal than a chicken roasted then eaten cold with tomatoes, cos lettuce, wholemeal crusty rolls and some fruit. If you have a large number to cater for, bread rolls are much easier to use than all the work of cutting up sandwiches. Make some good fillings -I like the following:
Tomato and Cheese
Skin and squeeze one or two tomatoes to get rid of most of the pips, then chop roughly. Pound or crush and mix well with grated cheese, seasoning with salt and pepper and add a little chopped basil.

Sardines
Skin and bone the sardines, crush or pound to a paste, season with salt and a pinch of cayenne pepper, a few drops of Worcestershire sauce and lemon juice and a small amount of grated carrot

Ham, Chicken or Corned Beef

These are always favourites. Shred or chop the meat finely, mix with a little mustard and chopped watercress.

Eggs

Hard boil the eggs, run under a cold tap to cool quickly then chop. Mix the chopped egg with chopped chives or the green stem of a spring onion or a sprig or two of parsley. Season well and mix with a little salad cream or mayonnaise.

Bananas

For a sweet roll, try mashing up bananas and chopped nuts or dates with a little cottage cheese.

All these fillings should be kept in a cool place to become firm before they are used. Many sandwich fillings freeze well: cooked egg yolk, peanut butter, cooked or canned meats, poultry or fish, roquefort or blue cheeses and pickles. Not recommended are mayonnaise, jam, whites of hard-boiled eggs, lettuce, tomatoes, celery, cucumber or watercress.